A·N·N·U·A·L E·D·I·T·I·O·N·S

Educating Exceptional Children

03/04

Fifteenth Edition

EDITOR

Karen L. Freiberg

University of Maryland, Baltimore County

Dr. Karen Freiberg has an interdisciplinary educational and employment background in nursing, education, and developmental psychology. She received her B.S. from the State University of New York at Plattsburgh, her M.S. from Cornell University, and her Ph.D. from Syracuse University. She has worked as a school nurse, a pediatric nurse, a public health nurse for the Navajo Indians, an associate project director for a child development clinic, a researcher in several areas of child development, and a university professor. Dr. Freiberg is the author of an award-winning textbook, *Human Development: A Life-Span Approach*, which is now in its fourth edition. She is currently on the faculty at the University of Maryland, Baltimore County.

McGraw-Hill/Dushkin

530 Old Whitfield Street, Guilford, Connecticut 06437

Visit us on the Internet
http://www.dushkin.com

Credits

1. **Inclusive Education**
   Unit photo—Courtesy of Barbara Mabbett/New Zealand Ministry of Education.
2. **Early Childhood**
   Unit photo—© 2003 by Cleo Freelance Photography.
3. **Learning Disabilities**
   Unit photo—© 2003 by PhotoDisc, Inc.
4. **Speech and Language Impairments**
   Unit photo—United Nations photo by Marta Pinter.
5. **Developmental Disabilities**
   Unit photo—United Nations photo by L. Solmssen.
6. **Emotional and Behavioral Disorders**
   Unit photo—Courtesy of Redison Rice Corporation.
7. **Vision and Hearing Impairments**
   Unit photo—United Nations photo by O. Monsen.
8. **Multiple Disabilities**
   Unit photo—United Nations photo by L. Solmssen.
9. **Orthopedic and Health Impairments**
   Unit photo—© 2003 by Cleo Freelance Photography.
10. **Giftedness**
    Unit photo—Courtesy of Pamela Carley.
11. **Transition**
    Unit photo—United Nations photo by S. Dimartini.

Copyright

Cataloging in Publication Data
Main entry under title: Annual Editions: Educating Exceptional Children. 2003/2004.
1. Exceptional children—Education—United States—Periodicals. 2. Educational innovations—United States—Periodicals
I. Freiberg, Karen L., *comp.* II. Title: Educating Exceptional Children.
ISBN 0–07–254847–9   658'.05   ISSN 0198–7518

Fifteenth Edition

Cover image © 2003 PhotoDisc, Inc.
Printed in the United States of America   1234567890BAHBAH543   Printed on Recycled Paper

Editors/Advisory Board

Members of the Advisory Board are instrumental in the final selection of articles for each edition of ANNUAL EDITIONS. Their review of articles for content, level, currentness, and appropriateness provides critical direction to the editor and staff. We think that you will find their careful consideration well reflected in this volume.

EDITOR

Karen L. Freiberg
University of Maryland, Baltimore County

ADVISORY BOARD

Elizabeth Begley
Ithaca College

Erin Brumbaugh
Marietta College

MaryAnn Byrnes
University of Massachusetts - Boston

Lorna Catford
Sonoma State University

Jozi De Leon
New Mexico State University

Sheila Drake
MidAmerica Nazarene University

Colleen Finegan-Stoll
Wright State University

Mark B. Goor
George Mason University

Robin I. Herman
Central State University

Thomas J. Long
Catholic University of America

Mack McCoulskey
Angelo State University

Sharon A. Merrill
Xavier University

Susan M. Munson
Duquesne University

Gael L. Ragle
Arizona State University - West Campus

Marcia J. Reinholtz
Greensboro College

Joyce M. Smith
SUNY College, Oswego

Linda A. Svobodny
Minnesota State University, Moorhead

Ruth Thompson
Edinboro University

Kathleen S. Whittier
SUNY at Plattsburgh

Steve L. Williams
California State University, Hayward

Staff

To the Reader

In publishing ANNUAL EDITIONS we recognize the enormous role played by the magazines, newspapers, and journals of the public press in providing current, first-rate educational information in a broad spectrum of interest areas. Many of these articles are appropriate for students, researchers, and professionals seeking accurate, current material to help bridge the gap between principles and theories and the real world. These articles, however, become more useful for study when those of lasting value are carefully collected, organized, indexed, and reproduced in a low-cost format, which provides easy and permanent access when the material is needed. That is the role played by ANNUAL EDITIONS.

Since the shock of September 11, 2001, when homeland security was threatened in America, citizens have become more child- and family-oriented. After the terrorist attacks, many couples withdrew their plans to divorce, travel was curtailed, and hearth and home became treasured. Parents tried to find ways to comfort their children and reassure themselves.

In homes where families were raising children with disabilities or conditions of exceptionality, the question of how to proceed had special poignancy. Overprotection is not desirable. Where should the balancing fulcrum be placed between challenges and cautions? Parents, teachers, police, firefighters, doctors, nurses, social workers, psychologists, security guards—all people in public service occupations became more concerned about the needs of families and children.

The education of America's children has remained a priority in both the United States and Canada since September 11, 2001, despite the astronomically high costs of the war against Al Qaeda and new security measures at airports, border crossings, ports, power plants, and even schools. President George Bush still envisions new schools, new teachers, higher salaries for teachers, reductions in class size, improved curricula, and more school supplies, including computers. Will Congress be able to appropriate the funds to fulfill his wish list?

President Gerald Ford signed the Individuals with Disabilities Education Act (IDEA) into law in 1975. It required that all students, including those with disabilities, be provided a free and appropriate education in the least restrictive environment. For most of America's children, this now means education in regular classrooms. The number of children with disabilities requiring special services has jumped about 50 percent since the advent of IDEA. This is due to better diagnostic and assessment techniques; more children being kept alive after premature, low birth weight; "at-risk" births; earlier education; later education or transition services until age 21; and more awareness of conditions of disability. Current costs for special education in the United States are about $51 billion a year, about 20 percent of total school spending. As the use of vouchers for special services in private schools becomes more widespread, these costs may escalate considerably.

IDEA requires schools to work with parents as partners in the education of individuals with disabilities. Educational services must be provided to persons with special needs from time of diagnosis (birth, if applicable) through age 21. Educators, in collaboration with parents and other service providers, are required to provide individualized family service plans (IFSPs) to infants and young children who are at risk of developing disabilities or who acquire disabilities before they enter public school. Individualized transition plans (ITPs) must be provided for older students. For this reason, one-quarter of all the articles in *Annual Editions: Educating Exceptional Children 03/04* deal with family involvement.

Every child with a disability who is enrolled in public school has an annually updated individualized education plan (IEP). This describes how the child will receive special services and where, when, why, and what services will be provided. It is team-written by teachers, the student, parents, and all applicable service providers. IDEA directs IEPs to be outcomes-oriented. Most IEPs direct that education be carried out in regular education classes.

Annual Editions: Educating Exceptional Children 03/ 04 includes articles discussing the pros and cons of inclusion. It explains how IDEA provisions are being implemented in all areas of special education. Selections have been made with an eye to conveying information, giving personal experiences, and offering practical suggestions for implementation.

To help us improve future editions of this anthology, please complete and return the postage-paid article rating form on the last page. Your suggestions are valued and appreciated.

Karen Freiberg

Karen L. Freiberg
Editor

Contents

UNIT 1
Inclusive Education

Four articles present strategies for establishing positive interaction between students with and without special needs.

Unit Overview   **xviii**

UNIT 2
Early Childhood

Three unit articles discuss the implementation of special services to preschoolers with disabilities.

Unit Overview   **24**

The concepts in bold italics are developed in the article. For further expansion, please refer to the Topic Guide and the Index.

UNIT 3
Learning Disabilities

The assessment and special needs of students with learning disabilities are addressed in this unit's three selections.

Unit Overview   **44**

The concepts in bold italics are developed in the article. For further expansion, please refer to the Topic Guide and the Index.

UNIT 4
Speech and Language Impairments

In this unit three selections examine communication disorders and suggest ways in which students can develop their speech and language.

UNIT 5
Developmental Disabilities

Three articles in this section discuss concerns and strategies for providing optimal educational programs for students with developmental disabilities, and Down Syndrome.

The concepts in bold italics are developed in the article. For further expansion, please refer to the Topic Guide and the Index.

UNIT 6
Emotional and Behavioral Disorders

Ways to teach emotionally and behaviorally disordered students are discussed in the unit's three articles.

UNIT 7
Vision and Hearing Impairments

Three selections discuss the special needs of visually and hearing impaired children within the school system.

The concepts in bold italics are developed in the article. For further expansion, please refer to the Topic Guide and the Index.

UNIT 8
Multiple Disabilities

The implications of educational programs for children with multiple impairments are examined in this unit's three articles.

The concepts in bold italics are developed in the article. For further expansion, please refer to the Topic Guide and the Index.

UNIT 9
Orthopedic and Health Impairments

In this unit, three articles discuss how health problems and mobility impairments have an impact on a child's education.

UNIT 10
Giftedness

Three articles examine the need for special services for gifted and talented students, assessment of giftedness, and ways to teach these students.

The concepts in bold italics are developed in the article. For further expansion, please refer to the Topic Guide and the Index.

UNIT 11
Transition

The three articles in this section examine the problems and issues regarding transitions within school or from school to the community and workforce.

The concepts in bold italics are developed in the article. For further expansion, please refer to the Topic Guide and the Index.

Topic Guide

This topic guide suggests how the selections in this book relate to the subjects covered in your course. You may want to use the topics listed on these pages to search the Web more easily.

On the following pages a number of Web sites have been gathered specifically for this book. They are arranged to reflect the units of this *Annual Edition.* You can link to these sites by going to the DUSHKIN ONLINE support site at *http://www.dushkin.com/online/.*

ALL THE ARTICLES THAT RELATE TO EACH TOPIC ARE LISTED BELOW THE BOLD-FACED TERM.

Assessment

2. Standards for Diverse Learners
5. Identifying Paraprofessional Competencies for Early Intervention and Early Childhood Special Education
8. Providing Support for Student Independence Through Scaffolded Instruction
10. Successful Strategies for Promoting Self-Advocacy Among Students With LD: The LEAD Group
11. For the Love of Language
15. Don't Water Down! Enhance: Content Learning Through the Unit Organizer Routine
16. Identifying Depression in Students With Mental Retardation
17. Wraparound Services for Young Schoolchildren With Emotional and Behavioral Disorders
24. Loneliness in Children With Disabilities: How Teachers Can Help
25. Using Technology to Construct Alternate Portfolios of Students With Moderate and Severe Disabilities
28. Chaos in the Classroom: Looking at ADHD
29. Uncommon Talents: Gifted Children, Prodigies and Savants
30. Using the Internet to Improve Student Performance
31. Gifted Students Need an Education, Too
34. Choosing a Self-Determination Curriculum

Autism

14. The Secrets of Autism

Brain diseases and disorders

15. Don't Water Down! Enhance: Content Learning Through the Unit Organizer Routine
16. Identifying Depression in Students With Mental Retardation
33. Listening to Student Voices About Postsecondary Education

Collaboration

2. Standards for Diverse Learners
7. The Itinerant Teacher Hits the Road: A Map for Instruction in Young Children's Social Skills
17. Wraparound Services for Young Schoolchildren With Emotional and Behavioral Disorders
21. Seeking the Light: Welcoming a Visually Impaired Student
23. Training Basic Teaching Skills to Paraeducators of Students With Severe Disabilities
25. Using Technology to Construct Alternate Portfolios of Students With Moderate and Severe Disabilities
30. Using the Internet to Improve Student Performance
32. Transition Planning for Students With Severe Disabilities: Policy Implications for the Classroom

Computers

9. Graphic Organizers to the Rescue! Helping Students Link—and Remember—Information
13. Young African American Children With Disabilities and Augmentative and Alternative Communication Issues
21. Seeking the Light: Welcoming a Visually Impaired Student
22. Visual Teaching Strategies for Students Who Are Deaf or Hard of Hearing
25. Using Technology to Construct Alternate Portfolios of Students With Moderate and Severe Disabilities
30. Using the Internet to Improve Student Performance

Conflict resolution

17. Wraparound Services for Young Schoolchildren With Emotional and Behavioral Disorders
24. Loneliness in Children With Disabilities: How Teachers Can Help

Cultural diversity

2. Standards for Diverse Learners
5. Identifying Paraprofessional Competencies for Early Intervention and Early Childhood Special Education
13. Young African American Children With Disabilities and Augmentative and Alternative Communication Issues

Developmental disabilities

14. The Secrets of Autism
15. Don't Water Down! Enhance: Content Learning Through the Unit Organizer Routine
16. Identifying Depression in Students With Mental Retardation
25. Using Technology to Construct Alternate Portfolios of Students With Moderate and Severe Disabilities
29. Uncommon Talents: Gifted Children, Prodigies and Savants
32. Transition Planning for Students With Severe Disabilities: Policy Implications for the Classroom
33. Listening to Student Voices About Postsecondary Education

Early childhood education

6. Language Flowering, Language Empowering: 20 Ways Parents and Teachers Can Assist Young Children
7. The Itinerant Teacher Hits the Road: A Map for Instruction in Young Children's Social Skills
11. For the Love of Language
12. Literacy-Based Planning and Pedagogy That Supports Toddler Language Development

Elementary school

8. Providing Support for Student Independence Through Scaffolded Instruction
9. Graphic Organizers to the Rescue! Helping Students Link—and Remember—Information
10. Successful Strategies for Promoting Self-Advocacy Among Students With LD: The LEAD Group
17. Wraparound Services for Young Schoolchildren With Emotional and Behavioral Disorders
18. Making Choices—Improving Behavior—Engaging in Learning
26. Mobility Training Using the MOVE Curriculum: A Parent's View
28. Chaos in the Classroom: Looking at ADHD
31. Gifted Students Need an Education, Too

Emotional and behavioral disorders

14. The Secrets of Autism
16. Identifying Depression in Students With Mental Retardation
17. Wraparound Services for Young Schoolchildren With Emotional and Behavioral Disorders
18. Making Choices—Improving Behavior—Engaging in Learning
19. Homeless Youth in the United States
24. Loneliness in Children With Disabilities: How Teachers Can Help
28. Chaos in the Classroom: Looking at ADHD
29. Uncommon Talents: Gifted Children, Prodigies and Savants

Schools

Self-esteem

Speech and language impairments

Talented children and youth

Technology

Transition

Visual impairments

World Wide Web Sites

The following World Wide Web sites have been carefully researched and selected to support the articles found in this reader. The easiest way to access these selected sites is to go to our DUSHKIN ONLINE support site at *http://www.dushkin.com/online/*.

AE: Educating Exceptional Children 03/04

The following sites were available at the time of publication. Visit our Web site—we update DUSHKIN ONLINE regularly to reflect any changes.

General Sources

Consortium for Citizens With Disabilities
http://www.c-c-d.org

Included in this coalition organization is an Education Task Force that follows issues of early childhood special education, the president's commission on excellence in special education, issues of rethinking special education, 2001 IDEA principles, and many other related issues.

ERIC Clearinghouse on Disabilities and Gifted Education
http://www.ericec.org

This ERIC clearinghouse has information on everything important to special education professionals. It links also to The Council for Exceptional Children and the National Clearinghouse for Professions in Special Education.

Family Village
http://www.familyvillage.wisc.edu/index.htmlx

Here is a global community of disability-related resources that is set up under such headings as library, shopping mall, school, community center, and others.

National Information Center for Children and Youth With Disabilities (NICHCY)
http://www.nichcy.org/index.html

NICHCY provides information and makes referrals in areas related to specific disabilities, early intervention, special education and related services, individualized education programs, and much more. The site also connects to a listing of Parent's Guides to resources for children and youth with disabilities.

National Rehabilitation Information Center (NARIC)
http://www.naric.com

A series of databases that can be keyword-searched on subjects that include physical, mental, and psychiatric disabilities, vocational rehabilitation, special education, assistive technology, and more can be found on this site.

President's Commission on Excellence in Special Education (PCESE)
http://www.ed.gov/inits/commissionsboards/whspecialeducation/

The report stemming from the work of the PCESE, *A New Era: Revitalizing Special Education for Children and Their Families* can be downloaded in full at this site.

School Psychology Resources Online
http://www.schoolpsychology.net

Numerous sites on special conditions, disorders, and disabilities, as well as other data ranging from assertiveness/evaluation to research, are available on this resource page for psychologists, parents, and educators.

Special Education News
http://www.specialednews.com/disabilities/disabnews/povanddisab031200.html

This particular section of this site discusses the problems of coping with both poverty and disability. Explore the rest of the site also for information for educators on behavior management, conflict resolution, early intervention, specific disabilities, and much more.

Special Education Exchange
http://www.spedex.com/main_graphics.htm

SpEdEx, as this site is more commonly known, offers a wealth of information, links, and resources to everyone interested in special education.

UNIT 1: Inclusive Education

Consortium on Inclusive Schooling Practices
http://www.asri.edu/cfsp/brochure/abtcons.htm

The Consortium represents a collaborative effort to build the capacity of state and local education agencies to provide inclusive educational services in school and community settings, focusing on systemic reform rather than on changes in special education only.

Institute on Disability/University of New Hampshire
http://iod.unh.edu

This site includes Early Childhood, Inclusive Education, High School and Post-Secondary School, Community Living and Adult Life, Related Links, both state and national, and information on technology, health care, public policy, as well as leadership training and professional development.

Kids Together, Inc.
http://www.kidstogether.org

Based on the IDEA law about teaching children with disabilties in regular classrooms, this site contains all the information on inclusion you might need to know.

New Horizons for Learning
http://www.newhorizons.org

Based on the theory of inclusion, this site is filled with information on special needs inclusion, technology and learning, a brain lab, and much more, presented as floors in a building.

UNIT 2: Early Childhood

Division for Early Childhood
http://www.dec-sped.org

A division of the Council for Exceptional Children, the DEC advocates for the improvement of conditions of young children with special needs. Child development theory, programming data, parenting data, research, and links to other sites can be found on this site.

Institute on Community Integration Projects
http://ici.umn.edu/projectscenters/

Research projects related to early childhood and early intervention services for special education are described here.

National Academy for Child Development (NACD)
http://www.nacd.org

The NACD, an international organization, is dedicated to helping children and adults reach their full potential. Its home page presents links to various programs, research, and resources into such topics as learning disabilities, ADD/ADHD, brain injuries, autism, accelerated and gifted, and other similar topic areas.

National Early Childhood Technical Assistance System
http://www.nectas.unc.edu

An exceptionally complete site on children with special needs, NECTAS explores many areas, including the IDEA and inclusion, and includes a projects database.

Special Education Resources on the Internet (SERI)
http://seriweb.com

SERI offers helpful sites in all phases of special education in early childhood, including disabilities, mental retardation, behavior disorders, and autism.

UNIT 3: Learning Disabilities

Children and Adults With Attention Deficit/Hyperactivity Disorder (CHADD)
http://www.chadd.org

CHADD works to improve the lives of people with AD/HD through education, advocacy, and support, offering information that can be trusted. The site includes fact sheets, legislative information, research studies, and links.

The Instant Access Treasure Chest
http://www.fln.vcu.edu/ld/ld.html

Billed as the Foreign Language Teacher's Guide to Learning Disabilities, this site contains a very thorough list of resources for anyone interested in LD education issues.

Learning Disabilities Online
http://www.ldonline.org

This is a good source for information about all kinds of learning disabilities with links to other related material.

Learning Disabilities Association of America (LDA)
http://www.ldanatl.org

The purpose of the LDA is to advance the education and general welfare of children of normal and potentially normal intelligence who show handicaps of a perceptual, conceptual, or coordinative nature.

National Center on Self Determination
http://www.selfdeterminationohsu.org/home/Projects_at_the_Center/ Community_Solutions_Project

The community solutions project described at this site focused on the unique needs of minority adolescents with disabilities as they transitioned from high school to adulthood.

Teaching Children With Attention Deficit Disorder
http://www.kidsource.com/kidsource/content2/add.html

This in-depth site defines both types of ADDs and discusses establishing the proper learning environment.

UNIT 4: Speech and Language Impairments

Speech Disorders WWW Sites
http://www.socialnet.lu/handitel/wwwlinks/dumb.html

A thorough collection of Web sites, plus an article on the relationship between form and function in the speech of specifically language-impaired children, may be accessed here.

UNIT 5: Developmental Disabilities

Arc of the United States
http://www.thearc.org

Here is the Web site of the national organization of and for people with mental retardation and related disabilities and their families. It includes governmental affairs, services, position statements, FAQs, publications, and related links.

Autism Society Early Interventions Package
http://www.autism-society.org/packages/early_intervention.pdf

Answers to FAQs about early intervention in cases of autism as well as online help with obtaining early intervention services, reading lists, and organizations to contact for further information are located on this Web site.

Disability-Related Sources on the Web
http://www.arcofarizona.org/dislnkin.html

This resource's many links include grant resources, federally funded projects and federal agencies, assistive technology, national and international organizations, and educational resources and directories.

Gentle Teaching
http://www.gentleteaching.nl

Maintained by the foundation for Gentle Teaching in the Netherlands, this page explains a nonviolent approach for helping children and adults with special needs.

UNIT 6: Emotional and Behavioral Disorders

Resources in Emotional or Behavioral Disorders (EBD)
http://www.gwu.edu/~ebdweb/

At this page, link to a collection of Web resources for teachers of students with serious emotional disturbances.

UNIT 7: Vision and Hearing Impairments

Info to Go: Laurent Clerc National Deaf Education Center
http://clerccenter.gallaudet.edu/InfoToGo/index.html

Important for parents and educators, this Web site from Gallaudet University offers information on audiology, communication, education, legal, and health issues of deaf people.

The New York Institute for Special Education
http://www.nyise.org/index.html

This school is an educational facility that serves children who are blind or visually impaired. The site includes program descriptions and resources for the blind.

UNIT 8: Multiple Disabilities

Activity Ideas for Students With Severe, Profound, or Multiple Disabilities
http://www.palaestra.com/featurestory.html

The Fall 1997 issue of the *Palaestra* contains this interesting article on teaching students who have multiple disabilities. The complete text is offered here online.

UNIT 9: Orthopedic and Health Impairments

Association to Benefit Children (ABC)
http://www.a-b-c.org

ABC presents a network of programs that includes child advocacy, education for disabled children, care for HIV-positive children, employment, housing, foster care, and day care.

www.dushkin.com/online/

An Idea Whose Time Has Come
http://www.boggscenter.org/mich3899.htm
   The purpose of community-based education is to help students in special education to become more independent. Here is an excellent description of how it is being done in at least one community.

Resources for VE Teachers
http://cpt.fsu.edu/tree/ve/tofc.html
   Effective practices for teachers of varying exceptionalities (VE) classes are listed here.

UNIT 10: Giftedness

The Council for Exceptional Children
http://www.cec.sped.org/index.html
   This page will give you access to information on identifying and teaching gifted children, attention-deficit disorders, and other topics in gifted education.

Kenny Anthony's Gifted and Talented and General Educational Resources
http://www2.tsixroads.com/~kva/
   In addition to definitions and characteristics of giftedness and needs of the gifted, an excellent list of education resources for the gifted can be found at this site.

National Association for Gifted Children (NAGC)
http://www.nagc.org/home00.htm
   NAGC, a national nonprofit organization for gifted children, is dedicated to developing their high potential.

UNIT 11: Transition

Building Partnerships Between Centers for Independent Living and Schools
http://cdrc.ohsu.edu/csd1/home/Projects_at_the_Center/Networks/ BUILDING_PARTNERSHIPS
   This article overviews the Take Charge approach to transitioning young people with disabilities into their future. The model uses coaching to assist youth to learn self-determination and transition planning skills.

National Center on Secondary Education and Transition
http://www.ncset.org
   This site coordinates national resources, offers technical assistance, and disseminates information related to secondary education and transition for youth with disabilities in order to create opportunities for youth to achieve successful futures.

We highly recommend that you review our Web site for expanded information and our other product lines. We are continually updating and adding links to our Web site in order to offer you the most usable and useful information that will support and expand the value of your Annual Editions. You can reach us at: *http://www.dushkin.com/annualeditions/*.

UNIT 1
Inclusive Education

Unit Selections

1. **Revamping Special Education**, Wade F. Horn and Douglas Tynan
2. **Standards for Diverse Learners**, Paula Kluth and Diana Straut
3. **More Choices for Disabled Kids: Lessons From Abroad**, Lewis M. Andrews
4. **What's Good? Suggested Resources for Beginning Special Education Teachers**, Sharon A. Maroney

Key Points to Consider

- How would you revamp special education to meet the needs of children with disabilities and their teachers in the new century?

- What conditions are needed to teach using a standards-based curriculum? What has the inclusion movement contributed to diverse classroom climates?

- Describe the model approaches to inclusive education and parental choice in Denmark, New Zealand, and the Netherlands. What will be the effect on public schools if vouchers to private schools are allowed for students with special needs?

- What does the 1997 reauthorization of IDEA require of states that fail to include children with disabilities in regular education classes? What impact will this have on twenty-first century education?

 **Links: www.dushkin.com/online/**
These sites are annotated in the World Wide Web pages.

Consortium on Inclusive Schooling Practices
http://www.asri.edu/cfsp/brochure/abtcons.htm

Institute on Disability/University of New Hampshire
http://iod.unh.edu

Kids Together, Inc.
http://www.kidstogether.org

New Horizons for Learning
http://www.newhorizons.org

One of the weaknesses of American schools, public and private, is professional development. Regular education teachers are expected to know how to provide special educational services to every child with an exceptional condition in their classroom, despite not having had course work in special education. The numbers of students with exceptionalities who are being educated in regular education classes are increasing annually. During its 25 years in existence, the Individuals with Disabilities Education Act (IDEA) has reduced the numbers of special needs students being educated in residential centers, hospitals, homes, or special schools to less than 5 percent. Children who once would have been turned away from public schools are now being admitted in enormous numbers. Without adequate preparation and support, regular education teachers feel overwhelmed. Their abilities to educate all of their students, those with, and those without, disabilities, suffer grave consequences.

The trend toward inclusive education necessitates more knowledge and expertise on the part of all regular education teachers. Educating children with exceptionalities can no longer be viewed as the job of special-education teachers. This trend also mandates knowledge about collaboration and advisory activities on the part of all special educators. Teamwork is essential as special education and regular education are becoming more and more intertwined.

Public schools have an obligation to provide free educational services in the least restrictive environment possible to all children who have diagnosed conditions of exceptionality. Although laws in Canada and the United States differ slightly, all public schools have an obligation to serve children with exceptional conditions in as normal an educational environment as possible. Inclusive education is difficult. It works very well for some students with exceptionalities in some situations and marginally or not at all for other students with exceptionalities in other situations.

For inclusion to succeed within a school, everyone must be committed to be part of the solution: superintendent, principal, teachers, coaches, aides, ancillary staff, students, parents, and families. Special education teachers often find their jobs involving much more than instructing students with special needs. They serve as consultants to regular education teachers to assure that inclusion is meaningful for their students. They collaborate with parents, administrators, support personnel, and community agencies as well as with regular education teachers. They plan curriculum and oversee the writing of Individualized Family Service Plans (IFSPs), Individualized Education Plans (IEPs) and Individualized Transition Plans (ITPs). They schedule and make sure that services are provided by all team-involved persons. They keep up with enormous amounts of paperwork. They update parents even when parents are too involved, or not involved enough. They keep abreast of new resources, new legal processes, and new instructional techniques. They make projections for the futures of their students and set out ways to make good things happen. They also struggle to be accountable, both educationally and financially, for all they do.

The term "least restrictive environment" is often mistakenly understood as the need for all children to be educated in a regular education classroom. If students can learn and achieve better in inclusive programs, then they belong there. If students can succeed only marginally in inclusive education classrooms, some alternate solutions are necessary. A continuum of placement options exists to maximize the goal of educating every child. For some children, a separate class, or even a separate school, is still optimal.

Every child with an exceptional condition is different from every other child in symptoms, needs, and teachability. Each child is, therefore, provided with a unique individualized education plan. This plan consists of both long- and short-term goals for education, specially designed instructional procedures with related services, and methods to evaluate the child's progress. The IEP is updated and revised annually. Special education teachers, parents, and all applicable service providers must collaborate at least this often to make recommendations for goals and teaching strategies. The IEPs should always be outcomes-oriented with functional curricula.

The first article in this inclusive education unit addresses the questions of how special education should be revamped to meet the needs of children with disabilities, and their teachers, in the twenty-first century. New U.S. laws are reviewed and their successes and their deficiencies examined. School districts and states have enough autonomy so that inclusive education is far from uniform from shore to shore. A downside of all inclusive special educational programming is the sense of entitlement of families and children receiving special services. The authors suggest steps for reform that can benefit everyone.

The second article discusses standards-based curriculum. The inclusion education movement has contributed to some very diverse classroom climates, where standards-based curricula must be flexible and developmental. There is no longer such a thing as a "grade" where one lesson-plan fits all, even in rural areas. Teaching to standards requires careful assessments, access to different levels of meaningful content, and assistance from all stakeholders in education—parents, teachers, and community members.

The third article addresses a future where school vouchers become commonplace. Parents will feel freer to move their special-needs children from school to school as often as necessary to ensure that educational goals are being met. The author discusses the comparative successes and the relative failures of voucher-based education in New Zealand, the Netherlands, Sweden, Denmark, and Australia. Much can be learned from the lessons of our world neighbors and their educational policies.

The fourth article included in this unit suggests resources for beginning special education teachers. Experienced educators have given their expertise to Sharon Maroney to pass on to novice teachers. Advice is included on developing professionalism, instructing effectively, managing behavior, and using special techniques. The author also counsels readers to try new things and have fun in their chosen professions. Educating exceptional children is challenging. It should also be exciting, and fun!

All of these selections are concerned with making regular education work when children with special needs are integrated into the classroom for a portion of, or the complete, school day. They speak to the requirement for accountability in education that produces a degree of excellence while allowing educators to feel pride in their achievement in their chosen profession.

Revamping special education

WADE F. HORN & DOUGLAS TYNAN

PRIOR to the 1950s, the federal government was not routinely involved in the education of children with special needs. A few federal laws had been passed to provide direct educational benefits to persons with disabilities, mostly in the form of grants to states for residential asylums for the "deaf and dumb, and to promote education of the blind." These laws, however, were in the tradition of providing residential arrangements for persons with serious disabilities, services that had existed since colonial times.

Absent federal law, how—and even whether—children with disabilities were to be educated within the public schools was left to the discretion of the states and their local school districts. Although some public schools undoubtedly provided exceptional services to children with disabilities, others did not. Indeed, as recently as 1973, perhaps as many as one million students were denied enrollment in public schools solely on the basis of their disability.

This state of affairs changed dramatically in 1975 with the passage of the Education of All Handicapped Children Act (PL 94-142). Renamed the Individuals with Disabilities Education Act (IDEA) in 1990, this landmark legislation mandated that children with disabilities receive a free and appropriate public education in the least restrictive environment. Critical components of the law include requirements for an initial evaluation to determine eligibility for services and accommodations, individual education planning, the provision of individualized services, and procedural safeguards to ensure the active involvement of a child's parents.

The good news is that IDEA has been largely successful in opening up educational opportunities for children with disabilities. The bad news is that IDEA, as too frequently happens with public-policy initiatives, has had some unintended negative consequences as well.

The growth of special education

In 1999–2000, 6.1 million children ages 3 to 21 years were found eligible for special-education services and accommodations, up from 3.7 million in 1976–77—an increase of 65 percent. The growing number of children in special education is not solely a function of an increase in the overall student population but also of a growth in the proportion of students claiming to be in need of special education. Specifically, 12.8 percent of the resident student population received special-education services and accommodations in 1997–98, compared to 8.3 percent of the resident student population in 1976–77.

There are several reasons why both the number and percentage of children identified as qualifying for special education under IDEA have grown so rapidly in recent decades. First, since passage of PL 94-142, both Congress and the Department of Education have responded to pressure from advocacy groups by broadening the definition of students eligible for special education. For example, children who are three to five years old are now eligible for services under the IDEA, as are children with autism and traumatic brain injuries.

Even more significantly, in 1991 the Department of Education issued a "policy clarification" indicating that children diagnosed with attention deficit disorder (ADD) and attention deficit hyperactivity disorder (ADHD) may be eligible for special-education services and accommodations under the "other health impaired" category of IDEA. On March 12, 1999, the department codified this policy clarification into law when it published regulations that, among other things, revised the definition of the "other health impaired" disability category by adding both ADD and ADHD as qualifying conditions. Given the extraordinary increase in the number of children diagnosed in recent years as having ADD or ADHD, the inclusion of these two diagnoses under "other health impaired" virtually assures continued growth in the number of students served through special education.

Second, the number of children identified under the category "specific learning disability," or SLD, has increased enormously. SLD is not a single disorder, but a category of special education that includes disabilities in any of seven areas: listening, speaking, basic reading of words, reading comprehension, written expression, mathematics problem-solving, and mathematics calculations. SLD is not synonymous with reading disability or dyslexia, although it is frequently misinterpreted as such, probably because the vast majority of children identified with SLD have reading deficits.

In 1976–77, at the inception of IDEA, 796,000 children, or 22 percent of the total special-education population, were identified as having a specific learning disability. By 1997–98, that number had grown to 2,726,000, or 46 percent of the total number of students in special education—an increase of 233 percent since 1976–77. In contrast, the number of children in all of the other disability categories combined increased only 13 percent during the same time period.

The increase in the number of students diagnosed with SLD would not be a problem if, in fact, we were simply better today at identifying students with SLD than in the past. There is, however, no universally accepted, validated test or diagnostic criteria to determine the presence or absence of learning disabilities. Nor is there a clear line of demarcation between students who have milder forms of SLDs and those who do not have SLDs. This lack of clear definitions and objective diagnostic criteria makes it possible to diagnose almost any low- or underachieving child as having an SLD. According to James Ysseldyke, director of the National Center on Educational Outcomes at the University of Minnesota, over 80 percent of all schoolchildren in the United States could qualify as having an SLD under one definition or another.

Third, many suspect that some school districts place nondisabled but low-achieving students into special-education classes in order to obtain state and federal funds that are available only after a child is identified as disabled under IDEA. While it is unlikely that children without any learning difficulties are being placed in special education, not every low-achieving child is also disabled. But when services are provided to low-achieving, nondisabled students in regular education, local school districts cannot claim reimbursement for the cost of these services, even if they are exactly the same as those provided to students with disabilities. This funding structure provides an enormous financial incentive for local school districts to identify merely low-achieving students as disabled.

Fourth, recent education reform efforts to hold schools more accountable for student outcomes may also be responsible for some of the increase in the population of special-education students. Until recently, students identified as receiving services under special education were not generally required to participate in state-wide assessments. Given that merit raises, promotions, and bonuses for both principals and teachers often ride on the results of state-wide exams, the temptation exists for local school districts to raise their scores artificially by excluding the participation of low-achieving special-education students in state-wide assessments. Although the 1997 amendments to the IDEA were intended to prohibit this practice, three states (Kentucky, Louisiana, and South Carolina) that recently enjoyed large gains on national reading tests also saw large increases in the percentage of special-education students excluded from taking the tests.

Finally, parents themselves have contributed to the growth in special education. Not long ago, being in special education carried with it a certain amount of social stigma. Today, due in large part to the success of disability advocacy groups, this stigma has lessened considerably. Instead, what special education offers today is the possibility of such attractive accommodations as the assistance of a personal tutor, a laptop computer, extra or even unlimited time on classroom tests and college entrance exams, a personal note-taker, and immunity from punishment when the student violates rules because of his disability.

The fact that eligibility for special education entitles one to an array of often expensive services and accommodations may help explain why, for example, nearly one in three high school students are officially designated as disabled in affluent Greenwich, Connecticut. It may also explain why clinicians in wealthier suburban communities frequently report upsurges in parental requests for diagnostic evaluations, especially for SLD and ADD, just as high school students are preparing to take college entrance exams. Indeed, while children from families with more than $100,000 in annual income account for just 13 percent of the SAT test-taking population, they make up 27 percent of those who receive special accommodations when taking the SAT.

Rising costs

As might be expected, the consequence of these trends is the skyrocketing cost of special education, often at the expense of regular education. According to the National School Boards Association, the per-pupil cost of special education is 2.1 times the cost of regular education. Since the average per-pupil expenditure in the United States is about $6,200, the average cost for students in special education is about $13,000 annually. Hence, the average *excess* cost of special education is $6,800 per pupil. Since IDEA covers 6.1 million children ages 3 to 21, the total cost of special education for these children is $79.3 billion, which is $41.5 billion more than a regular education would cost for them.

Under IDEA, the federal government is supposed to pay 40 percent of the costs of special education. In reality, federal funding has never exceeded 12.5 percent. Today,

Washington provides $5 billion in total funding to local school districts, or about 12 percent of the costs of special education. On average, states pay 56 percent of the costs, with a range of 11 percent to 95 percent. The remaining average of 32 percent is paid for by local school districts. Thus, IDEA is perhaps the largest unfunded federal mandate for education ever placed on state and local government. Recently, Senator Jim Jeffords of Vermont has called for an increase in federal funding over the next five years from the current 5 billion dollars annually to 37 billion dollars, which would approach the 40 percent funding suggested in 1975. To date, Senator Jeffords' efforts have resulted only in a nonbinding resolution, and not actual dollars.

Making matters worse, since special education (unlike regular education) is a federal mandate, schools can be sued for not providing the services that parents think their child deserves. This has led some school districts to spend extraordinary sums on special-education placements, services, and accommodations in order to avoid even more costly lawsuits. The Economic Policy Institute estimates that each year special education absorbs 38 cents of every new tax dollar raised for the public schools.

A particularly expensive result of qualifying a child for special education is the possibility that in doing so, a public school may be obligating itself to pay for all or part of a child's private school tuition in the event that public schools cannot accommodate their needs. In fact, public school districts today pay for the private school tuition of more than 100,000 special-education students at an estimated cost of $2 billion annually, and part of the cost of private schooling for an additional 66,000 special-education students. An extreme example of this is a southern California school district that, as reported in the *Washington Monthly*, pays for a severely brain-damaged boy to attend a specialized school in Massachusetts, flying his parents and sister out for regular visits, at an annual cost of $254,000.

One consequence of these escalating costs may be the eventual weakening of public support for special education. As ever increasing numbers of children are determined eligible for ever more expensive special-education services, the public's confidence in the special-education system may gradually erode. If so, the public may overreact and demand the abandonment of special education, leaving severely disabled children once again without public education. Indeed, in a recent Phi Delta Kappa/Gallup poll, 65 percent of parents said that the extra attention paid by instructors and classroom assistants to disabled students came at the expense of their own children.

Training for a lifetime of entitlement

Another consequence of the expansion of disability categories is that low- and underachieving students are being handled by an "accommodation model," when other approaches—prevention, intervention, and compensatory strategies—would better suit their needs. When initially passed in 1975, PL 94-142 was largely intended to ensure that students with significant physical and sensory disabilities were not denied a free and appropriate public education. For these students, the right approach was, and remains, to make public education accessible through the use of access ramps for those in wheelchairs, books written in Braille for the blind, and sign-language interpreters for the deaf. There was no expectation that special education would, by itself, ameliorate the physical or sensory handicap, thereby making these accommodations no longer necessary.

There are, however, subgroups of students with disabilities for whom it is reasonable to expect that special education will help them overcome or compensate for their handicapping condition, so that they no longer need special services or accommodations. For example, special education ought to ameliorate emotional and behavioral disorders so that students with these disorders no longer need alternative placements. Similarly, when working with students with SLD, ADD, and ADHD, the goal should be to help them learn self-directed compensatory strategies so they can succeed without the aid of special services. For example, children with ADHD could be taught, through guided practice and positive reinforcement, how to use an assignment pad and how to better organize their backpacks or desks. An accommodation strategy would merely assign an aide to keep track of the student's work. In other words, for many in special education the goal can—and should—be independence, rather than a lifetime of dependence on special accommodations, often at taxpayers' expense.

Unfortunately, special education has largely failed to help most of its students achieve such independence. Instead, most special-education students under IDEA can expect to receive its services and accommodations until they leave school. According to data collected from 16 states in 1993 by the Department of Education, only 1 to 12 percent of special-education students over the age of 14 years are declassified each year. Other policy developments, such as the accommodations provided under the Americans with Disabilities Act, reinforce the tendency toward permanent accommodations for disabilities, even those that can be remediated.

Contributing further to this problem is the focus within both the federal and state systems on due process requirements and fiscal management rather than educational results. Local schools are told they are "doing it right" when they strictly adhere to the procedures that govern eligibility for services and, once a child is found eligible, the development of an Individual Education Plan (IEP). A committee comprised of school personnel and the child's parents puts together the IEP, which sets specific goals for the child and identifies settings in which the child is to achieve those goals. Current oversight efforts also focus on whether schools provide parents with proper procedural safeguards and responsibly draw down funds. Federal accountability systems pay little attention to whether students in special education are advancing in core subjects or acquiring the skills to make special education no longer necessary.

It's questionable whether many of the accommodations typically provided to special-education students are even doing what proponents advocate. For an accommodation to be useful, it should demonstrate "differential advantage" for special-education students. That is, the accommodation—whether giving extended time to complete a test, allowing students to have the instructions and test questions read aloud to them, or using large-print or Braille forms of the test—should improve the scores of students with disabilities above and beyond improvements that students without disabilities might achieve if they were provided with the same accommodation. We know, for example, that the use of large print does provide a differential advantage to students with vision impairment. When students with vision impairment and those without take the same large-print test, their scores are comparable. If they take a standard small-print test, those with vision impairment do worse. Clearly, the use of large print helps to level the playing field.

Unfortunately, some accommodations routinely provided to special-education students have not demonstrated such differential advantage. Take, for example, the provision of extra time to take tests. According to research by Lynn Fuchs and her colleagues at Vanderbilt University, giving more time on conventional math and reading tests does not help grade school students diagnosed with learning disabilities any more than it does non-learning-disabled students, although it may provide a differential advantage on more complicated math tests that require extensive reading and writing. Moreover, although studies by the College Board have found that providing extended time on the SATs increases the scores of students with learning disabilities by an average of 45 points on verbal and 38 points on math, no studies have yet been done to determine whether giving more time on the SATs satisfies the requirement for differential advantage.

Another way to determine whether an accommodation is appropriate is to examine its effects on the test's predictive validity—the extent to which accommodation enhances or reduces the test's ability to predict an outcome or measure the underlying ability it was designed to measure. One danger in providing accommodations to special-education students is that the altered test may no longer validly assess the ability or skill it was created to assess, or predict the outcome it was designed to predict. This seems to be the case for at least some accommodations routinely provided to special-education students. Research has generally found, for example, that giving students with learning disabilities extra time on the SAT tends to predict greater college success than these students actually achieve.

Disciplinary immunity

What these various accommodations do seem to accomplish is this: Students in special education come to believe that they are entitled to operate under a different set of rules from everyone else. Nowhere is this more evident than in how school disciplinary rules are differently applied to students in special education and those in regular education.

According to the "stay put" provisions of IDEA, once placement in special education has begun, it can only be changed by the IEP committee. If the student's parents do not consent to a change in placement and request a hearing, the student must "stay put" in the current placement until the hearing process is concluded. Suspensions that last longer than 10 days (or have the cumulative impact of more than 10 days) and expulsions are considered a change in placement and hence prohibited under the "stay put" provisions of the IDEA.

There are two exceptions to this. First, disciplinary sanctions of 10 days or less are not considered a change in placement and consequently are not subject to this restriction (although if the current suspension combined with earlier suspensions would total over 10 days, the student could not be suspended). Second, a school can propose disciplinary sanctions greater than 10 days and expulsions if it believes the misbehavior is not related to the disability. If, however, the parent disagrees and requests a hearing, the student must "stay put" in his or her current placement.

The "stay put" provision can lead to situations in which two students, one in regular education and the other in special education, both bring weapons or an illegal substance to school, yet only the student in regular education is suspended or expelled. This situation is not merely hypothetical. Several years ago, a group of six students in Fairfax County, Virginia, brought a .357 magnum handgun onto school property. Five of the students were expelled. The sixth was not. The reason? He was classified as "learning disabled" with a specific weakness in "written language skills."

This is not an isolated episode. In another case, also in Fairfax County, five gang members used a meat hook to assault another student. Only three of the perpetrators were expelled. The other two were special-education students. When then Virginia governor George Allen tried to challenge the wisdom of using federal law to protect violent special-education students, the Clinton administration threatened to pull millions of dollars in federal education spending from the state.

Due to these and other examples of problems arising from the "stay put" provision, Congress in 1997 passed amendments to IDEA giving schools more latitude in disciplining violent special-education students. For example, in situations involving a "substantial likelihood" of injury, a hearing officer may unilaterally place a student involved with weapons or drugs in an alternative educational setting. For this to occur, however, the school must show that it had made reasonable efforts to minimize the risk of harm in the current placement, "including the use of supplementary aids and services." Furthermore, if the recommendation is expulsion, the IEP team must conduct a review to determine whether the misconduct was a manifestation of the child's disability. If so, no expulsion.

These qualifications continue to ensure that special-education students are treated differently from regular students in cases of serious violations of school rules. Indeed, in April 1999, the National School Boards Association urged federal lawmakers to further amend IDEA to provide greater flexibility to suspend, expel, or reassign students whose misconduct jeopardizes safety or unreasonably disrupts classroom learning.

Unrealistic expectations

The end result of special education's focus on process rather than outcome, accommodations rather than prevention and intervention, and exceptions to disciplinary codes rather than uniform enforcement is that many special-education students see their disability as a rationale for a lifetime of entitlements. This expectation brings its own negative consequences. For example, while it is true that many colleges offer accommodations to students with disabilities under Section 504 of the Rehabilitation Act, the extensive supports of special education required under IDEA generally do not apply to colleges and universities. Thus many students with disabilities, having grown used to special accommodations in primary and secondary schools, are confronted with a harsher reality when they enter college or the workforce.

Take, for example, the case of *Bartlett v. New York Board of Law Examiners* (1997). In this case, Marilyn Bartlett, a former special-education student who had failed to pass the New York bar exam on five previous occasions, argued that she was entitled to unlimited time to take the bar exam because her reading disorder qualified her for special accommodations under the Americans with Disabilities Act. The U.S. Second Court of Appeals subsequently ruled that she was not entitled to unlimited time to take the bar exam because, as evidenced by the fact that she had standardized reading test scores in the average range, she had successfully compensated for her reading disability.

What this case illustrates is that special education has largely lost sight of the appropriate "end game." As originally intended, IDEA was designed to integrate children with special needs into the mainstream of American life. Today, in far too many instances, special education serves to separate, not integrate, through the use of exceptional rules and procedures not available to nondisabled students. In effect, special education has ceased to see its mission as teaching compensatory and coping skills so

that students can participate fully in the mainstream of American society. Instead, it encourages a sense of lifetime entitlement to special accommodations.

Three levels of disability

The first step toward reform of special education is to recognize that the system currently includes three fundamentally distinct populations: (1) those with significant developmental disabilities and sensory and physical handicaps; (2) those with milder forms of neurological conditions, such as learning disabilities and attention deficit disorder; and (3) those with conduct or behavioral problems. Currently, despite some carefully developed individual programs, over 90 percent of children in special education receive similar services. The interests of all students would be served if special education were redesigned to better address the very different needs of its subgroups.

The first group, for which the original law was passed, consists of children born with birth defects, serious sensory or physical disabilities, and significant cognitive delays. In the vast majority of such cases, these children are identified as disabled during infancy and the preschool years, frequently by health-care professionals or early-childhood education specialists, and begin receiving intervention services before they enter elementary school. For these children, there is no need for an elaborate identification process within the schools. Long before they enter kindergarten, we know who they are and to a large extent understand their medical, rehabilitation, and educational needs.

The key to educating these students, who comprise fewer than 10 percent of all children in the special-education system, and less than 1 percent of all children in school, is to adequately fund appropriate accommodations (e.g., interpreters for the deaf, curb cuts for those in wheelchairs, books written in Braille for the blind, and so forth), while including them as much as possible in the education mainstream. To a large extent, this is what special education currently provides these students. Their right to have access to a free and appropriate education must be maintained under any change in the structure of special education.

The second, and by far the largest, group of students currently in special education comprises those with mild forms of neurological dysfunction, such as mild mental retardation, learning disabilities, and ADD. The question that needs to be asked about these students, especially given the emphasis under the 1997 IDEA amendments on their inclusion in the regular classroom, is: What is so "special" about the special education they receive?

In many cases, the answer is not much, except that they are classified differently from their peers. Research shows that the most effective educational strategies for this group of students are the same ones that help most students in regular education. These include frequent individualized monitoring and feedback and intensive direct instruction. What this group of special-education students needs is not an entirely different teaching approach or set of strategies, but good teaching—albeit with greater consistency, intensity, and slower pacing than other students are likely to require.

Thus, rather than perpetuating the myth that students with relatively mild disabilities are receiving a different kind of instruction compared to nondisabled students, we should adjust regular education so as to keep these students in the regular classroom. Indeed, Robert Sternberg and Elena Grigorenko of the Yale Child Study Center, as well as Reid Lyon of the National Institutes of Health, assert that reading disabilities, the most common form of learning disability, are the result not so much of neurological dysfunction as of the method by which most schools currently teach reading. If all schools were to teach phonological awareness, sound-symbol relationships, and reading comprehension, and do so effectively and early, most reading problems could be avoided. For those relatively few children who develop reading problems despite this approach, the regular education teacher could implement in-class interventions, perhaps with the assistance of a reading specialist. In this way, reading problems would be addressed in a regular classroom, rather than being referred to special-education programs.

This approach is in marked contrast to the current system, which emphasizes identification rather than intervention, and which hardly involves the classroom teacher. If, for example, a child is falling behind in reading, under the current system a referral is made for testing his reading level and establishing an estimate of his IQ. A psychologist and a reading specialist typically do this evaluation, not the teacher who sees the child each day. From the start, the process is largely disengaged from what goes on in the classroom.

An alternative model would involve a functional analysis of reading done by the teacher, perhaps with the help of a psychologist and reading specialist. Instead of being concerned with documenting an IQ-achievement discrepancy score, time would be spent analyzing the particular reading problem experienced by an individual child. By using actual classroom samples of reading, supplemented by some additional testing materials, the child's reading ability could be assessed in far less time and with far less expense than the current system of formal educational and IQ testing. This model aims at helping the child to develop the skills and coping mechanisms necessary to achieve at higher levels in school, not simply accommodating his disability.

A similar approach could be used for children with ADD and ADHD. A recently published large-scale treatment study of students with ADHD found the best outcomes among those children who received a combination of relatively low doses of medication, a classroom behavior-modification program, and behavioral family therapy to help the parents better manage their child's home behavior. Rather than being taught to rely on medication to manage their symptoms, the children in the combination treatment were taught, both at home and in school, the skills necessary to maintain behavioral control even in the absence of medication. These results suggest that students with ADD would benefit more if schools adopted obvious rules and boundaries with clear consequences for good and bad behavior, rather than relying on medication alone to enhance educational performance.

The third major subgroup of students currently receiving special education comprises those with conduct or behavioral problems. Students with these types of disorders, when seen in the mental-health system, are usually diagnosed as having either "oppositional defiant disorder" or "conduct disorder," characterized by refusals to comply with requests, emotional overreaction to situations, and failure to take responsibility for their own actions.

Effective treatment of these disorders involves making these individuals strictly accountable for their behavior, insisting on compliance with requests, and helping them learn to cope calmly with stressful situations. Unfortunately, once these students are identified as in need of special education, many of the accommodations routinely provided to them—most especially a lowered standard of acceptable behavior—actually undermine these desirable goals. This sets up these students for later failure, as they frequently come to expect the same kinds of accommodations outside the school as well. They will be disappointed, since most non-academic spheres—from job markets to the criminal justice system—are far less accommodating of disruptive behavior.

An alternative approach would be to develop school- and system-wide efforts to reduce these problems overall, rather than classifying and then segregating individual students. For example, staff training for public school teachers and administrators undertaken by the May Institute in New England resulted in a considerable improvement in behavior and a reduction in referrals to special education. In one city, a school-wide program to reinforce compliance with rules resulted in a 40 percent drop in detentions. In a second, the need for special-education placements was reduced almost three-fold after implementation of a positive reinforcement program for rule compliance, at a cost of less than $10 per year per child. At another school, a program incorporating positive reinforcement for compliance and close monitoring of behavior was implemented at a cost of only $30 per elementary school student. The result was a 30 percent reduction in disciplinary referrals to the principal.

It is questionable whether students who persist in defying rules despite such efforts should be included within the framework of special education at all. It is a fine line to distinguish between a psychiatric disorder that can be treated and criminal behavior that should be adjudicated, a distinction made even more difficult in the high school years.

Funding reforms

Currently, schools draw down special-education funds based on the number of students identified as having a qualifying disability under IDEA. As noted earlier, this creates an incentive to identify low-achieving students as disabled. If the current system resulted in substantial improvements in educational outcomes for these students, there would be less need for reform. But evidence is mixed at best as to whether student performance is enhanced by placement in special education.

One reform advocated by some is to move to census-based funding for special education. Under such a scheme, funding for special education would be based not on the number of children identified as in need of special education but on total student enrollment. Census-based funding has the advantage of providing schools with the flexibility to set up school-wide programs to enhance learning and good behavior. (Although the 1997 amendments to the IDEA allowed some movement in this direction, identification and classification remain the focus of the system.) Critics, however, worry that census-based funding provides schools with little incentive to provide the more expensive accommodations and services needed by the severely disabled, and does not necessarily lead to better results for students with disabilities.

Moreover, census-based funding does not take into account differences that may exist across school districts in the percentage of students with severe disabilities requiring intensive special-education services. An imbalance can occur, for example, when parents of severely disabled children move their children into a school district near a specialized medical facility. Even a quirk of fate can cause an overrepresentation of students with severe disabilities in some school districts. For example, a Pennsylvania school district of only 400 K–12 students includes a pair of severely autistic twins and a child with a severe head injury. Under census-based funding, such districts would be unfairly penalized financially. One remedy would be for schools to identify that relatively small group of children who have severe special needs and have state government help fund local programs for this population.

To increase accountability for improving educational outcomes for disabled students, funding could be based on the number of students who achieve the goals set forth in their Individual Education Plans, rather than simply the number of students identified as in need of special education. This, however, may result in the lowering of IEP goals. An alternative would be to use the current state-wide assessment tests and differentiate the scores of students in regular education from the scores of students in special education. Under the assumption that the purpose of special education is to improve the academic performance of these students, schools would be held accountable for measurable gains over time in the special-education population relative to those in regular education.

Reforms with results

Special education today is costly and ineffective. The elaborate eligibility and classification systems set up in response to well-meaning federal legislation have not translated into improved results for students with special needs. Moreover, by focusing on weaknesses and accommodations, we have given these children unreasonable expectations of how the larger community will respond to their academic weaknesses. As a result, many special-education students have a rude awakening in store for them when they arrive at college or enter the job market.

A major overhaul of special education is needed to ensure that the original goal of offering an appropriate education for all children is achieved, while, at the same time, as many students as possible are integrated into the mainstream of American life. To accomplish this, we must first recognize that special education, as currently constructed, really serves three distinct groups of students: those with significant physical, cognitive, and sensory handicaps, those with milder forms of neurological dysfunction such as SLD and ADD, and those with behavioral disorders. An improved education system would take into account the differing needs of these subgroups of special-education students and would encourage the development of coping and compensatory strategies. Our approach to disabilities must be reformed so that the principle of equal access to education translates into better practical results for students with special needs. In short, it is time to make special education "special" once again.

A longer version of this essay appears in Rethinking Special Education for a New Century *(Washington, D.C.: Progressive Policy Institute and Thomas B. Fordham Foundation, 2001).*

Standards for Diverse Learners

*Standards-based lessons create rich and challenging
learning experiences for all students.*

Paula Kluth and Diana Straut

Education standards receive much attention these days from political leaders, parents, and educators. Many of these stakeholders are concerned about what the standards movement means for the pluralistic classroom.

What kind of diversity exists in U.S. classrooms? Every kind.

- Students are no longer either Catholic, Jew, or Protestant; in fact, the fastest growing religion in the United States is Islam (Hodgkinson, 1998).

- Most of the 5.3 million U.S. students with disabilities spend some part of their day in classes with nondisabled students (Kaye, 1997).

- By 1995, bilingual programs were operating in nearly 200 U.S. schools (Rethinking Schools, 1998).

- At least one-third of the school-aged population in the United States is non-white (Marlowe & Page, 1999).

- 43 million people in the United States move every year (Hodgkinson, 1998), creating an increasingly mobile student population.

In addition, trends such as multicultural education, antitracking pedagogy, inclusive education, dual bilingual programs, magnet schools, and multi-age classrooms are contributing to the rich diversity of U.S. schools.

The standards movement will have little meaning if it cannot respond to the needs of all these students. Can we develop standards *and* make curriculum, instruction, and assessment responsive to learning differences?

Five Conditions

Doing so is not only possible, but vitally important; every student must be able to participate in standards-based education. To make standards inclusive, however, educators must support and cultivate five conditions.

- *Standards are developmental and flexible.* Standards should not be a one-size-fits-all approach to education. A student cannot and should not be expected to know and do exactly the same things as his or her peers. Developmental and flexible standards provide different students in the same classroom with opportunities to work on a range of concepts and skills according to individual abilities, needs, and interests (Reigeluth, 1997).

By adopting a personalized approach, teachers can use standards to "allow a range of acceptable performance" so that

> all students may continue to work toward student-outcome goals such as graduation or literacy, but within each goal area knowledge and skill standards may vary based on student-ability levels. (Geenen & Ysseldyke, 1997, p. 222)

For example, students can share how to solve an arithmetic problem in many ways. Some students may use sign language or communication boards to show understanding, others may write a paragraph explaining the process, and still others may express their knowledge through drawings. In addition, students in the same classroom can focus on problems that range in complexity, with some students describing the process for reducing frac-

tions and others designing and explaining binomial equations.

To teach standards effectively in a diverse classroom, educators need to adapt the curriculum to meet the individual needs of learners and make alternatives available for instructional materials, teaching strategies, curricular goals, learning environments, instructional arrangements, and lesson formats (Udvari-Solner, 1996). For example, some students might use protractors and a compass to study obtuse and acute angles, whereas others may need to use a geometry software program. Experiential projects that encourage vocalizing and moving can meet the needs of active students who like to get out of their seats, investigate problems, and manipulate materials.

Some teachers believe that implementing adaptations in a standards-based classroom will diminish curriculum and instruction. The opposite is true. Creative adaptations can make curriculum more relevant, make abstract concepts more concrete, and connect the instructor's teaching style more effectively to students' different learning styles (Udvari-Solner, 1996). The following lesson illustrates how rich and challenging standards-based lessons can be for students with various learning profiles.

> Mr. Lee drafted daily lessons based on the standards he was teaching. For example, Mr. Lee decided to read every other chapter of [a historical novel] aloud to the students. They would read the opposite chapters in partners. He also decided to use learning centers with cooperative groups. Each center focused on an aspect of World War II and engaged students via one of the multiple learning styles. For example, one

of the centers involved journal writing, based on actual diaries from the Holocaust. Another center focused on geography and involved mapping the progress of war based on listening to actual radio broadcasts recorded during World War II. (Fisher & Roach, 1999, p. 18)

Mr. Lee's careful planning and conscientious design of the curriculum and instruction invites all learners to participate in an engaging and age-appropriate curriculum and also responds to a variety of learning styles. Mr. Lee's classroom does not expect one size to fit all students.

- *Standards require a wide range of assessment tools*. Professional literature and the popular media have linked standards with high-stakes testing. Standards and testing, however, are not the same. Educators must separate testing from the standards in conversations, in the design of curriculum, and in classroom instruction.

We believe that high-stakes assessment models are harmful and exclusive. Under the guise of accountability, several U.S. states and some individual school districts have implemented standardized testing programs that sort, eliminate, or stratify students from kindergarten through 12th grade. When students struggle with standardized tests, we only find out that they cannot perform effectively with such an assessment tool. When students do achieve high test scores, we do not necessarily know that they have learned more, learned better, or become more skilled or knowledgeable. These tests provide plenty of information about how skilled students are at taking standardized tests on a given day, but the tests do not provide much information about whether students have actually met the standards.

Standards do need some type of consistent and comprehensive assessment system, however. The most effective way to gather information about what students know and are able to do is to use a range of data collection strategies, including portfolios, interviews, observations, anecdotal records, self-evaluation questionnaires, journals, and learning logs (Lopez-Reyna & Bay, 1997; Pike & Salend, 1995). Students charged with explaining the ideas embodied in the Declaration of Independence, for example, could demonstrate their understanding by interviewing a peer, participating in a group skit, or writing an essay on the topic.

Kentucky has resisted high-stakes testing and has found a way to include all students in the formal assessment process (Kearns, Kleinert, & Kennedy, 1999). Most students in Kentucky undergo both traditional and alternative assessments. Students with significant disabilities participate in the statewide assessment by working on alternative portfolios that are tailored to their needs and strengths. Kentucky designed this range of assessments because many students struggle with traditional assessments and, more important, because a reliance on one kind of assessment does not provide a meaningful analysis of any student's abilities or progress.

In contrast to standardized measures, authentic assessments offer a fuller picture of student learning because they relate directly to what students are learning, are continuous and cumulative, occur during actual learning experiences, are collaborative, and clearly communicate proficiency to all stakeholders (Pike, Compain, & Mumper, 1994; Pike & Salend, 1995; Valencia, 1990). And because standards ask students to perform a range of competencies, we need a range of assessments to measure the learning of these competencies.

- *Standards allow equitable access to meaningful content*. If there were some alternative to standards that could ensure that all students—regardless of learning profile, race, ethnicity, or proficiency in English—had access to challenging academic content, then perhaps we could dismiss the standards movement. The truth is that we have not done a good job of giving all students—particularly those students with unique learning characteristics—access to an appealing, thought-provoking, and stimulating curriculum.

For example, Reese, a student with significant disabilities, works in an inclusive general education 4th grade classroom. While the general education students work in small groups to investigate fossils, Reese sits in the corner of the classroom and completes a counting worksheet with a paraprofessional.

Had Reese been expected to participate in a standards-based curriculum, he could be meeting his individual goals of "interacting appropriately with peers" and "classifying objects by at least three different characteristics." At the same time, he would have the opportunity to use interesting materials, work with peers, and learn about geography and history. Sorting fossils into categories or building a model di-

nosaur with a cooperative group would be both more meaningful and more content-based than filling in a worksheet that taught no science and did nothing to include Reese in the classroom community.

A set of standards, articulated across the state or district, can give parents, teachers, and administrators a common language for talking about student goals and progress. More crucial, attention to a set of common outcomes can serve as a challenge to view students as capable and to respect them with an appropriately rigorous curriculum.

- *It takes a community to implement standards*. Teaching to the standards is part of classroom teachers' responsibilities, but it is not their job alone. Teachers should receive assistance from all stakeholders in the school and community.

Collaboration among general and special educators can provide students with more opportunities to address the standards and to practice related skills. All students benefit from the different teaching approaches, instructional styles, and perspectives offered by two or more educators working in the same classroom (Cook & Friend, 1995).

> The standards movement can provide teachers with a compass for crafting a rich curriculum and appropriate instruction.

Teaming across classrooms can also bring students closer to mastering the standards. For example, one physical education teacher helps kindergarten students recognize shapes by asking students to name the shapes of tumbling mats, hula-hoops, and floor scooters. While students learn new skills like hopping, galloping, and following rules, they are also engaged in an impromptu, cross-curricular, standards-based lesson with almost no up-front planning from the classroom teacher.

Teachers are not the only adults who can support a standards-based curriculum. The school secretary, recess monitor, lunchroom aides, teaching assistants, and family visitors can help. In one school, a custodian practices spelling words with students as they wait in line for lunch. Imagine the benefit of this fun exchange.

Students, the most important stakeholders in the standards movement, often know the least about implementing standards. Teachers should share information about standards in ways that students can understand; students are more likely to hit targets when they can see them (Strong, Silver, & Perini, 1999). Acting as allies in their own learning, students can develop personal strategies for meeting standards, and older students can even assist in developing standards-based lessons.

- *Standards are a catalyst for other reforms.* Some proponents of standards market them as the savior of public education, and many hope that this singular initiative will solve a wide range of educational and societal ills. At the same time, misconceptions about standards—as one-size-fits all, inequitable monsters that subject students and teachers to high-stakes tests—are creating a backlash that could reduce educators' commitment to designing learning opportunities for all students.

Standards are not the only route to educational excellence, but they can help us address the most pressing issues that stand in the way of students having a quality educational experience. For standards to work, schools need caring learning communities; skilled and responsive teachers; adequate financial, human, and material resources; effective partnerships with families; and concerned and visionary leadership. The standards movement should motivate political leaders to work for increased funding, smaller class sizes, better staff development opportunities, increased teacher planning time, and more social supports in schools, such as counselors and family liaisons.

The standards movement can provide teachers with a compass for crafting a rich curriculum and appropriate instruction, offering new opportunities and setting high expectations for all students in the multicultural, heterogeneous, dynamic classrooms of the 21st century.

References

Cook, L., & Friend, M. (1995). Coteaching: Guidelines for creating effective practices. *Focus on Exceptional Children, 28*(3), 1–15.

Fisher, D., & Roach, V. (1999). *Opening doors: Connecting students to curriculum, classmates, and learning.* Colorado Springs, CO: PEAK Parent Center.

Geenen, K., & Ysseldyke, J. E. (1997). Educational standards and students with disabilities. *The Educational Forum, 61*(1), 220–229.

Hodgkinson, H. L. (1998). Demographics of diversity for the 21st century. *The Education Digest, 64*(1), 4–7.

Kaye, H. S. (1997). Education of children with disabilities. *Disability Statistics Abstracts, 19.* San Francisco: Disability Statistics Center.

Kearns, J. F., Kleinert, H. L., & Kennedy, S. (1999). We need not exclude anyone. *Educational Leadership, 56*(6), 33–38.

Lopez-Reyna, N. A., & Bay, M. (1997). Enriching assessment: Using varied assessments for diverse learners. *Teaching Exceptional Children, 29*(4), 33–37.

Marlowe, B. A., & Page, M. L. (1999). Making the most of the classroom mosaic: A constructivist perspective. *Multicultural Education, 6*(4), 19–21.

Pike, K., Compain, R., & Mumper, J. (1994). *New connections: An integrated approach to literacy.* New York: Harper Collins.

Pike, K., & Salend, S. J. (1995). Authentic assessment strategies: Alternatives to norm-referenced testing. *Teaching Exceptional Children, 28*(1), 15–20.

Reigeluth, C. M. (1997). Educational standards: To standardize or to customize learning? *Phi Delta Kappan, 79*, 202–206.

Rethinking Schools. (1998). Number of language-minority students skyrockets. *Rethinking Schools Online, 12.* Milwaukee, WI: Rethinking Schools. Available: www.rethinkingschools.org/Archives/12_03/langsid.htm

Strong, R., Silver, H., & Perini, M. (1999). Keeping it simple and deep. *Educational Leadership, 56*(6). 22–24.

Udvari-Solner, A. (1996, July). Examining teacher thinking: Constructing a process to design curricular adaptations. *Remedial and Special Education, 17*, 245–254.

Valencia, S. (1990). A portfolio approach to classroom reading assessment: The why, whats, and hows. *The Reading Teacher, 43*(4), 338–340.

Authors' note: An expanded version of this article will appear in *Access to Academics for ALL Students* by P. Kluth, D. Straut, & D. Biklen (Eds.) (Mahwah, NJ: Lawrence Erlbaum Associates Publishers, in press).

Paula Kluth (pkluth@syr.edu) and **Diana Straut** (dmstraut@syr.edu) are Assistant Professors of Teaching and Leadership, Syracuse University, 150 Huntington Hall, Syracuse, NY 13244.

More Choices For Disabled Kids

Lessons from abroad

By Lewis M. Andrews

If THE OPPONENTS of school choice could have their way, the national debate over the use of public money to subsidize private schooling would turn on the subject of special education. With research demonstrating the overall success of school voucher programs in Milwaukee and Cleveland, and with the constitutional issue of public funding of religiously affiliated schools headed for resolution in a seemingly God-tolerant Supreme Court, defenders of the educational status quo have been reduced to fanning fears that government support of greater parental choice would transform public schools into dumping grounds for difficult-to-educate students.

Sandra Feldman, president of the American Federation of Teachers, repeatedly warns that, with private education more accessible to the poor and middle class, good students will "flee" to independent and parochial schools, leaving behind those kids who are physically and emotionally handicapped, are hyperactive, or have been involved with the juvenile justice system. "[P]rivate schools... don't have to take [the learning-disabled]," agrees Tammy Johnson of the liberal activist group Wisconsin Citizen Action, so public schools would be left "to deal with those children." Even if private schools were required to take a certain percentage of disabled students, adds *Rethinking Schools*, an online publication of teachers opposed to school choice, they "tend not to provide needed services for children with special education needs or for children who speak English as a second language." NAACP president Kweisi Mfume predicts that the true cost of private education will always exceed what the government can afford to cover, so "those in the upper- and middle-income brackets will be helped the most... as long as their kids don't have personal, behavioral, or educational challenges that cause the private school to pass them by."

Given the large number of parents who have come to rely on special education services provided through America's public schools, this strategy of conjuring a worst-case scenario for learning-disabled students would at first appear a promising one. According to the *Seventeenth Annual Report to Congress on the Implementation of the Individuals with Disabilities Education Act*, over 5.37 million children—97 percent of American students diagnosed with "special needs"—currently participate in public school special education programs; their parents, many of whom have become adept at using the legal system to access an estimated $32 billion in annual services, are a potent political force. The vast majority of these parents have come to believe that their own son or daughter benefits most from being educated in the same classes as normal students—a remedial philosophy known as "inclusion"—and would vigorously oppose any policy that threatens to isolate special-needs children in separate schools for the learning-disabled.

Over 5.37 million children participate in public school special education programs; their parents are a potent political force.

The argument that school choice must inevitably create special education ghettos would appear to have been strengthened by the recent adoption of market-based education reforms in New Zealand. In the late 1980s, that country's Labour government undertook a sweeping reorganization of its highly centralized education system, replacing the Department of Education and its 4,000 employees with a new Ministry of Education staffed by only 400 people and putting each local school under the control of a community board of trustees. At the same time, the government abolished school zoning, allowing children to transfer freely between schools, even to private schools, at state expense.

A recent book on these New Zealand reforms by school choice opponents Edward Fiske and Helen Ladd, *When Schools Compete: A Cautionary Tale*, makes much of a flaw in the initial legislation, which permitted the more popular public schools to reject students who would be costly to educate or whose disabilities might drag down the test averages. The authors argue that this "skimming" or "creaming" of the better students—which did happen in some cases—is an inevitable consequence of any school choice program, a conclusion widely publicized in the United States by our teachers union.

Yet a closer look at how learning-disabled students are actually faring under a variety of school choice programs worldwide suggests that the special education card may not play out exactly as the opponents of market-based education reform are hoping. Take the case of New Zealand itself, which has largely remedied its original legislation with two amendments: a 1999 supplemental voucher program targeted at the country's indigenous population, the Maori, and a law requiring all schools accepting state funds to adopt a non-discriminatory admissions policy. Under the new Special Education 2000 policy, schools also receive supplemental funding for each learning-disabled child they take in; principals are free to spend the money on what they and the child's parents determine are the most appropriate services. And if the special-needs child leaves the school for any reason, the supplemental funding follows the child to his or her new placement. As a result of these modifications to the initial law, school choice now enjoys nearly universal public support, says Roger Moltzen, director of special education programs in the Department of Education at New Zealand's University of Waikato, and "is unlikely to be repealed."

The Dutch experience

To SEE MORE CLEARLY the impact of school choice on the treatment of learning disabilities, it is useful to compare the experience of three northern European countries: the Netherlands, Sweden, and Denmark. Each has adopted school choice as part of its national education policy, but with very different provisions in the area of special education. Consider first the Netherlands, where public funding of parental choice has been national policy since 1917 and where almost two-thirds of Dutch students attend private schools.

Until about 15 years ago, universal school choice for mainstream students coexisted with a separate, complex, and cumbersome arrangement for educating the learning-disabled. The Dutch had actually maintained 14 separate school systems, each geared to a particular learning disability—deafness, physical handicaps, mild mental retardation, severe mental retardation, multiple disabilities, and so on—and each mimicking as closely as possible the grade levels of conventional public and private schools.

This separate-but-parallel system did employ private providers; it also tested children regularly to determine whether any might be eligible for transfer to mainstream

schools. But by the late 1980s the Dutch began to notice a disturbing increase in the percentage of pupils classified as learning-disabled. (The number of learning-disabled students actually remained constant, but this represented a sharp percentage increase, given the steady decline in the total number of school-age children.) There was widespread concern that the special education bureaucracy was expanding its services at the expense of children with mild-to-moderate learning problems, who were not being adequately integrated into mainstream society. The key to reform, many believed, was to create a financial structure that gave parents of special-needs children the same educational choices as other parents.

Under a "Going to School Together" policy adopted by the Netherlands in 1990, it became the stated intention of the Ministry of Education that parents of children with disabilities should… be able to choose between [any] ordinary or a special school for their child." Children who required additional services for serious learning disabilities were awarded "a personal budget," which under Dutch law parents could spend at either a special or a mainstream school. To ensure equality of opportunity for all students, supplemental funding was provided to both public and private schools in economically depressed districts, where the percentage of learning-disabled students tends to be higher.

Today the Dutch educational structure enjoys strong support from all political quarters, but especially from advocates of greater inclusion for the learning-disabled. Already the number of separate special school systems has been reduced from 14 to only four.

The Swedes and the Danes

COMPARE THE EVOLUTION of special education services in the Netherlands with Sweden, which in March 1992 adopted a "Freedom of Choice and Independent Schools" bill. It gave parents "the right and opportunity to choose a school and education for one's children" by granting all independent schools a municipal subsidy equal to 85 percent of the public school per-pupil cost multiplied by that private or parochial school's enrollment. Independent schools that received this funding were free to emphasize a particular teaching method, such as Montessori, an ethnic affiliation, or even a religious affiliation—but all had to be licensed by the national authority, Skolverket.

Like the Dutch, the Swedes had adopted a universal choice policy, but with one important limitation: The parents of special education students were not effectively granted the same freedom as parents of normal children. This omission was due in large part to Sweden's long history of pedagogic paternalism, which for decades had lowered testing standards, altered textbooks, and micromanaged both classroom and extracurricular activities—all in an effort to avoid making the learning-disabled feel in any way inferior. ("A handicap," according to official publications of the Swedish National Agency for Special Needs Education, "is not tied to an individual but is created by the demands, expectations, and attitudes of the environment.") When the Swedes finally adopted school choice for mainstream children, they were reluctant to risk letting learning-disabled students "flounder" in this new, more competitive educational marketplace.

The result today is that the majority of Sweden's deaf students are still educated in separate institutions. Other special-needs students, who supposedly have been integrated into the educational mainstream, continue to suffer under a centrally managed system in which support services are negotiated between school principals and municipal finance officers, with parents having little input. In theory, all conventional schools are supposed to have an action plan outlining a program of support for their special-needs students. According to a 1998 study by Sweden's National Agency for Education (NAE), however, only half of the country's schools maintain any such plans and fewer than 20 percent of affected parents feel they are able to participate.

Today the Dutch educational structure enjoys strong support from advocates of greater inclusion for the learning-disabled.

One interesting consequence of this lingering paternalism is that the percentage of Swedish children classified as needing special education services is high relative to other industrialized countries and continues to grow at a disproportionate rate. Between the school years 1992–93 and 1996–97, according to the NAE, the number of students registered in schools for the mentally impaired rose by one-fifth. Furthermore, the severity of disabilities tends to be ranked higher within categories. For example, only 25 percent of Sweden's mentally retarded are considered mild cases, while 75 percent are labeled "moderate-to-severe." In the United States, by way of contrast, the proportions are exactly reversed. To what extent this reflects the failure of Sweden's centralized management of special education—or simply the tendency of a large bureaucracy to expand its client base—is unclear at present, but the failure of Sweden to make school choice truly universal has clearly undermined the government's stated goal of promoting greater inclusion.

Finally we come to Denmark, where political support for private education dates back to 1899 and where 11 percent of students attend more than 400 private schools with municipal governments covering 80–85 percent of the cost. Compared to Sweden and the Netherlands, the Danish education ministry has the longest history of, in its own words, letting "resources follow the [special-needs] child." Parents normally have the final say over what school their learning-disabled son or daughter attends, and if an independent school is chosen, the Ministry of Education pays a sum per pupil to the receiving school, with the student's hometown ultimately reimbursing the ministry. The Ministry of Education provides supplemental resources—such as classroom aids, extra courses, and after-hours tutoring—through special grants on a case-by-case basis.

The startling result is that only 0.7 percent of Denmark's 80,000 learning-disabled students are confined to specialized institutions—as compared to five times that percentage in the United States. The Paris-based Organization for Economic Cooperation and Development (OECD), which tracks special education statistics internationally, has praised the Danes for their exceptionally "strong commitment to inclusive education" and for years has held up Denmark's approach to schooling as a model to the rest of the world.

One obvious conclusion to be drawn from the three-way comparison of the Netherlands, Sweden, and Denmark—as well as from the experience of New Zealand—is that inclusion is not only possible under school choice, but with the right policy adjustments, may succeed to an extent not even imagined by American educators. The critical variable appears to be the willingness of legislators to extend freedom of choice to all parents, including the parents of the learning-disabled. In Australia, a school choice country where supplemental funding to support special education is provided to both private and public schools by the national government—but where individual territories have wide discretion in directing how the money is spent—those regions which provide the most flexibility to parents of the learning-disabled also have the best record of mainstreaming. From 1990 to 1995, the percentage of special-needs students successfully integrated into schools in New South Wales more than doubled, while the number of Schools for Special Purposes (the Australian euphemism for segregated special-needs schools) declined sharply. By contrast, West Australia retained most of its separate schools during that same period.

Inclusion is not only possible under school choice, but may succeed to an extent not even imagined by American educators.

It is also worth noting that, regardless of the degree to which choice has been offered to parents of the learning-disabled, the subsidy of private education in foreign countries has not turned government schools into the "special education ghettos" American critics have predicted; rather it has led to a general increase in standards for all schools. According to studies by the European Agency for Development in Special Needs Education (EADSNE), the choice of an independent school in countries subsidizing private education is based far less on academic status than on a school's denominational affiliation, its political or social leanings, and, in some cases, the school's mix of instructional languages.

In a recently published review of education in Denmark, the Netherlands, and Sweden, EADSNE notes that private schools in these countries are "not generally considered elite" and that attending one confers "no added status or advantages." It is true in the case of the Netherlands that private schools have the legal right to impose admissions criteria, but in practice the vast majority follow an unrestrictive admissions policy. Sweden has seen a large increase in its number of private and religious schools since legalizing choice—an average annual growth of 15 percent—but this is from an extraordinarily low base created by a steeply progressive tax code that, prior to 1992, had made private education prohibitively expensive for all but the wealthiest families. Australia has a number of elite private boarding schools, which cater to parents of children from Hong Kong, Singapore, and Malaysia; but the domestic reality is that nearly half the enrollment in Australia's non-government schools is from families with a combined income of less than $27,000 (U.S.). In none of the 18 countries that in any way subsidize private or parochial education could the increase in the number of independent schools be described as a "massive flight" of the most capable students from public education.

Upon thoughtful consideration, the failure of school choice policies abroad to harm public education is not surprising. In the United States the concept of public funding of private education has become synonymous with the idea of a voucher system whereby parents receive a tuition coupon from the government for each of their children, which they are free to redeem at a school of their choosing. This equivalence between choice and vouchers in the American mind has allowed opponents of school choice to conjure up fearful scenarios in which wealthier families combine vouchers with their own resources to bid up and buy out limited slots at the most prestigious private schools.

There are many ways to finance school choice, with as many protections for the poor and disabled as the state is willing to entertain.

Even if we put aside the appropriate counterargument—namely, that a free education marketplace would create as many good private schools as the public demanded—we have already seen that there are many ways other than vouchers to finance school choice, with as many protections for the poor and disabled as the state is willing to entertain. In Australia, where school choice was actually adopted as a populist reform in 1973 by a liberal-leaning Labor government, subsidies for private education are based on what is called a Social Economic Status (SES) model. Students attending private schools from wealthy towns receive assistance amounting to less than 25 percent of tuition, while students from poorer areas in the western part of the country can be reimbursed up to 97 percent. Technically speaking, school choice refers only to a method for making educators more accountable to parents—by empowering parents to choose their children's

schools—not to any ideological bias involved in selecting among them any options for financing this method.

If there is a cautionary lesson to be learned from the experience of foreign countries, it comes from the United Kingdom, where in 1981 the parliament adopted the Assisted Places Scheme with the aim of providing private school tuition scholarships to 11-, 12-, and 13-year-old children from low-income families. By 1992 there were more than 26,000 voucher students attending almost 300 independent schools throughout England and Wales—and a separate parallel system had been established in Scotland.

Yet in spite of the program's apparent success, the annual enrollment cap of 5,000 was not raised, nor was there a serious effort to include children in their younger, more formative years. Instead, in 1988, Parliament enacted a more limited form of school choice, very similar to what Connecticut Sen. Joseph Lieberman and other Democrats are now advancing in the United States as a "moderate" alternative to a freer education marketplace. Under this "open enrollment" system all students were allowed to transfer between government-run schools on a space-available basis, but no funding could follow a student to private (what the English call "public") or religious schools, thus inhibiting the ability of education entrepreneurs to offer students real academic options.

Britain's attempt to limit parental choice to government schools has created the very special education ghettos that opponents fear.

The result of Britain's attempt to limit parental choice to government schools has been to create the very special education ghettos that opponents of school reform say they are against. "Popular schools in wealthy communities have devised many subtle ways to keep out expensive-to-educate students," observes Philip Garner, research professor in special education at Nottingham Trent University. Children with learning disabilities "are confined to failing schools in poorer districts, such as Liverpool, Tower Hamlets, and Hackney." In a telling indication of popular dissatisfaction with England's "moderate" approach to choice, the number of appeals brought before that country's special education tribunal reached 3 per week in the school year 1995–96. It was not until just before the last election, with polls showing a growing public anger over declining social services, that Parliament finally passed legislation allowing private companies and foundations to take over management of what the tabloids were calling "Britain's sink schools."

Inclusion and achievement

So FAR WE HAVE SEEN that school choice is not only compatible with inclusion but may, under the right circumstances, be the most effective means of implementing it.

Yet social inclusion is not a synonym for academic achievement. How, we must also ask, does a more competitive educational marketplace affect the intellectual development of learning-disabled students?

One clue comes from, of all places, the United States, where the same administrators who oppose choice for mainstream and moderately impaired children in their own schools tend overwhelmingly to favor private placements over public institutions for their towns' most difficult-to-educate students. According to Department of Education statistics, over 2 percent of the nation's learning-disabled population—100,700 students—are contracted out by local school boards to independent institutions, many operated by Catholics, Jews, Mennonites, Quakers, Lutherans, Baptists, Methodists, Presbyterians, and Episcopalians. Ironically, the states that rely most on private providers to teach the severely disabled have been among the staunchest opponents of market-based education reform: California, Connecticut, Illinois, Maryland, Massachusetts, New Jersey, New York, and Rhode Island.

American public school administrators are far less inclined to use private providers to teach students within their own walls; yet when they do, the results are instructive. In the school year 1999–2000, the school board of Hawthorne, California, hired Sylvan Learning Systems to offer remedial reading services to its learning-disabled students, while continuing to tutor normal children with regular teachers. According to the Hawthorne district's own standardized test, the special education students exceeded the gains of the non-special education students by five points for a total Normal Curve Equivalent (NCE) gain of nine. (NCEs are a common standard for measuring student progress in reading.) Special education students who completed a similar program in Compton, California, during the same school year made similar gains.

School systems characterized by multiple service providers and accountability to parents "seem to be the most successful."

The overall academic success of special-needs students in school choice countries has led the European Agency for Development in Special Needs Education to conclude that the policy mechanisms for providing services to the learning-disabled may be just as important to their intellectual and social development as any teaching technique. In its recently published *Seventeen Country Study of the Relationship Between Financing of Special Needs Education and Inclusion*, EADSNE found that monopolistic public school systems characterized by "direct input funding"— that is, upping the budget for every increase in the number of learning-disabled students—produced the least desirable outcomes. Conversely, school systems characterized by multiple service providers, decentralization, accountability to parents, and an emphasis on teaching over such bureaucratic procedures as diagnosis and cate-

gorization "seem to be the most successful" at helping the learning-disabled to grow into happy, productive adults.

Again, it is useful to consider specific countries. In Sweden—where, as we have seen, choice is encouraged only for mainstream students—a telling split has developed in measures of parental satisfaction with the educational system. In 1993, a poll conducted by Sweden's National Agency of Education concluded that "85 percent of Swedes value their new school choice rights," a clear indication that parents of mainstream children were pleased with the academic results. On the other hand, studies by the same agency showed that the confidence of parents of learning-disabled children in Sweden's special education services was eroding at a rapid pace. It is "alarming," concluded the NAE in its 1998 report, *Students in Need of Special Support*, "that parents of more than 100,000 schoolchildren feel that the school system does not have the means to give their children the support they may need."

Halfway around the world in New Zealand, where exceptional efforts have been made in recent years to ensure that special-needs students benefit from school choice, experts such as Dr. David Mitchell of the School of Education at the University of Waikato record significant progress in the treatment of learning disabilities. Over the past three years, he notes, New Zealand's special education system has moved "from being relatively ad hoc, unpredictable, uncoordinated, and nationally inconsistent to being relatively coherent, predictable, integrated, and consistent across the country. It is moving away from... seeing the reasons for failure at school as residing in some defect or inadequacy within the student to seeing it as reflecting a mismatch between individual abilities and environmental opportunities."

In Australia, a 1998 study funded by the national Department of Education, Training, and Youth Affairs found that many intellectually and physically disabled students who received an inclusive education under the nation's school choice program were "achieving in literacy and [math skills] at the same levels as their peers and, in some cases, much better than their classmates." Because the overwhelming percentage of non-government schools in that country are religiously affiliated, the internationally respected Schonell Special Education Research Centre at the University of Queensland has begun a previously unthinkable study to determine the extent to which faith improves academic achievement in the learning-impaired.

Current dissatisfactions

ALL OF WHICH suggests that the more American parents of learning-disabled children become knowledgeable about the benefits of school choice around the world, the more the advocates of the status quo may regret ever trying to exploit the issue of special education in the first place. After all, notes Thomas B. Fordham Foundation president Chester E. Finn, it's not as if parents of learning-disabled children are anywhere near being satisfied with the services public schools now provide. "America's special education program has an urgent special need of its own," he writes. "It is, in many ways, broken." Jay Matthews, education reporter for the *Washington Post*, agrees, noting that journalists, himself included, "have done a terrible job telling this story. Special education systems are often too confusing, too bureaucratic and too bound by privacy rules to yield much useful information." What research is available, he adds, "suggests that the special education system has led to widespread, if well-intentioned, misuse of tax dollars and has failed to help kids."

To appreciate the unexpected way in which parental dissatisfaction with current services may shape domestic education policy, consider the surprising evolution of the "A+ Plan," the statewide voucher program adopted by the Florida legislature in 1999. Although initially regarded by some as a muted reform because children were not entitled to a private education unless their public school had failed to meet minimum academic standards in only two of four years, the law did authorize a sweeping pilot program for learning-disabled students in Sarasota County. Under this test project, the only requirement for a special-needs child to transfer to a private school was that his parents express dissatisfaction over his progress at meeting the goals of his individualized instructional plan.

So popular was the pilot program that just one year later, state senator John McKay was able to pass an amendment to the original A+ Plan, allowing the Sarasota County provision to apply to the entire state. According to the new law, known as the McKay Scholarship Program, private schools taking on a special-needs child could recover from the government from $6,000 to $20,000, depending on the severity of the child's disability. The only caveat was that any school wanting to participate in the program had to accept all learning-disabled applicants. In the school year 2000–01, 105 private schools in 36 of Florida's 67 districts signed up to enroll more than 900 special education students. Over the current academic year (2001–02), Florida state officials estimate the number of learning-disabled students receiving assistance will quadruple to 4,000, while the number of participating schools will triple to more than 300.

Although researchers have yet to identify the precise reasons the expansion of the McKay Scholarship Program

had such easy political sailing, anecdotal evidence suggests strong backing from the largest group of eligible families: those with moderately disabled children who, while continuing to be promoted with their classmates, were nevertheless floundering academically. "My child needed a choice, an alternative. [She] was lost in middle school," says the mother of a scholarship recipient from the western part of the state. "She was held back early on, and the district did not want to keep holding her back, so even though she was not learning, she was moved along." Black clergy from Florida's cities, where the percentage of fourth-graders unable to read can soar as high as 60 percent, were also outspoken advocates of the McKay Scholarship Program.

Interestingly, a similar alliance of middle-class parents and minority clergy seems to have coalesced behind President Bush's recently enacted "No Child Left Behind" education bill. While stripped of its initial tuition voucher proposal for mainstream schools, the legislation nevertheless retained its "supplemental services" provision, which makes parents at over 3,000 poorly performing schools nationwide eligible for federal funding of remedial tutoring at an independent school or even a private company of their choice. Essentially a remedial education voucher program, it lets parents decide how and where the funds will be used.

While the prospect of advocates for the learning-disabled leading the charge for school choice here in the United States will doubtless come as a shock to the teachers unions and their political allies, it is hardly without precedent. Much of the shift toward the privatization of public education in Europe and elsewhere has come from political activism on behalf of special-needs students.

Indeed, it can be argued that opponents of school choice and parents of the learning-disabled were never very likely to stick together in the first place. Unlike mainstream students, most of whom can survive one bad year of mediocre instruction, a special-needs child can be permanently damaged by a single incompetent teacher, whose tenured position is protected by the current public school monopoly. In the end, the parents of learning-disabled students have the same goal as all market-oriented school reformers: to make every educator accountable to the highest possible standards.

Lewis M. Andrews is executive director of the Yankee Institute for Public Policy in Hartford, Connecticut. This study was supported by a grant from the Milbank Foundation for Rehabilitation. Yankee Institute associates John Canali, Douglas Carlson, William Dick, and Douglas Lake provided research assistance.

What's Good?
Suggested Resources for Beginning Special Education Teachers.

"What's good?" "What do I need?" "What will I actually use?"
"What should I buy with my limited budget?"

Sharon A. Maroney

These are the questions most often asked by beginning teachers when seeking advice on acquiring materials and locating resources for classroom use. Faced with too many responsibilities and too little time, wanting to be fully prepared but not knowing exactly how, seeing catalogs filled with teaching materials but having no experience with any, and having limited financial resources, beginning teachers need assistance in selecting teaching resources. Teachers need strategies that are effective, efficient, easy to use, practical, and adaptable. Information must reflect current best practices in education.

SPECIAL EDUCATION TEACHERS CAN DEVELOP PROFESSIONALISM THROUGH MEMBERSHIP IN PROFESSIONAL ORGANIZATIONS AND KNOWLEDGE OF THE LEGAL REQUIREMENTS OF THE FIELD.

This article includes a set of classroom resources identified by experienced teachers as recommended resources for beginning teachers. The resources are grouped into six areas of priority for beginning special education teachers: (a) developing professionalism, (b) basics for effective instruction, (c) academic instruction, (d) cognitive-behavioral instruction, (e) behavioral management, and (f) classroom extras.

Developing Professionalism

We need to view teaching as a profession, not just a job. Teachers continually work to become true professionals by obtaining access to information, keeping current with the developments in the field, and being knowledgeable of what it means to be a professional special educator. Special education teachers can develop professionalism through membership in professional organizations and knowledge of the legal requirements of the field.

As newly established special education professionals, beginning teachers should become members of a professional organization that advocates for special educators, special education, and the students and families who receive special educa-

tion services. With membership in The Council for Exceptional Children (CEC), teachers have access to high-quality, timely information and the CEC Web site (http://www.cec.sped.org); reap the benefits of CEC's advocacy activities; and receive the following publications: *TEACHING Exceptional Children* (6 issues/year), *Exceptional Children* (4 issues/year), *CEC Today* (10 issues/year), and *Research Connections in Special Education* (2 issues/year). Membership in the CEC offers opportunities to become involved in the profession at the local, state, national, and international levels through professional development, leadership, advocacy, publications, and networking activities. Membership is also available in the 17 divisions of CEC, representing areas of interest within special education.

Special education teachers should be proficient in using the resources of the federally-funded Educational Resources Information Center—the ERIC system. This includes knowing how to search the ERIC database and use the resources of the ERIC Clearinghouses. The ERIC Clearinghouse on Disabilities and Gifted Education is located at The Council for Exceptional Children in Reston, VA.

All special education teachers should have copies of current district, state, and federal rules, regulations, and policies for special education. This is especially important for beginning teachers, who are expected to be knowledgeable of and adhere to rules and regulations immediately. As soon as beginning teachers accept positions, they should contact the director of special education within the school district, the intermediate special education agency, and the state department of special education to request and obtain this information. All teachers need to have their own copy of the rules and regulations so [as] not to rely on others for the interpretation of or access to these documents.

THE WEB SITE OF THE U.S. OFFICE OF SPECIAL EDUCATION PROGRAMS PROVIDES ACCESS TO INFORMATION ON FEDERAL INITIATIVES, LEGAL ISSUES, AND NATIONAL RESOURCES IN SPECIAL EDUCATION.

The book, *IDEA 1997: Let's Make It Work* (1998) uses a question-and-answer format to present the content of the Individuals with Disabilities Education Act (IDEA) of 1997. Recently a first-year special education teacher shared that although she had prepared for and completed several individualized education program (IEP) meetings, she still felt that the other professionals on the IEP team understood the IEP process much better than she did. This teacher found *IDEA 1997: Let's Make It Work* (1998) to be especially useful, understandable, and full of the information she needed.

The compact disk, *Discover IDEA CD '99* (1999), allows teachers to access the actual text of the IDEA 1997, in addition to providing a frequently asked questions (FAQs) section and

keyword search capability. This resource is especially useful for locating exact wording and references to specific topics throughout the law. Teachers can visit the IDEA Practices Web site (http://www.ideapractices. org) to preview this CD and learn about the IDEA Partnerships Projects of the U.S. Department of Education.

Several Web sites devoted to special education currently exist on the Internet. The National Center for Children and Youth with Disabilities (NICHY) Web site (http://www. nichy.org) and Special Education Resources on the Internet (SERI; http// www.hood.edu/seri) are two teacher- and parent-friendly Internet resources for information on special education and people with disabilities. The NICHY site distributes numerous publications and information sheets on different disabilities and topics in special education. SERI posts information and links to several other Web sites on special education and related topics. The Web site of the U.S. Office of Special Education Programs (http://www.ed.gov/ offices/OSERS/OSEP/index.html) provides access to information on federal initiatives, legal issues, and national resources in special education.

The *Survival Guide for the First Year Special Education Teacher* (Cohen, Gale, & Meyer, 1994) is a teacher-friendly book that many beginning teachers have found extremely helpful. Teachers especially liked the use of lists and the good basic advice and information. Survival topics include shunning the need to be superman or superwoman, preparing emergency lesson plans for when all else fails, the dos for working with general educators, and hints for positive report card comments. This resource can provide an informal approach to address the responsibilities required of special education teachers.

Effective Instruction

Research has identified several strategies that constitute effective teach-

ing that can be applied to academic and behavioral instruction; special education and general education classrooms; and individual, small-group, and large-group instruction. Because students currently identified as needing special education services typically experience severe deficits in several academic and behavioral skills, teachers need to be knowledgeable of and able to implement effective teaching strategies.

The First Days of School: How to Be an Effective Teacher (Wong & Wong, 1998) is an excellent resource for first-year teachers and one that experienced teachers will use throughout their careers. The authors identify three characteristics of effective teachers: holding positive expectations for student success; being good classroom managers; and designing lessons to help students teach mastery. The book presents comprehensive, almost step-by-step information to enable teachers to attain all three characteristics. Sections titled "Your very first priority when class starts is to get the students to work" and "Are you an invitational or disinvitational teacher?" are examples of the common sense approach of this book.

An extensive collection of research-based techniques is presented in *Strategies and Tactics for Effective Instruction* (Algozzine, Ysseldyke, & Elliott, 1997) and *Time Savers for Educators* (Elliott, Algozzine, & Ysseldyke, 1997). The strategies are presented to address four components of effective instruction: planning instruction, managing instruction, delivering instruction, and evaluating instruction. Teachers will especially appreciate the reproducibles provided so strategies can be used immediately and with little preparation. An additional resource on research-based teaching strategies is the Educational Resources Information Center Clearinghouse on Teaching and Teacher Education (ERIC—on the Web: http://www.ericsp.org). The ERIC Clearinghouse, a program of the National Library of Education, U.S. Department of Education, is the largest database on teaching and teacher education.

THE MOST IMPORTANT ACADEMIC RESOURCES SPECIAL EDUCATION TEACHERS MUST HAVE ARE THE CURRENT GENERAL EDUCATION CURRICULAR MATERIALS, INCLUDING ALL STUDENT MATERIALS, TEACHER'S MANUALS, AND ANCILLARY MATERIALS.

Effective instruction also requires the effective use of time. As many special education teachers know, the time students spend waiting (wait time) can easily turn into disruption time. Beginning teachers can review resources such as *Five-Minute Warm-ups for the Middle Grades: Quick and Easy Activities to Reinforce Basic Skills* (Green, Schlichting, & Thomas, 1994) and create an index card file of activities that can quickly engage students during those 5–10 minutes of wait time. Although the title indicates application to the middle grades, the activities in this book can be adapted easily for other ability levels, grade levels, or content. This is a helpful resource for any teacher looking to decrease waiting time, increase student engagement, and prevent disruptive behavior.

Academic Instruction

Unfortunately for some beginning teachers, teacher training programs in special education often include limited course work in teaching methods and materials in academic curricula areas, especially science, social students, language arts, and the general education curricula. As a result, special education teachers frequently feel unprepared to teach all the academic content areas they are required to teach. Therefore, many beginning teachers must prepare themselves for this teaching responsibility.

The most important academic resource special education teachers must have are the current general education curricular materials, including all student materials, teacher's manuals, and ancillary materials. These materials are invaluable for beginning teachers in that they include a scope and sequence of skills to be taught, comprehensive lesson plans, and a variety of assessment tools. Many current curricula also include instructional strategies and accommodations for students with special needs. As mandated by IDEA 1997, all students receiving special education must have access to the general education curriculum. Special education teachers need to approach their school administrators and request their own copies of these materials. Limited access to these resources will decrease the effectiveness and efficiency of instruction.

TeachNet.com (http://www.teachnet.com) and Education World (http://www.education-world.com) are two Web sites suggested for teachers interested in accessing teaching resources on the Internet. These interactive sites are designed for classroom teachers and provide a variety of resources for teachers with varying interests and needs. TeachNet.com offers lesson plans, how-to information sheets, and a teacher-to-teacher message center. Education World offers resources and information in general education and special education, across curriculum areas, and links to related sites. Both of these sites are easy to navigate, and the information is clearly presented.

Motivating students is a challenge for all teachers, especially when students have had a history of academic difficulty. *If You're Going to Teach Kids to Write, You've Gotta Have This Book* (Frank, 1995) is an extremely entertaining approach to teaching and motivating students to write. This book is filled with creative, fun, motivating writing activities and illustrations while at the same time presenting a sound process for developing writing skills. A second re-

source to help motivate students to write is the *Scholastic Rhyming Dictionary* (Young, 1994). Some teachers have commented that after some of their students were introduced to this book, the students couldn't wait to use this dictionary to write rap lyrics in their free time.

TEACHERS NEED STRATEGIES THAT ARE EFFECTIVE, EFFICIENT, EASY TO USE, PRACTICAL, AND ADAPTABLE.

Cognitive-Behavioral Instruction

Cognitive-behavioral instruction involves teaching students to think before they act and to become aware of the role their thoughts play in determining their behavior. Many special education teachers successfully change student behavior by rewarding desired behavior, and many students demonstrate certain types of behavior in efforts to earn rewards. But what happens when there isn't someone available to reward behavior? Cognitive-behavioral instruction, on the other hand, enables students to control their own behavior independently and throughout their lives. The following are four cognitive-behavioral instruction curricula. Beginning teachers are advised to select one of these curricula and to use it earnestly. Cutting and pasting activities from different curricula is not recommended.

1. Clear Thinking (Nichols, 1998) is an instructional curriculum designed to teach adolescents and young adults cognitive restructuring for clearer and more logical thinking, as based on the rational emotive therapy model. Teachers of students with behavioral disorders have been pleased with this program and with how well students have received it. This program includes an instructor's guide, *Clear Thinking: Talking Back to Whispering Shadows* (Nichols, 1998) and a student text, *Whisper-*

ing Shadows; Think clearly & Claim Your Personal Power (Nicholas & Shaw, 1998).

2. For the elementary grades, *Thinking, Feeling, Behaving* (Vernon, 1989a, and 1989b) is a curriculum also based on rational emotive therapy. It is designed to teach students the connections between their thoughts, feelings, and behavior, and that rational thoughts lead to rational feelings and rational behaviors. This curriculum is available at two grade levels: *Thinking, Feeling, Behaving: An Emotional Education Curriculum for Children* (Vernon, 1989b) and *Thinking, Feeling, Behaving: An Emotional Education Curriculum for Adolescents* (Vernon, 1989a).

3. *I Can Problem Solve: An Interpersonal Cognitive Problem-Solving Program* (Shure, 1992), is an instructional curriculum containing 77 lessons designed to teach students how to think and to use thinking to solve their own problems. This program is available at three grade levels: pre-school, kindergarten and primary, and intermediate elementary grades.

4. The skillstreaming curriculum by Goldstein and McGinnis (1997) is a complete prosocial skills curriculum following a direct instruction approach involving teacher modeling and student role playing. Each curriculum provides teachers with assessment tools, strategies for conducting group lessons, and activities for generalization. This curriculum is available at three grade levels: *Skillstreaming the Elementary School Child* (McGinnis & Goldstein, 1997), *Skillstreaming the Adolescent* (Goldstein & McGinnis, 1997); and *Skillstreaming in Early Childhood* (McGinnis & Goldstein, 1997).

Behavior Management

When asked to identify the most important factor related to the success or failure of beginning teachers, school administrators frequently cite behavior management. Beginning special education teachers must be prepared with classwide and individual behavior management techniques that they can effectively and efficiently use. Teachers have found these resources helpful:

- *The Tough Kid Book* (Rhode, Jenson, & Reavis, 1993) materials provide beginning teachers with the basics in behavior management in a teacher-friendly, ready-to-use format. Both beginning and practicing teachers have found these materials extremely useful. *The Tough Kid Book* (Rhode, Jenson, & Reavis) presents several practical strategies to increase or decrease student behavior, as well as strategies for academic instruction. *The Tough Kid Tool Box* (Jenson, Rhode, & Reavis, 1994) provides the reproducibles for the implementation of the strategies presented in *The Tough Kid Book*.

- *The Teacher's Encyclopedia of Behavior Management: 100 Problems and 500 Plans* (Sprick & Howard, 1995) presents in-depth descriptions of three or more interventions for each of 100 kinds of common problem behavior. The step-by-step descriptions, with sample recording and evaluation materials, provide beginning teachers with the information they need to implement each intervention. The book serves as a model of the comprehensive application of several behavioral change strategies.

TEACHER TRAINING PROGRAMS IN SPECIAL EDUCATION OFTEN INCLUDE LIMITED COURSE WORK IN TEACHING METHODS AND MATERIALS IN ACADEMIC CURRICULA AREAS, ESPECIALLY SCIENCE, SOCIAL STUDENTS, LANGUAGE ARTS, AND THE GENERAL EDUCATION CURRICULA.

- *The Pre-referral Intervention Manual: The Most Common Learning and Behavior Problems Encountered in the Educational Environment* (McCarney & Cummins, 1988) is a book of ideas for classroom interventions. It can be extremely helpful when brainstorming ideas for prereferral interventions, classroom accommodations, and behavioral interventions for students. Included in this book are 193 academic and social behavior problems with approximately 20 or more intervention suggestions for each.

Internet Addresses for Suggested Web Sites

The Council for Exceptional Children (CEC): www.cec.sped.org
ERIC Clearinghouse on Disabilities and Gifted Education: www.ericec.sped.org
ERIC Clearinghouse on Teaching and Teacher Education: http://www.ericsp.org
Education World: http://www.education-world. com
IDEA Practices: http://www. ideapractices.org
National Information Center for Children and Youth with Disabilities (NICHY): http://www.nichy.org
Special Education Resources on the Internet (SERI): http://www.hood. edu/seri
TeachNet.com: http://www.teachnet. com

Classroom Extras

School should be academically focused, challenging, supportive, exciting, and fun. With the never-ending demands faced by beginning teachers and the uncertainty that goes along with beginning a career, some teachers forget to have fun in the classroom or feel they don't have the time to try something new. On the other hand, some very enthusiastic teachers quickly burn out by trying to do something new and different each day. Here's a more re-

Recommended Resources for Beginning Teachers

Clear Thinking: Talking Back to Whispering Shadows: Instructor's Guide (Nichols, 1998). ISBN 0-9649142-2-0, $30.

The Council for Exceptional Children (CEC). Membership information, 1-800-232-7733, annual fee $75–$85.

Discover IDEA CD '99 (1999). Available from IDEA Partnerships Projects, http://www.ideapractices.org, $10.

The First Days of School: How to Be an Effective Teacher (Wong & Wong, 1998). ISBN 0-9629360-0-0-6, $30.

Five-Minute Warmups for the Middle Grades: Quick and Easy Activities to Reinforce Basic Skills (Green, Schlichting, & Thomas, 1994). ISBN 0-86530-263-4, $10

I Can Problem Solve: An Interpersonal Cognitive Problem-Solving Program for the Intermediate Elementary Level (Shure, 1992). ISBN 0-87822-340-1, $40.

I Can Problem Solve: An Interpersonal Cognitive Problem-Solving Program for the Kindergarten and Primary Level (Shure, 1992). ISBN 0-87822-339-8, $40.

I Can Problem Solve: An Interpersonal Cognitive Problem-Solving Program for the Preschool Level (Shure, 1992). ISBN 0-87822-338-X, $40.

IDEA 1997: Let's Make It Work (1998). ISBN 0-86586-303-2. Available from CEC, 1-800-232-7733, $15.

If You're Going to Teach Kids to Write, You've Gotta Have This Book (Frank, 1995). ISBN 0-86530-317-7, $15.

Instructor, published by Scholastic Inc., 1-800-544-2917, $15 per year.

The Laughing Classroom: Everyone's Guide to Teaching with Humor and Play (Loomans & Kolberg, 1993), ISBN # 0-915811-44-8, $15.

The Pre-referral Intervention Manual: The Most Common Learning and Behavior Problems Encountered in the Educational Environment (McCarney & Cummins, 1988). ISBN 1-87837-211-4, $30.

Scholastic Rhyming Dictionary (Young, 1994). ISBN 0-590-49461-9, $13.

Skillstreaming the Adolescent (Goldstein & McGinnis, 1997). ISBN 0-87822-369-X, $18.

Skillstreaming in Early Childhood (McGinnis & Goldstein, 1997). ISBN 0-87822-321-5, $14.

Skillstreaming the Elementary School Child (McGinnis & Goldstein, 1997). ISBN 0-87822-372-X, $18.

Strategies and Tactics for Effective Instruction (Algozzine, Ysseldyke, & Elliott, 1997). ISBN 1-57035-119-8, $30.

Survival Guide for the First Year Special Education Teacher (Cohen, Gale, & Meyer, 1994). ISBN 0-86586-256-7. Available from CEC, 1-800-232-7733, $12.

The Teacher's Encyclopedia of Behavior Management: 100 Problems and 500 Plans (Sprick & Howard, 1995). ISBN 1-57035-031-0, $40.

Teaching Tolerance, available from Teaching Tolerance, 400 Washington Avenue, Montgomery, AL 36104, at no cost.

Thinking, Feeling, Behaving: An Emotional Education Curriculum for Adolescents (Vernon, 1989). ISBN 0-87822-306-1, $26.

Thinking, Feeling, Behaving: An Emotional Education Curriculum for Children (Vernon, 1989). ISBN 0-87822-305-3, $26.

Time Savers for Educators (Elliott, Algozzine, & Ysseldyke, 1997). ISBN 1-57035-118-X, $20.

The Tough Kid Book (Rhode, Jenson, & Reavis, 1993). ISBN 0-944584-55-1, $20.

The Tough Kid Tool Box (Jenson, Rhode, & Reavis, 1994). ISBN 1-57035-000-0, $20.

Whispering Shadows: Think Clearly & Claim Your Personal Power: Student Text (Nichols & Shaw, 1998). ISBN 0-9649142-1-2, $15

Note: All costs are approximate.

---

alistic plan for using the resources described in this section: First, plan one night each month to read one magazine, book chapter, or other resource; second, select one new idea or activity to try that month. Selecting, planning for, and implementing one new idea each month is a reasonable and achievable goal for a beginning teacher.

SCHOOL SHOULD BE ACADEMICALLY FOCUSED, CHALLENGING, SUPPORTIVE, EXCITING, AND FUN.

Of all the teacher-oriented magazines, *Instructor* consistently has much to offer beginning teachers: high-quality content, noteworthy educators as authors, and attractive and teacher-friendly presentation. *Instructor* magazine, available at the primary or intermediate level, includes monthly feature articles, posters for classroom use, student activity sheets, and information related to teachers and teaching. *Teaching Tolerance* magazine includes many articles on teacher and school developed programs to promote tolerance toward all types of diversity. Of special interest are the articles describing actual teachers and their projects, programs, and student activities. Beginning teachers find the activities and resources especially helpful for gathering ideas for culturally diverse classrooms.

The Laughing Classroom: Everyone's Guide to Teaching with Humor and Play (Loomans & Kolberg, 1993) is a collection of the authors' teaching experiences and reflections with several ideas for classroom activities. After an experienced special education teacher described how her attitude toward laughter and fun in classroom had changed as a result of this book, several other teachers purchased *The Laughing Classroom* and had similar positive experiences. This resource encourages teachers to reflect on their teaching and offers suggestions for change.

Final Thoughts

This article has described many useful resources for beginning teachers;

but these teachers will find themselves inundated with additional resources they will be *required* to use in the classroom. These materials will include curricula, benchmarks or standards, discipline plans, and other resources established by the school, district, or state. Beginning teachers should first consult building administrators, directors or coordinators of special education, and teaching colleagues to obtain these required resources and implementation information.

As beginning teachers obtain and use various resources, they should remember that *more is not always better*. It is preferable to have a few excellent resources and to study and use them completely and correctly, rather than to have several resources and become overwhelmed or confused by all the ideas presented.

References

Algozzine, B., Ysseldyke, J. E., & Elliott, J. (1997). *Strategies and tactics for effective instruction*. Longmont, CO: Sopris West.

Cohen, M. K., Gale, M., & Meyer, J. M. (1994). *Survival guide for the first year special education teacher* (Rev. ed.) Reston, VA: The Council for Exceptional Children.

The Council for Exceptional Children. (1998). *IDEA 1997: Let's make it work*. Reston, VA: Author.

Elliott, J., Algozzine, B., & Ysseldyke, J. E. (1997). *Time savers for educators*. Longmont, CO: Sopris West.

Frank, M. (1995). *If you're going to teach kids to write, you've gotta have his book* (2nd ed.). Nashville, TN: Incentive Publications.

Goldstein, A. P., & McGinnis, E. (1997). *Skillstreaming the adolescent* (2nd ed.). Champaign, IL: Research Press.

Green, B., Schlichting, S., & Thomas, M. E. (1994). *Five-minute warmups for the middle grades: Quick and easy activities to reinforce basic skills*. Nashville, TN: Incentive Publications.

Jenson, W., Rhode, G., & Reavis, H. K. (1994). *The tough kid tool box*. Longmont, CO: Sopris West.

Loomans, D., & Kolberg, K. (1993). *The laughing classroom: Everyone's guide to teaching with humor and play*. Tiburon, CA: H. J. Kramer Inc.

McCarney, S. B., & Cummins, K. K. (1988). *The pre-referral intervention manual: The most common learning and behavior problems encountered in the educational environment*. Columbia, MO: Hawthorne Press.

McGinnis, E., & Goldstein, A. P. (1997). *Skillstreaming the elementary school child* (2nd ed.). Champaign, IL: Research Press.

McGinnis, E., & Goldstein, A. P. (1997). *Skillstreaming in early childhood* (2nd ed.). Champaign, IL: Research Press.

Nichols, P. (1998). *Clear Thinking: Talking back to whispering shadows*. Iowa City, IA: River Lights Publishing.

Nichols, P., & Shaw, M. (1998). *Whispering shadows: Think clearly & claim your personal power*. Iowa City, IA: River Lights Publishing.

Rhode, G., Jenson, W., & Reavis, H. K. (1993). *The tough kid book*. Longmont, CO: Sopris West.

Shure, M. B. (1992). *I can problem solve: An interpersonal cognitive problem-solving program*. Champaign, IL: Research Press.

Sprick, R. S., & Howard, L. M. (1995). *The teacher's encyclopedia of behavior management: 100 problems and 500 plans*. Longmont, CO: Sopris West.

Vernon, A. (1989a). *Thinking, feeling, behaving: An emotional education curriculum for adolescents*. Champaign, IL: Research Press.

Vernon, A. (1989b). *Thinking, feeling, behaving: An emotional education curriculum for children*. Champaign, IL: Research Press.

Wong, H. K., & Wong, R. T. (1998). *The first days of school: How to be an effective teacher* (Rev. ed.). Sunnydale, CA: Wong Publications.

Young, S. (1994). *The Scholastic rhyming dictionary*. New York: Scholastic Inc.

Sharon A. Maroney *(CEC Chapter #682), Professor in Special Education, Western Illinois University, Macomb, Illinois.*

Address correspondence to the author at Western Illinois University, Special Education Department, 25 Horrabin Hall, Macomb, IL 61455 (e-mail: SA-Maroney1@wiu.edu).

From *Teaching Exceptional Children*, September/October 2000, pp. 22-27. © 2000 by The Council for Exceptional Children. Reprinted with permission.

UNIT 2
Early Childhood

Unit Selections

5. **Identifying Paraprofessional Competencies for Early Intervention and Early Childhood Special Education**, John Killoran, Torry Piazza Templeman, Joyce Peters, and Tom Udell
6. **Language Flowering, Language Empowering: 20 Ways Parents and Teachers Can Assist Young Children**, Alice S. Honig
7. **The Itinerant Teacher Hits the Road: A Map for Instruction in Young Children's Social Skills**, Faith Haertig Sadler

Key Points to Consider

- Describe the role of paraprofessionals in inclusive early childhood education. What are the eight competency areas that are critical to their training?

- Why is language fundamental to early childhood interventions? What are Alice Honig's suggestions for center-based or home-based activites that can empower young children with language arts?

- Describe the requirements that itinerant teachers who perform special educational services must meet to properly perform their tasks.

 **Links: www.dushkin.com/online/**
These sites are annotated in the World Wide Web pages.

Division for Early Childhood
http://www.dec-sped.org

Institute on Community Integration Projects
http://ici.umn.edu/projectscenters/

National Academy for Child Development (NACD)
http://www.nacd.org

National Early Childhood Technical Assistance System
http://www.nectas.unc.edu

Special Education Resources on the Internet (SERI)
http://seriweb.com

Public law 99-457 was a 1986 amendment (Part H) to PL94-142 (the Education for All Handicapped Children Act), which the U.S. Congress established as a grant incentive aimed at providing services for young children at risk of disability beginning at the age of 3. By 1991 this amendment to the now-renamed Individuals with Disabilities Education Act (IDEA) was reauthorized by PL102-119. It operates through "Child Find," which are organizational groups that look for babies, toddlers, and preschoolers with conditions of obvious disability (such as blindness, deafness, or orthopedic handicap). These young children can receive special educational services according to IDEA's mandate, "a free and appropriate education for all in the least restrictive environment." Many infants and young children are being found who are at "high risk" of developing educational disabilities (for example, low vision, hearing impairments, developmental delays) unless education begins before the age of 6. This outreach is having a profound impact on the care of families and children.

The United States is faced with multiple questions about the education of its future citizens—its young children. Many American babies are born preterm, small for gestational age, or with extremely low birth weight. This is a direct result of the United States' high rate of teenage pregnancy (nearly double that of most European countries and Canada) and its low rate of providing adequate prenatal care, especially for the young, the poor, or recent immigrant mothers. These infants are at high risk for developing disabilities and conditions of educational exceptionality. Early intervention can help these babies.

All services to be provided for any infant, toddler, or preschooler with a disability, and for his or her family, are to be articulated in an individualized family service plan (IFSP). The IFSP is to be written and implemented as soon as the infant or young child is determined to be at risk. IFSPs specify what services will be provided for the parents, for the diagnosed child, for siblings, and for all significant caregivers. Children with pervasive disabilities (such as autism, traumatic brain injuries, blindness, deafness, orthopedic impairments, severe health impairments, or multiple disabilities) may require extensive and very expensive early childhood interventions.

IFSPs are written in collaboration with parents, experts in the area of the child's exceptional condition, teachers, home-service providers, and other significant providers. They are updated every 6 months until the child turns 3 and receives an individualized education plan (IEP). A case manager is assigned to oversee each individual child with an IFSP to ensure high-quality and continuous intervention services.

In the United States, Child Find locates and identifies infants, toddlers, and young children who qualify for early childhood special education and family services. An actual diagnosis, or label of condition of exceptionality, is not required. Assessment is usually accomplished in a multidisciplinary fashion. It can be very difficult, but as much as possible, it is conducted in the child's home in a nonthreatening fashion. Diagnosis of exceptionalities in children who cannot yet answer questions is complicated. Personal observations are used as well as parent reports. Most of the experts involved in the multidisciplinary assessment want to see the child more than once to help compensate for the fact that all children have good days and bad days. In cases where the parents are non-English speakers and a translator is required, assessment may take several days.

Despite the care taken, many children who qualify for, and would benefit from, early intervention services are missed. Child Find associations are not well funded. There are constant shortages of time, materials, and multidisciplinary professionals to do assessments. Finding translators for parents who speak uncommon foreign languages adds to the problems. Occasionally the availability of funds for early childhood interventions encourages the overdiagnosis of risk factors in infants from low-income, minority, immigrant, or rural families.

A challenge to all professionals providing early childhood special services is how to work with diverse parents. Some parents welcome any and all intervention, even if it is not merited. Other parents resist any labeling of their child as "disabled" and refuse services. Professionals must make allowances for cultural, economic, and educational diversity, multiple caregivers, and single parents. Regardless of the situation, parental participation is the sine qua non of early childhood intervention.

At-home services may include instruction in the educational goals of the IFSP, and in skills such as discipline, behavior management, nutrition, and health maintenance. At-home services also include counseling for parents, siblings, and significant others to help them deal with their fears and to help them accept, love, and challenge their special child to become all he or she is capable of being. A case manager helps ensure that there is cooperation and coordination of services by all team members.

Most children receiving early childhood services have some center-based or combined center- and home-based special education. Center care introduces children to peers and introduces the family to other families with similar concerns. It is easier to ensure quality education and evaluate progress when a child spends at least a part of his or her time in a well-equipped educational center.

The first article in this unit provides specific tips on how to include paraprofessionals in early childhood special education programs. Trained personnel are in short supply and the needs of children are enormous. The authors suggest that knowing how to use subsidiary adults alongside teachers or other professionals can make them valuable stepping-stones rather than stumbling blocks. Areas of training, levels of mastery, and assessments of competencies are carefully explained.

The second article explains why language is fundamental to all early childhood interventions and how it becomes a critical factor in later school success. Preschool teachers and outreach programs need to expand their concern and expertise to families. Alice Honig gives specific suggestions for 20 center-based or home-based learning activities to empower young children with language arts.

The last article in unit 2 discusses the benefits of early intervention using itinerant teachers who travel from place to place to perform their special educational services. The extension of services from birth to the age of 3 in homes and local communities has given impetus to indirect service delivery models. An itinerant teacher can collaborate, consult, and provide technical assistance in many ways.

Identifying Paraprofessional Competencies for Early Intervention and Early Childhood Special Education

John Killoran, Torry Piazza Templeman, Joyce Peters and Tom Udell

Help! Paraprofessionals needed! This cry is going out across the United States, even as the increased demand is not seeing a corresponding supply of trained personnel.

Because few state institutions of higher education can produce the numbers of professionals needed to work with young children with disabilities and their families (Gallagher, Malone, Cleghorne, & Helms, 1997), it is only logical that state and local programs have increased their use of paraprofessionals in the delivery of needed services (see box, "The IDEA & Paraprofessionals"). In addition to the increased numbers of personnel currently needed to provide services, the training needs of these personnel are increasing. Here are factors contributing to the training needs of paraprofessionals:

- The changing nature and increased cultural and linguistic diversity of children and families.
- Advances in effective and researched-based practices.
- Changes in instructional models, such as the use of natural environments and community settings (Slobof, 1999; Stayton & Bruder,1999).

The role of the paraprofessional is dramatically different from that of the attendance taker of the past.

Despite these needs, few states, prior to the 1997 IDEA amendments, required demonstration of specific competencies or provided ongoing competency-based training for paraprofessionals.

This article provides a set of competencies for paraprofessionals and demonstrates ways to document the various mastery levels of paraprofessionals. We have found this structure useful; and it forms the foundation of Oregon's personnel development system for the state's early intervention/early childhood education special education services.

What are the competencies that paraprofessionals themselves have identified as critical in their roles and in which they are in need of training and support?

The Changing Role of the Paraprofessional

The role of the paraprofessional is dramatically different from that of the attendance taker of the past. Paraprofessionals are assisting and providing services that range

- From implementation of positive behavior strategies for children with disruptive behaviors to being part of schoolwide discipline programs.
- From assisting with fluoride treatments to conducting highly complex life-sustaining health procedures delegated by physicians and nurses for medically fragile children.
- From implementing articulation programs for groups of children to conducting tactile communication strategies for young children who are deaf-blind.

The paraprofessional has become the backbone of inclusive early childhood education and is frequently serving as a child's primary interventionist in inclusive and community settings (Hammeken, 1996; Winton, 1993). More frequently than ever before, paraprofessionals are performing not only instructional duties, but are also involved in daily administrative duties (Pickett,1990; 1996). As such, state and local Comprehensive System of Personnel Development (CSPD) models and technical assistance systems must address basic core competencies needed for paraprofessionals working with young children with disabilities and their families.

Identifying Paraprofessional Competency Needs

But what are the competencies paraprofessionals need? What are the standards, competencies, and skills that states should consider and that local agencies must ensure are demonstrated by their paraprofessionals? And perhaps most important, what are the competencies that paraprofessionals themselves have identified as critical in their roles and in which they are in need of training and support?

The Initial Identification of Competencies

To answer these questions, as well as many others related to the development and implementation of a statewide CSPD system for early intervention and early childhood special education (EI/ECSE) practitioners, the Oregon Department of Education, as the state lead agency for Part C and ECSE services, formed a multidisciplinary task force of more than 50 professionals to assist in identifying needed competencies and to recommend methods by which people could document their level of mastery for each of the identified competencies required for their position.

The task force members not only represented each of the disciplines linked with EI/ECSE services, but also included the professional organizations responsible for establishing licensing and preservice training requirements in the state.

The task force recommended and developed a portfolio-review process by which personnel could document their level of mastery of the competencies required for their roles.

The task force initially identified eight core competency areas (Figure 1), consisting of over 90 competencies. The core areas and the specific competencies identified by the task force were generic across four EI/ECSE personnel roles identified in the state's Part C federal application. These roles included supervisors, specialists, paraprofessionals, and related service providers.

The task force also defined five levels of mastery (Figure 2) and established a required level of mastery, based on the four personnel roles, for each competency. Mastery levels varied for each competency, depending on the specific role of personnel.

The IDEA & Paraprofessionals in Early Childhood Education

The 1997 Amendments to the Individuals with Disabilities Education Act (IDEA) have brought about many changes to special education and the provision of a free appropriate public education for young children with disabilities. Though many of these changes are subtle and fine-tune the process for serving children and their families (NICHCY, 1998), others are more significant and call for the development of new policies and initiatives within local and state education agencies and Part C lead agencies. One such change allows paraprofessionals, who have been appropriately trained consistent with state law, regulations, or written policy, to assist in the provision of special education and related services (Part B of IDEA) to children with disabilities and to provide early intervention services (Part C of IDEA) to infants, toddlers, and their families. Local agencies must now ensure that all personnel, including paraprofessionals providing early intervention and special education, are adequately and appropriately trained. As a result, states are not only faced with the task of developing a Comprehensive System of Personnel Development (CSPD) that is consistent and comparable across parts B and C but are also challenged with establishing policies, personnel standards, and training programs to ensure that currently employed paraprofessionals in early intervention and early childhood special education (EI/ECSE) are adequately and appropriately trained.

Simply stated, paraprofessionals are people who provide direct services to children and their families while under the supervision of teachers or other professionals (Pickett, 1999). Current literature supports the use of paraprofessionals in the delivery of services to children with disabilities and their families (Davis, 1995). It also illustrates, however, the task that many state and local programs face in implementing the new personnel requirements of IDEA '97. Few states have identified paraprofessional competencies or systematically train paraprofessionals even though they represent the largest group of personnel providing EI/ECSE services (Striffler, 1996).

The shortage of early intervention and special education personnel who are fully and appropriately trained is well-documented and consistently acknowledged in the professional literature (Gallagher, et al., 1997; Wischnowski, Yates, & McCollum, 1996). Gallagher et al. have pointed out that one fundamental challenge to the full implementation of IDEA remains the shortages of personnel faced by Part C programs and early childhood special education providers alike.

For example, specialists were required to demonstrate skills at higher levels of application and mastery (Level 4 or 5) whereas paraprofessionals demonstrated more skills at the awareness and knowledge level (Level 2 or 3). The task force also identified some competencies as not applicable for paraprofessionals.

Figure 1. Eight Core Competency Areas

1. Typical and Atypical Child Development
2. Assessment
3. Family
4. Service Delivery
5. Program Management
6. Service Coordination
7. Research
8. Professional Development, Values, Ethics

In addition to identifying the needed core areas, specific competencies, and their corresponding levels of mastery, the task force recommended and developed a portfolio-review process by which personnel could document their level of mastery of the competencies required for their roles. Ten methods of documenting competence, including performance evaluations, interviews, direct observation, work samples, formal coursework, inservice, written documents, videos, self-study, and letters of reference, were identified (see box "Suggested Portfolio Items for Documenting Competencies").

The draft competencies, their corresponding mastery levels and the portfolio process were disseminated to 400 reviewers. More than 100 reviewers returned the competencies and mastery recommendations with detailed feedback and suggestions for revision. The Oregon Department of Education and the Teaching Research Division at Western Oregon University synthesized and revised the competencies for piloting within EI/ECSE programs in the state.

Field-Testing the Identified Competencies and Portfolio Process

Researchers then conducted a pilot study in two of the state's largest EI/ECSE programs. The intent of the pilot was to further refine the competencies and their corresponding mastery levels, as well as to field-test the portfolio review and documentation process. One participating program was geographically located in a metro-urban area, and the second in a more rural portion of Oregon. Of the 186 pilot participants, 26% were paraprofessionals, 25% were specialists (teachers), and 43% were related services providers. Supervisors represented only 6% of the total pool of participants. The team developed workbooks for each of the four levels of personnel. The workbooks delineated the individual competency statements, the required mastery level for

each competency, and the required documentation. Each participant was responsible for developing his or her portfolios by gathering and submitting materials that would clearly document their acquisition of required competencies at the appropriate mastery level. Participants then submitted completed portfolios for review to a statewide panel of readers. The panel was comprised of university faculty, EI/ECSE program administrators and practitioners, and people representing a wide range of related service disciplines.

Eighty-six percent of the paraprofessionals participating in the pilot documented competence at the required levels. Researchers used the results of the pilot to further refine and significantly reduce the number of competencies from the original 96 to 57. This final listing of competencies became the basis of the state's EI/ECSE personnel standards and authorization process. Figure 3 illustrates the eight Core Competency Areas, their specific competencies, and their corresponding mastery level. Paraprofessionals are not required to document competencies whose mastery level is specified as N/A (not applicable) or unfamiliar.

Figure 2. Levels of Mastery

1. **Unfamiliar:** little or no information on this topic; the skill or information is new.

2. **Awareness:** The skill or information is familiar but more training is needed.

3. **Knowledge:** Can speak knowledgeably about the topic; able to discuss and use skill but more experience and feedback would be helpful.

4. **Application:** Can demonstrate skill in this area with guidance; able to use skill or knowledge in a variety of situations at a a satisfactory level.

5. **Mastery:** Can successfully and independently apply this skill in the workplace; can participate in the development; understands and uses the skill at an exemplary level.

The Identification of Specific Training Needs by Paraprofessionals

Subsequent to the work of the task force and the pilot study, the Teaching Research Division received federal funding (the Core project), which teamed the Teaching Research Division and the Oregon Department of Education in the development of regional professional development capabilities around Oregon's EI/ECSE Core Competencies. Oregon's EI/ECSE program is divided into eight service areas, based on a geographic, and to a lesser extent, population basis. Each service region has its own contractor and subcontractors, which administer the lead agency funds and provide EI/ECSE services.

Suggested Portfolio Items for Documenting Competencies

Following are 10 methods of documenting paraprofessional competence. We have identified the specific type of documentation required for each competency in the paraprofessional portfolio. Only one type of documentation must be submitted for each competency.

1. **Performance evaluations**, including comments, ratings, or observations within annual performance evaluations, and specific to the competency.

2. **Interviews** by two or more people—one in a similar role, and one in a supervisory capacity, which specifically address the competency.

3. **Observation** of the competency by a supervisor with a written record of observation.

4. **Written work samples** produced on the job or from a supervised practical experience.

5. **Coursework** documented by a written description of the course/training session and documentation of successful completion.

6. **Inservice** training documented through a description of the content, title, length of session, instructor date, and inservice objectives relative to the competency and a written description of how information is applied.

7. **Written document or summaries** of experience with specific examples related to the competency verified by a supervisor.

8. **A videotape** demonstrating the specific competency.

9. **Self-study**, independent study, or a completed professional development plan and a written description of how the self-study relates to the competency and how it has been applied.

10. **Letters of reference**, specific to the competency, from consumers, peers, or supervisors, which include examples.

Surveying Paraprofessional Training Needs

An initial activity of the CORE project effort was the development and administration of a survey to ascertain the respondents' perceptions of training needs in relation to each of the competencies, across the eight core areas. Core Project staff worked with key stakeholders within each of the eight regions to form regional training teams. These teams administered the survey to personnel from the aforementioned roles: supervisors, specialists, related services providers, and paraprofessionals.

Using the results of the surveys, the regional training teams then designed the continuing professional development plan for their specific service area. Community preschool and Head Start staff also completed the survey. Instructions were included with the survey, and Core Project staff demonstrated the survey administration. Respondents returned surveys directly to a central office in the region, not to their immediate supervisors.

The majority (83%) of the paraprofessionals surveyed served children from 3 through 5 years of age.

The team designed the survey to present each competency in the eight core areas with the corresponding level of mastery required for the role of the respondent. Respondents were asked to rate their perception of their individual training needs in relation to each competency as being a high, medium, or low training priority. In addition to identifying their training priorities, participants provided demographic data, included respondents' roles, the ages of children served, their current educational status, and their experience working in EI/ECSE. These data were entered into a database and queried across a variety of variables.

Paraprofessional Participation in the Survey

Of the 146 surveys returned, 64 (44%) were completed by paraprofessionals. These paraprofessionals worked in a variety of settings and capacities, some in self-contained settings where all of the children served had disabilities and some in home-based settings. Others worked in community preschool settings where children with disabilities received all of their services side-by-side with children without disabilities from the community. The majority (83%) of the paraprofessionals surveyed served children from 3 through 5 years of age. Their educational status data indicated that 73% of the paraprofessionals surveyed were high school graduates, 11% held a 2-year associate's degree, 13% held a bachelor's degree, and 3% held Master's degrees. The majority (69%) of the surveyed group had 6 or less years of experience working in EI/ECSE.

Results of the Survey

Not surprisingly, the 10 competencies identified by the paraprofessional respondents as their highest training need reflected the paraprofessionals' daily emphasis on service delivery and teaching (Figure 4). Six (60%) of the top 10 competencies identified fell within Core Competency Area 4: Service Delivery. This area is representative of the role of the paraprofessional who is now heavily involved in instructional tasks. Overall, the paraprofessional respondents also rated more items as a high priority for training than did any of the other respondent groups. Paraprofessionals indicated that their overall training needs were much higher than those of the other respondents, and they

Figure 3. Core Competency Areas, Individual Competencies, and Levels of Mastery

CORE COMPETENCY AREA AND INDIVIDUAL COMPETENCIES	MASTERY LEVEL
Area 1: Typical and Atypical Child Development	
• Knowledge and range of child development	Knowledge
• Knowledge of etiologies	Awareness
• Knowledge of impact of child's disability	Awareness
Area 2: Assessment	
• Functions of assessment	Unfamiliar
• Selection and administration of tests	NA
• Family interviewing	NA
• Observation techniques	Unfamiliar
• Assessment related confidentiality issues	Knowledge
• Various eligibility criteria	NA
Area 3: Family Issues	
• Working in partnerships	Knowledge
• Impacts of disabilities on families	Awareness
• Respect of families' culture and diversity	Awareness
• Advocating for families	Unfamiliar
• Sharing information with families	Knowledge
• Involving families	NA
• Strategies for flexible family involvement	NA
• Philosophies of family services	NA
• Effective communication	Application
• Assist families to embed goals and activities	Application
• Assist in accessing information	Unfamiliar
Area 4: Service Delivery	
• Knowledge of EI/ECSE best practice	Awareness
• Ability to create appropriate environments	Awareness
• Ability to effectively communicate with	Knowledge
• Ability to integrate therapeutic	Awareness
• Positive social interactions	Application
• Ability to design assessment based IFSPs	NA
• Ability to implement and evaluate progress	Application
• Ability to make program data-based changes	Awareness
• Ability to teach program implementation	Unfamiliar
• Ability to use adaptive equipment/techniques	Knowledge
• Effective communication skills	Knowledge
• Skills to communicate with others	NA
• Knowledge of different team formats	Awareness
Area 5: Program Management	
• Knowledge of eligibility regulations	Unfamiliar
• Knowledge of program goals and procedures	Knowledge
• Knowledge of staff evaluation process	Awareness
• Ability to manage/schedule daily operations	Awareness
• Ability to maintain safe environments	Application
• Maintenance/inventory	Knowledge
• Understanding of funding sources	NA
• Knowledge of labor and hiring laws	Awareness
• Responsive leadership	Awareness
Area 6: Service Coordination	
• Knowledge of public and private providers	NA
• Collaborative teaming	Awareness
• Ability to sue problem-solving	Awareness
• Development and implementation of inter-agency agreements	NA
• Development and implementation of effective transition plans	Awareness

Area 7: Research	
• Knowledge of research and its contribution	NA
• Use of current literature to modify practice	Unfamiliar
• Participates in program effectiveness activities	NA
• Participates in professional organizations	NA
Area 8: Professional Development, and Values and Ethics	
• Uses self-evaluation for professional growth	Knowledge
• Professional receives performance feedback	Application
• Provides feedback in a professional manner	NA
• Participates in continuing education	Awareness
• Adheres to identified codes of ethics	Application
• Assists other to establish and attain goals	NA

Note: EI/ECSE = early intervention/early childhood special education; IFSP = individualized family service plan

indicated a higher need for training on their tenth rated competency than any of the other respondent groups did for their number one rated competency.

Implications for Future Paraprofessional Training

Although there is certainly a need for paraprofessional training in many competencies that are transdisciplinary and cut across service roles, the study identified training designed specifically to meet paraprofessional service delivery and daily teaching needs as a high priority. This survey process provided a rich pool of information to base professional development activities and also indicated paraprofessionals' interest in and willingness to participate in training activities.

The identification of standards, levels of mastery, and methods to document individual competencies related to identified standards is critical to the development of a Comprehensive System of Personnel Development (CSPD) for paraprofessionals whether it be school-based or statewide. With the clear mandate within IDEA '97 to maintain a qualified work force, the process used in Oregon provided a solid foundation for long-term staff development that has been linked to professional competencies and state standards. The determination of a set of standards for knowledge and performance for those serving in the role of paraprofessional has provided a structure for the assessment of training needs, has yielded information that is highly relevant and useful in planning for training, and has served as the foundation of Oregon's EI/ECSE Comprehensive System of Personnel Development.

Although initially conceptualized and implemented for EI/ECSE paraprofessionals, it seems logical that teams could successfully use a similar process to identify paraprofessional competencies needed to work with a wider range of students. The process can be easily replicated at the local level, as well as serve as a starting point for other states as they approach the challenge of setting state standards for paraprofessionals and

Figure 4. The 10 Competencies Identified by Paraprofessionals as Their Highest Training Need

AREA	COMPETENCY
1. Child Development	• Knowledge of etiology and characteristics.
3. Family Involvement	• Assists families in accessing information and resources.
4. Service Delivery	• Knowledge of ECE and EI/ECSE best practice as defined by professional organizations.
	• Ability to create appropriate and stimulating environments to enhance learning.
	• Ability to effectively communicate with children.
	• Ability to integrate effective therapeutic practices into learning environments.
	• Ability to appropriately monitor child progress and to make program changes.
	• Ability to use adaptive techniques/equipment.
5. Program Management	• Knowledge of program vision, goals, guidelines and operating procedures.
8. Professional Development Values and Ethics	• Participation in continuing education and/or inservice training.

Note: ECE = early childhood education; EI/ECSE = early intervention/early childhood special education.

the personnel development system needed to make these standards a reality.

References

Davis, J. H. (1995). *A training program designed to develop knowledgeable paraprofessionals with improved job performance skills.* Ft. Lauderdale, FL: Fischler Center for the Advancement of Education, Nova Southeastern University. (ERIC Document Reproduction Service No. ED386 430).

Gallagher, P., Malone, D. M., Cleghorne, M.,& Helms, K. A. (1997). Perceived in-service training needs for early intervention personnel. *Exceptional Children, 64,* 19–29.

Hammeken, P. (1996). *Inclusion: An essential guide for the paraprofessional.* Menetonka, MN: Peytral Publications.

National Information Center for Children and Youth with Disabilities. (1998). *The IDEA Amendments of 1997, 26,* 1–39.

Pickett, A. L. (1990). *Paraprofessionals in education: Personnel practices that influence their performance.* Paper presented at the Rural Education Symposium of the American Council on Rural Special Education, Tucson, AZ.

Pickett, A. L. (1996). *Paraprofessionals in the educational workforce.* Washington, DC: National Education Association. (ERIC Document Reproduction Service No. ED337 329)

Pickett, A. L. (1999). *Strengthening and supporting teacher/provider-paraprofessional teams: Guidelines for paraeducator roles, supervision, and preparation.* New York: City University of New York.

Slobof, J. (1999). *Providing cross cultural support services to individuals with disabilities: Strategies for paraprofessionals who support individuals with disabilities.* Minneapolis: Institute on Community Integration, University of Minnesota. (ERIC Document Reproduction Service No. ED 398 695)

Stayton, V., & Bruder, M. B. (1999). Early intervention personnel preparation for the new millennium: Early childhood special education. *Infants and Young Children,12*(1), 59–69.

Striffler, N. (1996). The paraprofessional role. In D. Bricker & A. Widerstrom, *Preparing personnel to work with infants and young children and their families* (pp. 231–252). Baltimore: Paul H. Brookes.

Winton, P. J. (1993). Providing family support. In C. A. Peck, S. L. Odom, & D. C.Bricker (Eds.), *Integrating young children with disabilities into community programs: Ecological perspectives on research and evaluation.* Baltimore: Paul H.Brookes.

Wischnowski, M. W., Yates, T. J., & McCollum, J. A. (1996). Expanding training options for early intervention personnel: Developing a statewide staff mentoring system. *Infants and Young Children, 8*(4), 49–58.

John Killoran *(CEC Oregon Federation), Assistant Research Professor;* **Torry Piazza Templeman** *(CEC Oregon Federation), Associate Research Professor;* **Joyce Peters** *(CEC Oregon Federation), Associate Research Professor; and* **Tom Udell** *(CEC Oregon Federation), Assistant Research Professor, Teaching Research Division, Western Oregon University, Monmouth.*

For additional information, copies of the competencies, or materials related to this article please contact John Killoran, Teaching Research Division, Western Oregon University, 345 N. Monmouth Avenue, Monmouth, OR 97361 (e-mail: killorj@wou.edu; URL http:// www.tr.wou.edu/authoriz).

From *Teaching Exceptional Children,* September/October 2001, pp. 68-73. © 2001 by The Council for Exceptional Children. Reprinted by permission.

Language Flowering, Language Empowering: 20 Ways Parents and Teachers Can Assist Young Children

By Alice S. Honig

Parents, home visitors, and teachers in early childhood settings need tools for empowering young children to flourish in many domains. The domain of language development is fundamentally critical to later school success, social ease, and abstract thinking skills. To be wise mentors who use teaching tools and techniques well, we need understandings and insights about developmental progressions in each special child development area.

In some U.S. communities, as many as 45% of youngsters are "failing" kindergarten because their prereading language skills are not at a level that can prepare them for successful beginning reading in first grade. Some parents need far more help if they are to provide rich language support for their children's early school success (Payne, Whitehurst, & Angell, 1994). In many communities, such outreach supports are in rare supply. Fortunately, preschool teachers are gatekeepers into the rich territories of literacy. They need to expand their concern and expertise to families. Together the adults serve as primary guides who introduce children to the delights, byways, signposts, and fruitful gardens of the land of language learning.

What Do We Need To Know?

First, we need to know the *norms and windows* of language growth (Honig, 1989). How do language and competence in reading and writing grow from the infant/toddler period through the nearly school-age period? Knowledge of the normative *stages* of language development grounds our work (Cazden, 1981; Harris, 1990; Honig, 1983). For example, holophrasis (one-word speech) appears somewhere near the end of the first year, amid baby jargon and babbling sounds with intonations. Two-word (telegraphic) speech usually comes in before 24 months ("Want dat!" "Doggie dere." "My toy!" "Daddy fix." "Big moo-moo!"). The ability to form adult negatives ("I don't want meatballs" rather than "No me want dat") and to form full questions ("How do I draw that, teacher?") appear during the third year. During the later preschool years, children learn to interpret passive questions ("Was the car hit by the truck?") and to decode and answer "Why" questions accurately.

Some children find coordinating their tongue, lips, palate, and other language production parts difficult, while others

have an easier time, even with consonant clusters, such as *str* in *street*. As for pronunciation, usually by 4 years of age, about three fourths of child articulation is clear and intelligible.

Second, we need strong *research "ammunition"* to defend our developmentally appropriate practices (Committee on the Prevention of Reading Difficulties, 1997). Researches illuminate the quality of early support for literacy that caregivers *and* parents must provide to boost young children's language learning. Moerk, Snow, Tizard, Berko-Gleason, McQueen and Washington, the de Villiers, and many other researchers help us appreciate *how* adults facilitate and promote early passions for communication in turn-taking talk and conversations, passion for stories, and skills for spelling, writing, and reading (Greenberg, 1998).

Third, we need to consider how *language skills are special socially* for making friends and getting along well. Promoting early language competency during the infancy years could even serve to lessen the probability of harsh discipline with children. Families may be more frustrated and stressed in interactions with children who have receptive and expressive language delays. With teacher support for early child language skills and support for family language enrichment games with young children (Honig, 1982), some folks may then find it more appropriate to discipline with words rather than physical force.

Prisons are filled with adults who never learned to read or can read only at rudimentary levels. Thus, a fourth major emphasis must be on helpful *curriculum ideas* to enhance and promote early language competence from early infancy onward and to prevent school reading failures (Fowler, 1990; Honig, 1982; McCabe, 1992; Van Allen & Van Allen, 1982).

Girded with ideas, techniques, and reading materials, adults can effectively implement a language-rich curriculum to boost early literacy and motivation for early reading activities. More children will be likely to read fluently and read for pleasure in elementary grades. When networks of parents and professionals—caregivers, teachers, home visitors, and speech therapists—work together, then young children have seen greater chances for early language flowering. Effective teachers capitalize on the strengths and unique learning styles of each child, his/her special story interests, and oral fluency, to engage each youngster in book learning and book loving.

Techniques for Parents and Teachers

1. Offer Turn-Taking Talk with Babies. As you tenderly carry out daily routines with infants, verbally and responsively in "turn-taking talk," express your pleasure for their cooing and babbling with you (Devine, 1991; Honig, 1985).

2. Provide Prompts. Adults create early verbal *scaffolding* for emerging language (Bruner, 1983). Be particularly aware of the level at which a child is functioning. Some children use multiword sentences clearly by age 2. Others exhibit many articulatory substitutions (*bunny wabbit, shishy,* or *lellow* [for yellow], *dar* [for car]) and communicate mostly with two-word phrases. Tuned-in teaching adults know just how to *lure* little ones forward into further language competence by working in what Vygotsky called the "Zone of Proximal Development" (Brunner, 1984). With a teacher's insightful support, a child

reaches further understandings and learns more.

As you care for and talk with a child under 3, provide pauses to entice little ones to "finish" your phrases:

- Mary had a little ____.
- You need your toothbrush to brush your ____.
- I know a little gray mouse. He lives in a little gray ____.
- We go see saw up and down. We go up and ____.
- Baa baa, black sheep, have you any ____?
- Row row row your ____.
- First we put on your socks; then we put on your ____.

3. Be a Generous Word Giver. Label objects, actions, feelings, facial emotions, and events. If a toddler is now walking alone pretty well, exclaim admiringly: "You are walking, really getting up and walking now. You must be so proud of yourself!"

Use encouraging words and specific praise for new accomplishments, as when baby uses a spoon in self-feeding or wrinkles her nose to sniff a flower. When toddlers eagerly point out a barking doggy walking beyond the playyard gate, affirm cheerfully, "That doggy is going woof, woof, woof. Doggy is walking right by our yard!"

"The gerbil is twitching his whiskers" confirms for your preschoolers just what the animal is doing as each child reaches out to pet the gerbil gently. Your naming of events and things anchors reality in words and increases a young child's power to use linguistic symbols. How triumphant a 4-year-old on a museum trip feels as he looks up at the huge skeleton and informs you, "That's Tyrannosaurus Rex!"

When your toddlers and preschoolers are very sure of a label, play silly games on occasion. For example, hold up a green checker and say, "Is this purple?" Or pat a child's knee and say, "Oh, I'm patting your elbow!" Preschoolers love to catch a teacher making an absurd mistake once in a while!

4. Model and Expand on Infant/Toddler Language. Suppose a baby in bathtub exclaims "Wawa." Then cheerfully confirm: "Yes, that's water in your tub. You go splish splash in the water. You go swimmy swim in the water." All this while you "swim" the baby while holding her under her tummy. Suppose an infant says, "Ju!" Father then asserts, "You're right! Juice.

Orange juice. You love to drink orange juice, honey." Such tiny tidbits of language interactions expand and enrich an infant's language world.

5. Use Parallel Talk. Provide words to accompany child gestures (Honig, 1989). For example, as your 8-month-olds vigorously respond to music with their bodies, rejoice with them and exclaim, "You really like bouncing up and down to the music! Bounce, bounce, bounce!"

Your words *describe* what is going on, what children are doing or feeling. During parent group meetings, encourage family members to provide words for whatever they see their infant or toddler doing or trying to do. As a preschooler fills her pail with wooden beads, say clearly, "You are filling up the tub with those wooden beads. You are piling up the wooden beads in your tub."

If a child is lugging a basket of blocks, exclaim, "Those blocks sure are heavy to carry. The basket feels so heavy!" Keep on using parallel talk during outdoor playtime, as well as indoors. "You are taking turns climbing up the stairs of the slide" gives word power and reminds children of playground rules.

6. Use Self-Talk. Talk about *what* you are doing for a child or for the group and *how* you are doing it: "I am setting out a large piece of collage paper for every child. Now I will give you some pieces to paste on your collage paper. Here are some sprinkly glittery letters for you, Jo. Here are some tiny aluminum foil shapes, Kwanghee. You decide how you want them to go as you paste them down on your collage paper."

This principle is especially important in working with infants. For example, "I need to go get some clean diapers. So I'll carry you over to the diaper supply box. Here we go walking over to get some clean diapers." As you reach to get a jar of baby food down for a meal, say, "I am getting down some yum yum applesauce for your lunch."

7. Arrange for Children to Act Out Familiar Tales. Once preschoolers become deeply comfortable with a well known story, such as *Goldilocks and the Three Bears* or *The Three Billy Goats Gruff*, then they will be ready to act out the characters. Toddlers with few words can use pantomime at first to act out the characters. Sometimes children want to act out violent behaviors of favorite TV-show characters, such as Ninja Turtles. How can you keep

6. *Unit Relationships.* Students use this section to write the names of relationships that might be important to look for and the kinds of thinking required to learn the unit information. In Figure 3, for example, the teacher and students noted that the various areas of the nation must be described and then compared and contrasted to understand how their differences led to the Civil War.

7. *Unit Self-Test Questions.* Students use this section to generate and write questions related to different parts of the unit that they should be able to answer when the unit is complete. Later, when preparing for the unit test, students can ask themselves these questions to review the content of the unit. Figure 3 shows one of the questions that students generated about the Civil War: "What was sectionalism as it existed in the U.S. of 1860?"

8. *Unit Schedule.* The information in this section summarizes the schedule of required tasks, activities, or assignments that students must complete during the course of the unit. In this section, students write down their list of projects, homework assignments, and tests, rather than lesson topics for the unit. Figure 3, for example, shows dates in the square boxes and associated tasks and assignments in the adjacent rectangular boxes. Students should leave spaces in the schedule for items you or the students decide to add later during the unit.

9. *Expanded Unit Map.* After you introduce the unit, and you and your students complete the first page of the Unit Organizer, you can use the second page throughout and at the end of the unit to expand the unit map by adding critical subtopics, details, and key vocabulary in note form. Together, you and your students can identify and add these details daily to the expanded unit map as extensions of the original parts of the map. Students can use the expanded map as a note-taking device during daily lessons or during review at the end of each lesson. Figure 4 shows the expanded unit map for the unit on the "Causes of the Civil War."

10. *New Unit Self-Test Questions.* Use the space below the expanded unit map to write questions that you and your students identify as you explore the unit. For example, Figure 4 shows a question the teacher and students added to the expanded unit map: "How did national

events and leaders pull the different sections of the U.S. apart?"

Content Enhancement involves making decisions about what content to emphasize in teaching, transforming that content into learner-friendly formats, and presenting this content in memorable ways.

An Abbreviated Example of How to Use the Unit Organizer Routine

Using the Cue-Do-Review sequence (see box, above), lead students through the content of the unit by engaging them in the Unit Organizer Routine.

Cue

Hand out blank copies of the Unit Organizer device and explain that the class will be beginning a new unit, using the Unit Organizer. Show a blank Unit Organizer on an overhead projector and explain that you will complete that one as students complete their own. This should take only a few minutes. In addition, the first time the Unit Organizer is used, spend a few minutes talking about what it means to be organized at home, organized with schoolwork in a binder, and then talk about the value of the Unit Organizer for organizing class information. Each subsequent time that a Unit Organizer is used, it would still be valuable to review the benefits of using

the device and your expectations for student participation.

Do

Engage students in completing the Unit Organizer, using a set of Linking Steps. Linking Steps refer to the procedures a teacher uses to present the content of a unit in an interactive way to students. Linking Steps guide the way the Unit Organizer is used when introducing the unit (using Page 1 of the Unit Organizer), expanding the unit (using the Expanded Unit Organizer), and gaining closure on the unit. Although it would take less time to simply tell students what to write in each of the sections of the Unit Organizer, prompt student responses with questions that will enable them to actively use the device and will enhance their learning at each step.

First, help students to see the overall context of the unit and how the new unit is related to previous and future learning. Ask students to recall the name of the previous unit, prompt them to look at a text for the name of the current unit, and hypothesize the name of the next unit. Then ask them how the three units fit together, what they have in common, or the name of a larger category to which they might belong. Students seldom may be asked to think and respond to questions at that level, but even upper elementary students are able to provide reasonable responses when asked. With any group of students, it may be necessary to paraphrase a student's response to clarify the bigger picture. Complete Sections 1–4 of the Unit Organizer at this step when introducing the unit, and review the information in these sections at unit closure.

Second, discuss and complete information in the Unit Map in order to help students identify and see the structure of main ideas or parts of the unit. If a major part of the unit includes a textbook chapter, ask students to survey the chapter for major headings, discuss probable main ideas, and then write them on the Unit Map in Section 5 of the Unit Organizer. For younger students and for the benefit of those with poor motor skills, help students by showing them how to map out (i.e., draw) the total number of ovals or shapes that correspond to the number of main ideas that will be present on the completed Unit Map. Do so before discussing and writing the names of the main ideas in the ovals. Also, don't forget to include the lines and line labels! Throughout daily lessons in the unit, connect critical details and information to the

Cue It! Do It! Review It!

A Cue-Do-Review sequence is a simple formula for making the most of the Unit Organizer Routine (or any instructional strategy). You can use it to focus students' attention on the Unit Organizer device, implement the device, and check student understanding. Mark Twain might have referred to this as "You tell 'em what you're gonna tell 'em. You tell 'em. And you tell 'em what you told 'em." Here's how it works:

1. Provide a "Cue." As with any instructional device (e.g., globe, video, role play activity, graphic organizer), you will enhance students' understanding by (a) directing their attention to the device and explaining what it is (if it is not already obvious), (b) explaining your expectations, and (c) showing how using the device will help students succeed.

2. In the "Do" step, use a set of Linking Steps for (a) introducing, (b) using and expanding, and (c) gaining closure on a unit with the Unit Organizer.

3. In the "Review" step, use a simple review to check and clarify student understanding of information discussed, as well as the process for using the Unit Organizer.

main ideas on the Expanded Unit Map in Section 9. Review the information in both sections at unit closure.

Within the unit map, you should draw lines between the geometric shapes and the unit paraphrase and include "line labels" on each line to indicate the relationships between the parts and the main idea of the unit.

Third, after students see how the critical parts of the unit are structured, ask them to discuss and identify possible relationships or kinds of thinking required to understand the information in the main parts of the unit. Prompt students to analyze the Unit Map, the main ideas contained in it, and the relationships among the main ideas, and their relation to the Unit Paraphrase. Using the completed example in Figure 3, ask questions such as "We have one main

idea regarding the sections of the country. On a test, what might you be asked to do? How might you be asked to think about that information?" Write these unit relationships in Section 6 of the Unit Organizer when the unit is introduced, and be sure to review them at the end of the unit.

Fourth, prompt students to create some good questions that correspond to the different parts of the unit map and unit context. For a moment, students can pretend that they are the teacher and select test questions. Work with students to make sure that critical questions related to mastery of the content are included and recorded in Section 7 of the device. The Unit Relationships also may be clarified at this step as students recognize the kinds of thinking that are required (e.g., listing, explaining, comparing, predicting) to address the questions that they write.

As an alternative, some teachers have found it beneficial to write the Unit Self-Test Questions in Section 7 before analyzing the Unit Relationships in Section 6 because the latter step is less difficult for many students if the self-test questions can be identified first. For example, after writing the questions, some teachers prompt students to identify whether certain questions would require students to compare, explain, name, or problem-solve, or use other thinking skills, and then write students' responses into the Unit Relationships section.

As the unit progresses, record new questions in Section 10. Review the questions from Section 7 of the Unit Organizer and, later, from Section 10 of the Expanded Unit Organizer throughout the unit and at the end of the unit, before any test.

Finally, describe and create the list of assignments and due dates to assist stu-

dents in planning for, managing, and completing tasks and assignments related to the current unit. Prompt students to write these assignments in Section 8 of the Unit Organizer when the unit is introduced. Be sure to review the list throughout the unit.

Using the Unit Organizer, teachers ask students to discuss and identify possible relationships or kinds of thinking required to understand the information in the main parts of the unit.

When co-constructing the first page of the Unit Organizer device at the beginning of a new unit, the "Do" step may take an entire class period (i.e., 45–55 minutes) or more depending on student discussion and content difficulty.

Review

After introducing the unit, after adding daily information in the Expanded Unit

Organizer, and at the closure of a unit, it is important to check student understanding. After co-constructing the Unit Organizer at the beginning of a unit, take a few minutes to review the information contained in all eight parts of the device. Ask questions like these:

- What's the name of the new unit?
- What's another way of writing the name of the unit?
- How many main parts are there in the unit?
- What questions should we be able to answer by the time we finish the unit?
- What process did we go through to really understand this unit?
- When is your test?

Also, ask students to describe how the Unit Organizer helped them to learn.

The Unit Organizer Routine can provide a powerful and effective way for teachers to plan for and teach students with and without disabilities, in content area classes.

Tips, Suggestions, and Modifications

Planning Tips

First, when you are ready to use The Unit Organizer Routine, begin by selecting one class in which to try it out—perhaps your least demanding class in terms of diversity or classroom management. Also consider beginning with a unit that is fairly uncomplicated or one that includes more concrete information rather than more abstract information. For instance, a unit on mammals might be a better place to start than a unit on photosynthesis.

Second, collect the materials you plan to use in your unit, such as slides and textbooks.

Third, always construct a draft of the Unit Organizer device before introducing it to the class. The Unit Organizer truly does work well as a planning routine as well as a teaching routine. In fact, the first time you plan while using the Unit Organizer, you may find that it takes some extra time because you might realize ways to better organize unit information that you may have presented many times before.

Logistical Suggestions

When you are ready to introduce a new unit with the Unit Organizer, consider these suggestions:

- Copy and distribute to students two-sided copies of the Unit Organizer device with the main Unit Organizer on one side and the Expanded Unit Organizer on the second side.
- Cue students to take notes on the Unit Organizer.
- Use fine- or extra-fine-tip overhead transparency pens to add information to the Unit Organizer during presentations.
- Construct the Expanded Unit Map using different geometric shapes (e.g., ovals for main ideas, squares for first level details, and triangles for less important details).
- Vary the colors in construction of the Expanded Unit Map to reflect different levels of information of detail.
- When co-constructing the Expanded Unit Map with students, use "Inspiration" software, from Inspiration Software, Inc., to quickly and neatly lay out the critical and connected details with the use of technology.

Ideas for Modifications

In addition, consider these modifications for students with disabilities and others who are low achieving:

- Rather than constructing a Unit Organizer on an overhead projector, enlarge the device and create a laminated copy to post on the wall and construct it there.
- Create a blank Unit Organizer on a bulletin board, cut out geometric shapes from construction paper, and tack them up on the bulletin board to display unit information.
- Draw empty geometric shapes on a Unit Organizer or partially complete

the Unit Organizer before copying for students.

- Enlarge the Unit Organizer onto legal size (8"x14") paper for students to complete.
- As a review activity before a test, hand out 3"x5" index cards or colored Post-Its or "sticky notes" to small groups of students and prompt them to reconstruct the organization of unit main ideas and details on poster paper, as well as draw in the lines and line labels.

Students can pretend that they are the teacher for a moment and select test questions.

Assessment Considerations

When you are ready to assess student learning at the end of a unit, be sure that your test reflects the emphasis of your Unit Organizer and its sections. In other words, if you have previously used a particular unit test with the same unit in previous school years, evaluate the test to see whether the big ideas are emphasized over the smaller ones. Construct and weight test items that assess understanding of big ideas rather than rote recall of details. More specifically, consider including questions that relate to explaining the unit map and the relationships among critical pieces of information.

Final Thoughts

Research on the Unit Organizer Routine (Lenz, Schumaker, et al., 1993) has shown that teacher planning was enhanced and the performance of low-achieving students, students with learning disabilities, and average-achieving students improved substantially in regard to understanding and retaining information. In fact, the students of teachers who use the routine regularly and consistently scored an average of 15 percentage points higher on unit tests than did students of teachers who used it only irregularly (see box, "Research Supporting the Unit Organizer Routine").

Research Supporting the Unit Organizer Routine

Researchers conducted a study of the Unit Organizer Routine (Lenz, Schumaker, et al., 1993) in the U.S. Midwest across three high school and three middle school general education classrooms identified as being inclusive by the school district. The researchers collected data intensively through the use of single-subject, multiple-baseline designs on two high-achieving, two average-achieving, two low-achieving, and two students classified as having a learning disability. The researchers collected student performance data over a 7-month period.

Research has shown that use of the Unit Organizer Routine enhanced teacher planning and the performance of low-achieving students, students with learning disabilities, and average-achieving students. These students substantially improved their understanding and retention of information. In fact, among these groups, the students of teachers who used the routine *regularly* and consistently scored an average of 15 percentage points higher on unit tests than did students of teachers who used it only *irregularly*.

Teachers also reported that the Unit Organizer Routine helped those students with language problems and whose first language was not English acquire secondary content. Although the overall performance of high-achieving students did not substantially increase in these studies, the researchers observed increases in performance when the content became more difficult and abstract for individual students. Since the original study was conducted, teachers in many culturally and geographically diverse communities throughout the United States have replicated the results.

Teachers and students who achieve these kinds of results are truly winners. This winning attitude was expressed by one teacher who said, "Focusing on the 'big idea' questions enables me to think more clearly about what are the tools or things I can give students to have them see the patterns" (V. Arndt Helgesen, personal communication, 1993). Thus, the Unit Organizer Routine can provide a powerful and effective way for teachers to plan for and teach students with and without disabilities in content area classes because it focuses on quality rather than simply on quantity. Together, teachers and students can more successfully navigate each unit journey from beginning to end without watering down the learning outcomes.

References

Bulgren, J. A., Schumaker, J. B., & Deschler, D. D. (1993). *The concept mastery routine*. Lawrence, KS: Edge Enterprises.

Lenz, B. K., Marrs, R. W., Schumaker, J. B., & Deshler, D. D. (1993). *The lesson organizer routine*. Lawrence, KS: Edge Enterprises.

Lenz, B. K., Schumaker, J. B., Deshler, D. D., Boudah, D. J., Vance, M., Kissam, B., Bulgren, J. A., & Roth, J. (1993). *The unit planning routine: A guide for inclusive planning* (Research Report). Lawrence, KS: University of Kansas Center for Research on Learning.

Novak, J. D., & Gowin, D. B. (1984). *Learning how to learn*. New York: Cambridge University Press.

Daniel J. Boudah *(CEC Texas Federation), Assistant Professor, Department of Educational Psychology, Special Education Programs, Texas A&M University, College Station.* **B. Keith Lenz** *(CEC Chapter #665), Senior Research Scientist;* **Janis A. Bulgren** *(CEC Chapter #665), Senior Research Scientist;* **Jean B. Schumaker** *(CEC Chapter #665), Associate Director; and* **Donald D. Deshler** *(CEC Chapter #436), Director, Center for Research on Learning, University of Kansas, Lawrence.*

Address correspondence to Daniel J. Boudah, Department of Educational Psychology, Special Education Programs, Texas A&M University, 704 Harrington Education Center, College Station, TX 77843-4225 (e-mail: boudah@acs.tamu.edu).

Additional Resources

Lenz, B. K., Bulgren, J. A., Schumaker, J. B., Deshler, D. D., & Boudah, D. J. (1994). *The unit organizer routine*. Lawrence, KS: Edge Enterprises.

This teacher manual, as well as others in the Content Enhancement Series, are available with training. For more information, contact Janet Roth at The University of Kansas, Center for Research on Learning, 3061 Dole Building, Lawrence, KS 66045. Phone: 785-864-4790; e-mail: JRoth@quest.sped.ukans.edu

From *Teaching Exceptional Children*, January/February 2000, pp. 48-56. © 2000 by The Council for Exceptional Children. Reprinted by permission.

Identifying Depression
in Students with Mental Retardation

Laura M. Stough
Lynn Baker

The belief that people with mental retardation are always happy, carefree, and content is a misconception. In reality, students with mental retardation are at risk for the same types of psychological disorders as are students without cognitive deficits (Crews, Bonaventura, & Rowe, 1994; Johnson, Handen, Lubetsky, & Sacco, 1995; Sovner & Hurley, 1983).

As many as 10% of children with mental retardation suffer from depression, in contrast to the lower prevalence rate of 1%–5% in children without mental retardation

---

Many researchers have actually found a *higher* rate of depressive disorders in people with mental retardation (e.g., Borthwick-Duffy & Eyman, 1990; Menolascino, 1990; Reiss, 1990). Teachers should be aware of this increased risk for depression so that they can appropriately refer their students for diagnosis and treatment. In this article, we present suggestions for detecting and treating childhood depression.

Prevalence and Symptoms of Depression

Although little research has investigated the precise prevalence of depression in children with mental retardation, special education teachers will likely encounter students with depression. Several studies have suggested that these children exhibit symptoms of sadness, loneliness, and worry at a much higher rate than do their peers without disabilities (e.g., Matson & Frame, 1986; Reiss, 1985). These studies estimated that as many as 10% of children with mental retardation suffer from depression, in contrast to the lower prevalence rate of 1%–5% in children without mental retardation (Cantwell, 1990).

Clinical depression is usually determined by a psychologist or psychiatrist, who uses the *Diagnostic and Statistical Manual of Mental Disorders, Fourth Edition* (DSM-IV; American Psychiatric Association, 1994) to make the diagnosis. To be formally diagnosed as "depressed," a child must experience *five different clinical signs of depression* over a 2-week period. The primary symptom is that the student exhibits either an overall depressed mood or a loss of interest in daily activities (also called *anhedonia*). Some students may express

this depressed mood in the form of persistent irritability, rather than by sadness or withdrawal.

Figure 1.
Signs of Major Depression

Look for five or more of these symptoms in the same 2-week period. These symptoms should represent a *change* from the person's previous typical level of functioning:

- Depressed or irritable mood most of the day, nearly every day.
- Decreased interest in pleasurable activities.
- Significant weight loss or weight gain.
- Sleeping problems.
- Activity level has increased or decreased.
- Fatigue or energy loss.
- Feelings of worthlessness or guilt.
- Loss of concentration.
- Thoughts of death.

Source: Adapted from the *Diagnostic and Statistical Manual of Mental Disorders-Fourth Edition,* by the American Psychiatric Association, 1994, Washington, DC: Author.

The remaining four symptoms are expressed as *changes* in a student's usual functioning. These changes may be expressed as either an increase or decrease in any of the following areas: (a) appetite or weight; (b) sleep habits; (c) activity level; (d) energy level; (e) feelings of worthlessness or guilt; (f) difficulty thinking, concentrating, or making decisions; or (g) recurrent thoughts of death or suicidal ideations, plans, or attempts (see Figure 1).

Students with *mild* mental retardation seem to be at risk for depression because they often can perceive that their peers without disabilities are able to accomplish tasks that they themselves cannot

---

Causes of Depression

Students may experience depression as a result of a negative life event, such as the loss of a parent, stresses at home, or adjustment to a new environment. This type of reactive depression is normal and is not a cause for concern unless the depressive symptoms linger and significantly interfere with a student's typical level of functioning. In other cases, there may not be a clear precursor for the depression, yet the student consistently is in a depressed mood. It is when this mood persists over a 2-week period that a teacher should observe the child for other signs of depression.

Students with *mild* mental retardation seem to be at risk for depression because they often can perceive that their peers without disabilities are able to accomplish tasks that they themselves cannot (Eaton & Menolascino, 1982). They may also be aware, via negative peer experiences, that they are different and viewed negatively by society. These observations can then lead to a higher risk for depression and low

self-esteem. Conversely, people with *severe* mental retardation are not as likely to be diagnosed with depression as those with mild retardation, but this may be because of their limited ability to verbally express feelings of sadness or hopelessness, rather than an actual decreased risk for depression (Charlot, Doucette, & Mezzacappa, 1993; Pawlarcyzk & Beckwith, 1987). As a result, depression may be easily overlooked in people with severe mental retardation.

Difficulty of Detection and Diagnosis in Students with Mental Retardation

Teachers, parents, and direct care workers are usually the first to notice that a child with mental retardation is having a problem; however, they often find it hard to determine if the problem is behavioral or emotional (Borthwick-Duffy, 1994). Often, diagnosticians and psychologists tend to attribute symptoms of depression to a student's limited cognitive functioning, rather than to the depression that the student is experiencing. This underdiagnosis of depression is called *diagnostic overshadowing*, in that the depression is deemphasized because the student additionally is labeled as mentally retarded (Crews et al., 1994; White et al., 1995).

The lack of understanding that most psychologists have about students with mental retardation usually results from the lack of exposure that psychologists have had with this population. Phelps and Hammer estimated that fewer than 25% of professionals in the area of psychology receive information about mental retardation in their graduate programs (as cited by Nezu, 1994). As a result, the teacher's input to the psychologist about a student's emotional well-being is extremely important.

The classroom teacher continually monitors the cognitive, social, and emotional well-being of students. Although many students with mild

mental retardation can verbalize their feelings of depression, those with more severe limitations tend to express their depression primarily through changes in their behavior. The teacher can help detect these changes in students' behavior by being sensitive to variations in their overall mood or activity level. Teachers can help identify when a student's behavior has changed in its frequency, intensity, or duration.

For example, some students with mental retardation who are experiencing depression become more aggressive (Reiss & Rojahn, 1993). In these cases, the teacher can give valuable input about how typical the aggressive behavior is and when the behavior first was exhibited by the student. Such input can offset the previously mentioned "overshadowing" in correctly diagnosing depression in students with mental retardation.

Detecting Symptoms in the Classroom

Behavioral Markers

It is most common for a person who is depressed to exhibit an overall mood of sadness. Children with mental retardation, however, may express their sadness through withdrawing and decreasing their social interactions with their peers. Alternatively, they may change the way in which they interact with their peers, becoming irritable or even aggressive toward them. Also, teachers should pay attention when students exhibit new, inappropriate behavior, such as noncompliance or distractibility. In some cases, students may even begin to express their depression through self-injurious behavior. Although behavioral markers such as these may stand out, they may also be quite subtle: A depressed student may simply not seem to take pleasure in activities that he or she previously enjoyed.

Figure 2.
Ideas for Treating Students' Depression Across Life Settings

Skill Building

- Develop the student's communication skills.
- Try a social skills unit to develop interpersonal skills.
- Focus on problem-solving.
- Teach conflict resolution.

Resource Networking

- Work with the family to find needed community resources.
- Start a parent support group in your school.
- Obtain literature from a mental health center about depression.

Expression Opportunities

- Develop nonverbal means for student expression: music, dance, art.
- Role-play potentially stressful situations and appropriate solutions.
- Use films and stories to teach problem-solving.

Relationship Opportunities

- Have pets in class.
- Have students write or draw to pen pals.
- Provide appropriate peer-group opportunities.
- Invite volunteers from the community to develop supportive friendships.
- Find group activities outside the school setting appropriate for the student.

Physical Markers

People with depression usually experience changes in their *vegetative functioning*, or eating and sleeping patterns. Students with mental retardation may also exhibit these signs. Teachers should be aware of changes in overall activity level (either a decrease or an increase) in their students. A student who usually is calm and methodical may show signs of hyperactivity, whereas a student who usually maintains a high level of activity may become withdrawn and slow to respond to stimuli. Changes in weight or interest in food can also be markers of depression. Again, the teacher should look for changes in usual student patterns: the formerly thin student who puts on a substantial amount of weight quickly or the voracious eater who suddenly has no appetite.

Sleep behavior can also be a sign of depression, either increased sleeping or a decrease in the hours the student sleeps. A common occurrence for someone who is depressed is to have little difficulty going to sleep but then awaken in the early morning. Teachers should be aware that sleepy or lethargic students may be suffering from these sleep disturbances during the night.

Treatment of Depression in Children with Mental Retardation

The Individuals with Disabilities Education Act (IDEA) not only ensures the right to free and appropriate educational services, but also to related services, such as psychological assessment and counseling. Many times the school district has programs or staff that can help a student diagnosed as depressed. Once the student has been assessed, the teacher can work closely with the school psychologist or counselor to provide supportive therapy for the student.

The teacher can also discuss with the family any additional support needs that they might have as these needs may contribute to the stress that the student is experiencing. Loss of employment, death of a family member, or economic hardships can all affect the student's level of depression. Teachers should be aware of changes in their students' home environments to help determine if a student is depressed—as opposed to, for example, simple being oppositional. These support needs often occur across settings, for example, at family outings or at recreational activities (see Figure 2).

Examining the settings in which a student functions on a regular basis can help pinpoint obstacles or difficulties that the student is experiencing in these areas, for example, appropriately talking to peers at the community pool. Knowledge of these difficulties thus can help the teacher target instructional objectives for the student in the classroom, such as learning social skills training.

Psychological Services

Psychological services in the mental health community are limited for people with mental retardation. One reason for this may be the bureaucratic structure of these services. Typically, services for people with mental retardation and services for people with mental health needs are provided separately. This separation of services often results in a quandary between agencies as to who should provide services and, often, in a lack of services for the person who is "dually diagnosed."

The most popular forms of psychological services used for children without cognitive limitations experiencing depression may also be used with children with mental retardation. The most popular forms of therapy for children with depression are behavioral therapy, social and adaptive skills training, psychotherapy, and the use of psychiatric medications. These and additional treatment modalities are listed in Figure 3.

Because children with mental retardation are a heterogeneous group, the mental health provider must make modifications in these approaches and techniques. Rubin (1983) suggested that providers should consider the following characteristics of a child when providing psychological services to a student with mental retardation:

Figure 3. Possible Types of Therapy Appropriate for Use with Students with Depression

Individual psychotherapy: The student discusses issues with a counselor or psychologist on an individual basis. The focus is on the student's perceptions and behaviors. The student is usually guided to make his or her own interpretations and goals for change.

Group psychotherapy: Usually a group is formed around a common problem that each member of the group shares to some degree. Groups are usually facilitated by a professional counselor or psychologist. The involvement and support of the other group members are part of the therapeutic treatment.

Family therapy: The family meets with a psychologist or counselor who moderates while problems and solutions are generated by the family members. Family interactions, perceptions, and roles are the areas of focus and change.

Skills training: Building social skills allows the student to engage in social situations while he or she receives modeling and coaching from a therapist or teacher. These social situations allow the student to practice skills in particular deficit areas.

Psychodrama: Guided by a psychologist or counselor, the student acts out themes or roles that represent areas of concern and unresolved conflict. The drama provides emotional release and insight into these areas of concern.

Art therapy: A nonverbal therapy, usually directed by a psychologist, counselor, or art therapist, art therapy uses art as the milieu in which emotions and thoughts can be expressed freely.

Music therapy: A nonverbal therapy, usually directed by a psychologist, counselor, or music therapist, music therapy uses music to help students express and release emotions.

Play therapy: A psychologist or counselor works with the student as he or she plays with toys or other materials that permit expression of conflict issues.

Psychopharmacology: This type of therapy uses prescription drugs to treat medical problems associated with mental disorders.

- Intellectual aptitude.
- Capacity for relationships.
- Neurological functioning.
- Communication skills.

In addition, the mental health provider should always be apprised of the student's current medication intake and medical history.

> When we ignore signs of depression in children with mental retardation, these children become at risk for being misunderstood, underestimated, and untreated.

Final Thoughts

Intellectual functioning does not seem to offset depression; in fact, those with mild mental retardation seem to be at an even greater risk for depression. We say, "seem to be," because of the paucity of recent research in this important area. In addition, many treatment techniques for depression that have proven successful in persons without retardation remain untested in those with mental retardation (Sevin & Matson, 1994).

Children with mental retardation experience pain, loss, and depression as do other people. When we ignore signs of depression in children with mental retardation, these children become at risk for being misunderstood, underestimated, and untreated.

References

American Psychiatric Association. (1994). *Diagnostic and statistical manual of mental disorders* (4th ed.). Washington, DC: Author.

Borthwick-Duffy, S. A. (1994). Epidemiology and prevalence of psychopathology in individuals with mental retardation. *Journal of Consulting and Clinical Psychology, 62,* 17–27.

Borthwick-Duffy, S. A., & Eyman, R. K. (1990). Who are the dually diagnosed? *American Journal on Mental Retardation, 94,* 586–595.

Cantwell, D. P. (1990). Depression across the early life span. In M. Lewis & S. M. Miller (Eds.), *Handbook of developmental psychopathology* (pp. 293–310). New York: Plenum.

Charlot, L. R., Doucette, A. C., & Mezzacappa, E. (1993). Affective symptoms of institutionalized adults with mental retardation. *American Journal on Mental Retardation, 98,* 408–416.

Crews, W. D., Bonaventura, S., & Rowe, F. (1994). Dual diagnosis: Prevalence of psychiatric disorders in a large state residential facility for individuals with mental retardation. *American Journal on Mental Retardation, 98,* 688–731.

Eaton, L. F., & Menolascino, F. J. (1982). Psychiatric disorders in the mentally retarded: Types, problems, and challenges. *American Journal of Psychiatry, 139,* 1297–1303.

Johnson, C. R., Handen, B. L., Lubetsky, M. J., & Sacco, K. A. (1995). Affective disorders in hospitalized children and adolescents with mental retardation: A retrospective study. *Research in Developmental Disabilities, 16,* 221–231.

Matson, J. L., & Frame, C. L. (1986). *Psychopathology among mentally retarded children and adolescents* (Vol. 6). Beverly Hills: Sage.

Menolascino, F. J. (1990). The nature and types of mental illness in the mentally retarded. In M. Lewis & S. M. Miller (Eds.), *Handbook of developmental psychology* (pp. 397–408). New York: Plenum.

Nezu, A. M. (1994). Introduction to special section: Mental retardation and mental illness. *Journal of Consulting and Clinical Psychology, 62*(1), 4–5.

Pawlarcyzk, D., & Beckwith, B. E. (1987). Depressive symptoms displayed by persons with mental retardation: A review. *Mental Retardation, 25,* 325–530.

Reiss, S. A. (1985). The mentally retarded, emotionally disturbed adult. In M. Sigman (Ed.), *Children with emotional disorders and developmental disabilities: Assessment and treatment* (pp. 171–193). Orlando, FL: Grune & Stratton.

Reiss, S. A. (1990). Prevalence of dual diagnosis in community-based day programs in the Chicago metropolitan area. *American Journal on Mental Retardation 94,* 578–585.

Reiss, S. A., & Rojahn, J. (1993). Joint occurrence of depression and aggression in children and adults with mental retardation. *Journal of Intellectual Disability Research, 37,* 287–294.

Rubin, R. L. (1983). Bridging the gap through individual counseling and psychotherapy with mentally retarded people. In F. J. Menolascino (Ed.), *Mental health and mental retardation: Bridging the gap* (pp. 119–128). Baltimore: University Park Press.

Sevin, J. A., & Matson, J. L. (1994). An overview of psychopathology. In D. C. Strohmer & H. T. Prout (Eds.), *Counseling and psychotherapy with persons with mental retardation and borderline intelligence* (pp. 21–78). Brandon, VT: Clinical Psychology Publishing.

Sovner, R., & Hurley, A. (1983). Do the mentally retarded suffer from affective illness? *Archives of General Psychiatry 40,* 61–70.

White, M. J., Nicholas, C. N., Cook, R. S., Spengler, P. M., Walker, B. S., & Look, K. K. (1995). Diagnostic overshadowing and mental retardation: A meta-analysis. *American Journal on Mental Retardation, 100,* 293–298.

Read More About It

General Information on Depression and Mental Retardation

Borthwick-Duffy, S. A., & Eyman, R. K. (1990). Who are the dually diagnosed? *American Journal on Mental Retardation, 94,* 586–595.

Charlot, L. R., Doucette, A. C., & Mezzacappa, E. (1993). Affective symptoms of institutionalized adults with mental retardation. *American Journal on Mental Retardation, 98,* 408–416.

Matson, J. L., & Barrett, R. P. (1990). Affective disorders. In J. L. Matson & R. P. Barrett (Eds.) *Psychopathology in the mentally retarded* (pp. 121–146). New York: Grune & Straton.

Menolascino, F. J. (1990). The nature and types of mental illness in the mentally retarded. In M. Lewis & S. M. Miller (Eds.), *Handbook of developmental psychology* (pp. 397–408). New York: Plenum.

Treatment and Counseling

Hurley, A. D. (1989). Individual psychotherapy with mentally retarded individuals: A review and call for research. *Research in Developmental Disabilities, 10,* 261–275.

Nezu, C. M., Nezu, A. M., & Gill-Weiss, M. J. (1992). *Psychopathology in persons with mental retardation: Guidelines for assessment and treatment.* Champaign, IL: Research Press.

Petronko, M. R., Harris, S., & Kormann, R. J. (1994). Community-based behavioral training approaches for people with mental retardation and mental illness. *Journal of Consulting and Clinical Psychology, 62,* 49–54.

Schroeder, S. R., Schroeder, C. S., & Landesman, S. (1987). Psychological services in educational settings to persons with mental retardation. *American Psychologist, 42,* 805–808.

Laura M. Stough (*CEC Texas Federation*), *Senior Lecturer; and* **Lynn Baker,** *Doctoral Candidate, Department of Educational Psychology, Texas A&M University, College Station.*

Address correspondence to Laura M. Stough, Department of Educational Psychology, Texas A&M University, 704 Harrington Tower, College Station, TX 77843–4225 (e-mail: stough@acs.tamu.edu).

UNIT 6

Emotional and Behavioral Disorders

Unit Selections

Key Points to Consider

• How does the wraparound system work? What are some tips for teachers using this system?

• How have choice-making opportunities for students with emotional and behavioral problems helped break the cycle of negative responses that hinders their progression through the educational system?

• After reading the article by Jacqueline Smollar, what would you suggest as measures to reduce the number of homeless adolescents?

 **Links: www.dushkin.com/online/**
These sites are annotated in the World Wide Web pages.

Resources in Emotional or Behavioral Disorders (EBD)
http://www.gwu.edu/~ebdweb/

he definition of a student with emotional behavioral disorder (EBD) usually conjures up visions of the violence perpetrated by a few students who have vented their frustrations by taking guns to school. One of the hot topics in special education today is whether or not students with emotional and behavioral disorders are too dangerous to be included in regular education classes. The statistics show that students with EBDs are as likely to be the victims of violence or bullying by nondisabled classmates as to be the troublemakers. The definition of EBDs broadly includes all emotionally disordered students with subjective feelings such as sadness, fear, anger, guilt, or anxiety that give rise to altered behaviors that are outside the range of normal.

Should children with chronic and severe anger, already convicted of problem behaviors such as violent acts or threats of violence, be re-enrolled in inclusive regular education classes with individualized education plans (IEPs)? Although teachers, other pupils, and school staff may be greatly inconvenienced by the presence of one or more behaviorally disordered students in every classroom, the law is clear. The school must "show cause" if a child with EBD is to be permanently moved from the regular classroom to a more restrictive environment.

The 1994 Gun-Free Schools Act in the United States requires a one-year expulsion of a student who brings a firearm to school. The Individuals with Disabilities Education Act (IDEA) in its 1997 reauthorization made a compromise for students with EBDs or other conditions of disability. If bringing a gun to school is related to their disability (for example, as the result of being teased or bullied), they are exempt from the Gun-Free Schools Act legislation. They can be expelled, but only for 10 days while the school determines their degree of danger to others. If they are judged to really be dangerous, they can temporarily be given an alternate educational placement for 45 days, subject to reassessment. Their IEPs should not be rewritten to place them in a permanent restrictive setting unless their acts were clearly unrelated to their disabilities (hard to prove). This double standard is very controversial. Students without disabilities are expelled with no educational provisions for one full year.

The identification and assessment of students with emotional and behavioral disturbances are controversial. Labels are discouraged because of their effects on self-concept and self-esteem. A student can benefit more from an unlabeled IEP giving strengths, aptitudes, and achievements, plus a characterization of the dimensions of altered behavior in which he or she has specific needs. Each student's attitude toward change and progress should be assessed frequently.

For educational purposes, children with behavior disorders are usually divided into two main behavioral classifications: (1) withdrawn, shy, or anxious behaviors and (2) aggressive, acting-out behaviors. The debate about what constitutes a behavior disorder, or an emotional disorder, is not fully resolved. The Diagnostic and Statistical Manual of Mental Disorders (4th edition) (DSM-IV) sees serious behavioral disorders as a category first diagnosed in infancy, childhood, or adolescence. Among the DSM-IV disorders of childhood are disruptive behaviors, eating disorders, tic disorders, elimination disorders, separation anxiety disorders, and reactive attachment disorders.

The numbers of students identified as having disorders of emotions and behaviors (EBDs) help determine a state's eligibility for federal funding of special education each year. This categorization for statistical and monetary purposes does not describe the severity of the emotional or behavioral disorder. This category encompasses about 9 percent of the students served by special education in the United States each year.

An alliance of educators and psychologists proposed that IDEA remove the term "serious emotional disturbances" and instead focus on disordered behaviors that adversely affect educational performance. Conduct usually considered a sign of emotional disorder, such as anxiety, depression, or failure of attachment, can be seen as behaviorally disordered if it interferes with academic, social, vocational, and personal accomplishment. So, also, can eating, elimination, or tic disorders and any other responses outside the range of "acceptable" for school or other settings. Such a focus on behavior can link the individualized educational plan curriculum activities to children's behavioral response styles.

Inclusive education does not translate into acceptance of disordered behaviors in the regular education classroom. Two rules of thumb for the behavior of all children, however capable or incapable, are that they conform to minimum standards of acceptable conduct and that disruptive behaviors be subject to fair and consistent disciplinary action. In order to ensure more orderly, well-regulated classroom environments, many schools are instituting conflict management courses.

What causes students to act out with hostile, aggressive behaviors directed against school personnel or other students? An easy, often-cited reason is that they are barraged with images of violence on the news, in music, on videos, on television programs, and in movies. It is too facile: Media barrage is aimed at everyone, yet only a few decide that they want to become violent and harm others. Aggressive, bullying children commonly come from homes where they see real violence, anger, and insults. They often feel disconnected, rejected, and afraid. They do not know how to communicate their distress. They may appear to be narcissistic, even as they seek attention in negative, hurtful ways. They usually have fairly easy access to weapons, alcohol, and other substances of abuse. They usually do not know any techniques of conflict management other than acting out.

The first article addresses the need to identify children with EBDs as early as possible and do primary prevention using Uri Bronfenbrenner's ecological model. The authors suggest support services involving many team members and many components of intervention. Parents, children, and other team members work together at conflict management and social skills development in wraparound ways.

The second and third articles describe characteristics of students with EBDs. The authors of "Making Choices" suggest that allowing students to make choices and engage in their own education can help break the cycle of negative responses. Jacqueline Smollar then describes homeless youth. She suggests that helping students to develop a sense of connectedness to adults with whom they can engage in loving, positive, productive behaviors is essential.

Wraparound Services for Young Schoolchildren with Emotional and Behavioral Disorders

Susanna Duckworth • Sue Smith-Rex • Suzanne Okey • Mary Ann Brookshire • David Rawlinson Regenia Rawlinson • Sara Castillo • Jessie Little

- **Suspension cut in half.**
- **Almost one-half fewer absences.**
- **Referrals to the office reduced by two-thirds.**
- **Parent conferences increased four-fold.**

Would you like to see results like these for your students with emotional and behavioral disorders? This article shows how.

In communities across the United States, educators, mental health practitioners, parents, and students have come face to face with the fact that even young elementary schoolchildren can become a threat to society and to themselves. The reauthorization of the Individuals with Disabilities Education Act (Public Law 105-17, IDEA Amendments of 1997, P.L. 105-17, 300.520, 64 Stat. 12412 [199]) makes it less difficult to expel dangerous or violent students with special needs from general and special education classrooms. In addition, IDEA provides suggestions regarding alternative settings as a means for delivering appropriate educational interventions. Being removed from school, however, should be a last resort; and educators should explore every avenue before a child is either expelled or placed in an alternative setting.

This article describes a project we conducted in a suburban location in the southeastern United States and suggests ways other educators might develop such supports for children and their families.

A dynamic process involves establishing trust, relationship building, and continuous assessment.

Meeting the Needs of Children and Their Families

We designed this project to meet the needs of young elementary schoolchildren with severe and complex emotional and behavioral disorders (EBD). These were children who were often angry, violent, and vulnerable to abuse. The intervention project for this self-contained class of children with EBD began in January 1999 and continued until May 2000. At the beginning of the project, the class contained 8 male students, who had been identified as early as kindergarten or first grade. During the project, class enrollment ranged from 8 to 12 students, 11 males and 1 female, whose ages ranged from 6 to 9 years. A behavioral support team determined that the children should remain in school.

To increase the chances for these children to be included in a general education setting, we implemented a family-centered system using "wraparound" services for the children and their parents (see Clark & Clarke, 1996; Eber, Nelson, & Miles, 1997; Eber, Osuch, & Redditt, 1996; VanDenBerg & Grealish, 1996). A wraparound system is "a needs-driven process for creating and providing services for individual children and their families" (Eber et al., 1997). We used this definition to direct our project. To better understand how to use a wraparound system, we studied the application of systems theory (see box, "Systems Theory").

Our review of the literature led us to develop the following guiding questions, which then provided the impetus for our project:

- What are the features of a hands-on wraparound system of services to serve young children with EBD?

- How can we increase parents' participation in their child's educational program?

- What can we learn from parental needs and concerns that will help us to better serve children with EBD?

- How can we better prepare our future teachers to meet the behavioral challenges of the 21st century?

We then created a behavioral support team to plan and address the guiding questions. Figure 1 shows our conceptualization of a wraparound system. Note the integration of school, team, and community services "wrapping around" the group of children and parents involved in our 18-month intervention project.

Systems Theory and a Wraparound System

The most common framework for understanding family assets, needs, resources, and perceptions is systems theory. This theory spotlights family values, priorities, and needs within a responsive, hierarchical, and methodical environment (von Bertalanffy, 1968). As early as 1970, Hobbs applied systems theory concepts to "ecological strategies" in his program for children with emotional disturbance, Project Re-Ed. Bronfenbrenner's (1977; Bronfenbrenner & Nevill, 1994) systems theory model focuses on human development and renewing support for children and families.

Systems theory, using Bronfenbrenner's research, has been put into practice by Bailey, who has written extensively about preschool children with special needs (Bailey & Wolery, 1992). It is from Bailey's interpretation of Bronfenbrenner's work, as well as Brooks-Gunn (1995), that we took our ideas and developed a wraparound system of services for helping children with EBD and their parents.

Role of the Behavioral Support Team

Members of the behavioral support team were people who expressed an interest in working with one another to support young children with EBD and their parents. The team, which consisted of professionals from a local university, a public school district, and a mental health agency (see Figure 2), met monthly to plan, problem-solve, and determine answers to the guiding questions. Parents were considered members of the behavioral support team because of their knowledge of their own needs, as well as the needs of their children. Parents were also recipients of wraparound services.

We developed several components to achieve the goal of implementing successful interventions for young children with EBD:

- *Data-based behavioral instruction* was directed by data collected in an observation booth by university students, teachers, and other professionals. The observation booth was available to parents, who were invited to observe their children at any time during the school day.

Figure 2. Behavioral Support Team Members

- University Special Education Professors (2)
- University Education Majors Serving as Mentors (12)
- Special Education Teacher
- Teaching Assistant
- Guidance Counselor
- Principal
- Clinical Child Psychologist from Local Mental Health Agency
- Director of the Local Alternative School Program
- Parents of the Children with Emotional and Behavioral Disorders

- *An innovative suspension program,* provided by the school's principal, was called "The Therapeutic Day" (see box). This program reduced full-day suspensions.

- *Cost-free, direct services* in the classroom provided by a clinical child psychologist from the local mental health agency. In addition, free individual family counseling was available at the agency site.

- *A mentoring program* conducted by university education majors. Each mentor was assigned a student from the class. Mentoring options included having lunch, tutoring, and participating in outdoor activities such as touch football, basketball, and miniature golf.

- *The use of the research-based social skills curriculum, Second Step* (Committee for Children, 1999).

Figure 1. A Wraparound System

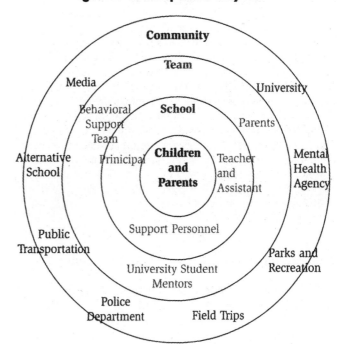

- *Monthly evening parent meetings,* scheduled with parental input, were held in the school library, with transportation provided as needed by the members of the behavioral support team. These meetings turned out to be the most important component of the program.

TO INCREASE THE CHANCES FOR THESE CHILDREN TO BE INCLUDED IN A GENERAL EDUCATION SETTING, WE IMPLEMENTED A FAMILY-CENTERED SYSTEM USING "WRAPAROUND" SERVICES

In addition, we visited consenting families in their homes so that the team could further clarify questions about the purposes of the project and of wraparound services.

We were enthusiastic with the process from the beginning, but we had to continuously remind ourselves to review and revise what we were doing with the children and their parents. We felt that if the project were to be successful, parents must be able to enhance their child-rearing skills and must be able to establish levels of trust with all members of the behavioral support team.

"The Therapeutic Day"

The purpose of "The Therapeutic Day" was to *increase* the amount of time a child would stay in school rather than to *increase* referrals to the principal and out-of-school suspensions. To these ends, the teacher used a cell phone programmed with the phone numbers of each child's parents so that phone calls could be immediate and, through conferencing and problem-solving, could increase parental participation for taking responsibility to help their children stay in school. The principal was a positive support, rather than symbolizing punishment.

Also, the principal coordinated with the university special education professors in providing opportunities for the education majors to serve as mentors—tutoring students, having lunch with them, and sponsoring a monthly "Fabulous Friday" event. Students earned points from a classroom behavior plan to participate in special events. As noted in Table 1, the discipline actions taken brought results.

The Participating Children and Their Parents

As the behavioral support team attempted to address our original guiding questions, which focused on parental needs and concerns about children with EBD and parental participation in educational programs, we reviewed some statistical data: 92% of the parents were single, and 92% of the students qualified for participation in the federal free lunch program. These data gave insight into parents' financial needs and their family structures. We asked ourselves how we could address the needs of parents who were single-handedly juggling employment issues and parental responsibilities while they were confronting pressures brought about by raising children with EBD.

We decided to have monthly parent meetings during which various behavioral support team members would present topics, such as effective discipline (Rawlinson, 1997), character building, behavior modification, mental health issues, and medications. We hoped that the topics would provide parents with an array of options to use at home that would support the educational program offered at school. We knew we could not conduct the parent meetings, however, without input from the parents themselves.

THE WRAPAROUND SYSTEM HELPED ANSWER THE PERENNIAL QUESTION, HOW CAN WE INCREASE PARENTS' PARTICIPATION IN THEIR CHILD'S EDUCATIONAL PROGRAM?

To that end, the first monthly meeting session began with a parental needs assessment. Outcomes from the assessment determined the topics selected for the subsequent meetings (see box, "Who Says My Child Has Behavior Problems in School?"). All participating members of the behavioral support team reviewed the needs-assessment findings, which demonstrated to all how parental requests for help were being honored. The following monthly discussion topics came out of the parental needs assessment:
- Feelings and attitudes.
- Who says my child has behavior problems in school?
- Family issues.
- How to handle stress.
- Losing a job.
- Finances.
- How to handle failure.
- Transportation problems.
- Dealing with unacceptable behavior.
- Trust-building and communication.
- Available community resources.
- How values are learned in life.
- How to communicate encouragement to your child.

During the sessions that followed, we began talking about feelings, attitudes, and character building. We also discussed situations arising at home, which cause children to behave inappropriately. We presented strategies to help parents with their children's problem behaviors; one source of strategies was *Second Step,* which uses a simple step-by-step method to modify behavior.

Behavioral support team members learned that parental needs, just as the students', were concrete. Issues of transportation, jobs, recreation, mental health, and childhood psychotropic medications were stresses in parents' lives. They had real survival needs that had to be addressed. Over 6 months, the parents listened to community representatives, as well as members of the behavioral support team, who could answer questions and facilitate meetings.

Who Says My Child Has Behavior Problems in School?

Steps that take place:

1. The *teacher* is usually the first to notice that a behavior problem interferes with a child's progress in the classroom. Some examples of behavior problems:

hitting	showing signs of depression
having tantrums	refusing to obey
being too quiet or withdrawn	using bad language
yelling	demonstrating uncontrolled anger

2. The *teacher* tells the *principal* or *school psychologist* about the child and the problem. This is called "referral."
3. The *school psychologist* observes the child in the classroom for several days.
4. The *school psychologist* gives the child several tests. Some examples of tests are behavior checklists, social/interaction tests, intelligence tests.
5. The *school psychologist* uses test results to see if the child's behavior fits the label "emotional disturbance," a category determined by the state education agency and used by the local school district.
6. If the child's behavior fits the label, the *school psychologist* sets up an individualized education program (IEP) meeting with the *parent, general education teacher, special education teacher, principal,* and others.
7. If all parties agree, *special education* services are provided for the child.

All behavioral support team members—including the parents—began to see one another as people with similar problems, hopes, and dreams. Trust was established. Many parents admitted that they, themselves, had experienced adjustment problems in school and that they continued to have little control over their own anger. They also admitted that there were serious problems at home with their children. The parents began to ask for help from people they now trusted. It became apparent that parents, as well as children, would not be open to learning unless it was relevant to their lives, presented in a meaningful way, and facilitated by someone who has taken the time to form a relationship of trust with them.

CELL PHONES AND AN OBSERVATION BOOTH WERE ESSENTIAL PARTS OF THE WRAPAROUND SERVICE

The Principal as a Major Key to Success

The school principal was a member of our behavioral support team. He was pivotal in getting the program off the ground. He had an in-depth knowledge of the students, their families, and the school's and communities' needs. Because of his associations and good communication with the school district office, he was able to obtain funds for the construction of the observation booth that helped us answer some of the wraparound systems' guiding questions dealing with parental participation and teacher preparation. The observation booth provided

- Opportunities for parents and professionals to observe children in their daily school setting.
- A specific milieu for university education majors to use observational recording techniques and to reflect on effective teaching practices.

---

10 Tips for Teachers

1. Use frequent positive reinforcement. Research says five positive reinforcements for *each* negative, (Beck & Williamston, 1993).
2. Ignore negative behavior that does not interfere with others' learning or influence others' behavior.
3. Tell children specifically what you want them *to do*, rather than what you want them *to stop doing*. For example, if a child is swinging his arms around and bothering another child, tell him to put his hands in his pockets or fold his arms instead of telling him to stop swinging his arms.
4. Use lots of humor.
5. Once you have stated that a certain consequence will follow a specific action, you *must* follow through with the consequence.
6. Give students the choice of two options, *both* of which are acceptable to you.
7. Change the physical environment, that is, rearrange the desks, and so forth.
8. Elicit support from parents in the form of "pep talks" before behavior is out of control.
9. Use masking tape on the floor to delineate personal space.
10. Spend plenty of time teaching procedures, and review them frequently during the year.

The principal provided essential leadership in finding alternative methods of support for the classroom teacher when the students' behaviors were violent and unacceptable. As the project progressed, he no longer viewed full-day suspension as the preferred option. Through the use of "The Therapeutic Day" (see box), students were able to remain in school or the classroom for at least a half-day and often for the entire day, instead of being suspended (see Table 1).

Table 1. Discipline Report from the Osiris Database

Discipline Actions Taken	1998–1999	1999–2000	% Decrease or Increase
Referrals to the office	128	46	- 64
Absences—partial day	78	18	- 230
Absences—full day	182	102	- 44
Suspensions	84	41	- 49
Parent Conferences	19	79	+ 415

As noted in Table 1, there was a significant decrease in referrals to the office, school absences, and suspensions. "The Therapeutic Day" technique was used in building cultural competence. For students to be culturally competent, they must have appropriate adaptive behavior and academic skills.

The Teacher as the Creator of Cultural Competence

Another member of the behavioral support team was the special education teacher in the self-contained class. Her role was to provide daily academic and behavioral instruction that would build *cultural competence* in the students (see box, "10 Tips for Teachers").

Academic Instruction

Academic instruction was based on each student's IEP. The teacher individualized all work and used a variety of instructional formats, including direct instruction. The students closely followed the general education curriculum, with allowances for their strengths and weaknesses. As well, the teacher used state curricular standards and a variety of instructional materials.

Behavior Management and Social Skills Development

Use of behavior management strategies, such as those found in "10 Tips for Teachers," and the administration of the *Second Step* program allowed the teacher to devote more class time to academic instruction, thereby enhancing the development of cultural competence. The teacher obtained documentation of student adaptive and academic behavior outcomes by means of a point-based behavior plan. Students and parents were able to monitor performance by reviewing total daily points that students earned for appropriate behaviors demonstrated in school.

The *Second Step* curriculum is a research-based program that teaches strategies for behavior management and appropriate social interaction. Mastery of the *Second Step* strategies leads children toward cultural competence. Topics in the curriculum include
- Developing empathy.
- Controlling impulses.
- Managing anger.

Instruction is teacher directed, based on posters, activities, and scripts provided by the publisher. Students with EBD are encouraged to generalize and transfer strategies learned in the *Second Step* program to other situations. For example, in our project, the teacher encouraged students to use *Second Step* role-playing activities to demonstrate empathy after reading a story about a student who had lost her home in a fire. Students who displayed appropriate social skills were allowed to participate in art, music, and physical education classes with their general education peers. To be effective with children with EBD, the teacher was committed to addressing academic, social, and behavioral needs.

What We Learned

In search of answers to the wraparound system's guiding questions, we gained insight and drew the following conclusions:
- The features of an ideal wraparound system of services for young children with EBD should include
  –A systems theory framework.
  –A continuing pledge by a behavioral support team to improve the lives of children and their parents.
  –A data-based program design that includes planning, problem-solving, and implementing interventions.
  –Creative and positive administrative leadership
  –Use of preferred practice based on research ("*OSEP Provides Solutions*,", 2000).

OUR BEHAVIORAL SUPPORT TEAM CONSISTED OF PROFESSIONALS FROM A LOCAL UNIVERSITY, A PUBLIC SCHOOL DISTRICT, AND A MENTAL HEALTH AGENCY—AND PARENTS OF THE CHILDREN IN THE CLASS.

- To increase parent participation in a child's educational program,
  –Trust must be established.

–Parent meetings must be perceived as meaningful and enjoyable.

–The school must project a supportive tone for children and their families.

- We can learn from parents that they have as many needs as their children do, and that parents must trust the school before change can occur.

- To better prepare teachers to address the challenging behaviors of children in the 21st century, teacher education programs must include
  –Access to data-collection opportunities.
  –Preferred practices that are research based.
  –Instruction in trust-building skills.
  –A long-term commitment to intervention programs.

We must overcome other obstacles if we are going to educate children with EBD in their least restrictive environment. Students' success will be significantly increased if schools consider using a wraparound system of services, attempt to build programs that increase parental trust and support, and identify alternatives to the expulsion of students with severe and complex emotional and behavioral disorders. As school districts continue to examine means of helping children with EBD and their parents, we must create systems of services that are supportive, are family-centered, and address the needs of educators.

References

Bailey, D. B., & Wolery, M. (1992). *Teaching infants and preschoolers with disabilities* (2nd ed., p. 66). Englewood Cliffs, NJ: Prentice-Hall.

Beck, R., & Williamston, R. (1993). *Project Ride for preschoolers: Responding to individual differences in education.* Longmont, CA: Sopris West.

Bronfenbrenner, U. (1977). Toward an experimental ecology of human development. *American Psychologist, 32,* 513–531.

Bronfenbrenner, U., & Nevill, P. R. (1994). America's children and families: An international perspective. In S. L. Kagan & B. Weissbourd (Eds), *Putting families first: America's family support movement and the challenge of change* (pp. 3–27). San Francisco: Jossey-Bass.

Brooks-Gunn, J. (1995). Children in families in communities: Risk and intervention in the Bronfenbrenner tradition. In P. Moen, G. H. Elder, Jr., K. Luscher, & H. E. Quick (Eds.), *Examining lives in context: Perspectives on the ecology of human development* (pp. 467–519). Washington, DC: American Psychological Association.

Clark, H. B., & Clarke, R. T. (1996). Research on the wraparound process and individualized services for children with multiple-system needs. *Journal of Child and Family Studies, 5*(1), 1–5.

Committee for Children. (1999). *Second Step Program,* Seattle, WA: Author.

Eber, L., Nelson, C. M., & Miles, P. (1997). School-based wraparound for students with emotional and behavioral challenges. *Exceptional Children, 63,* 539–555.

Eber, L., Osuch, R., & Redditt, C. A. (1996). School-based applications of the wraparound process: Early results on service provision and student outcomes. *Journal of Child and Family Studies, 5*(1), 83–99.

Hobbs, N. (1970). Project Re-Ed: New ways of helping emotionally disturbed children. In Joint Commission on Mental Health of Children (Ed.), *Crisis in child mental health: Challenge for the 1970s.* New York: Harper & Row.

IDEA Amendments of 1997, Public Law 105-17, 300.520, 64 Stat. 12412 (199). [ERIC document Reproduction Service]

OSEP provides solutions to improve student behavior. (2000, March). *CEC Today, 6*(6), 1–15.

Rawlinson, R. M. (1997). *From discipline to responsibility: Principles for raising children today.* Minneapolis, MN: Educational Media Corporation.

VanDenBerg, J. E., & Grealish, E. M. (1996). Individualized services and support through the wraparound process: Philosophy and procedures. *Journal of Child and Family Studies, 5*(1), 7–21.

von Bertanlanffy, L. V. (1968). *General systems theory.* New York: George Brazilles.

Making Choices— Improving Behavior— Engaging in Learning

Kristine Jolivette, Janine Peck Stichter, and Katherine M. McCormick

Do you have students who display inappropriate types of behavior, or who seem depressed, or who lack friends? Perhaps these are students with emotional and behavioral disorders (EBD; see box), and maybe the students present challenges that you find difficult to deal with and that interfere with their educational progress.

This article highlights one strategy, providing opportunities to make choices, that is effective in increasing appropriate behaviors for students with EBD (Munk & Repp, 1994), most notably when used by classroom teachers during ongoing classroom routines (Jolivette, Wehby, Canale, & Massey, 2001b; see also the box, "What Does the Literature Say?" for a link between the research literature on choice and related behavioral characteristics of students with EBD.)

We present a hypothetical case example to show how a teacher might incorporate choice-making opportunities for a student with EBD who is failing math in school. In the course of this article, we suggest practical strategies that both special and general education teachers may use in their academic curricula to encourage students to make appropriate choices. These opportunities may have benefits that long outlast the particular task or situation, to enhance relationships within the classroom, engage stu- dents in learning, and promote a positive classroom environment.

Opportunities to Make Choices

Choice-making opportunities provide students the opportunity to make decisions that may affect their daily routines (e.g., choice of academic task). For example, a student may choose

- From a list of explorers which explorer to write a report on.
- To begin another game with a different peer during free time.
- To use colored markers while illustrating a picture as part of a book report.
- The type of medium (poster, costume, movie) to use for a presentation on a country in social studies.

These varied choice-making opportunities occur frequently in most classrooms. They may seem trivial at first glance, but such choices can have significant implications for the type and level of student participation (Jolivette, Stichter, Sibilsky, Scott, & Ridgely, 2001a).

Several recent classroom investigations into the use of "choice" for students with EBD have shown that this strategy is effective in increasing (or decreasing) specific behaviors in school (Cosden, Gannon, & Haring, 1995; Dunlap et al., 1994; Jolivette et al., 2001b). These re- sults suggest that providing students with EBD the opportunity to make

What Are Characteristics of Students with Emotional and Behavioral Disorder?

Students with EBD often have these characteristics:

- An inability to learn that cannot be explained by intellectual, sensory, or health factors.
- An inability to build or maintain satisfactory interpersonal rela- tionships with peers and teach- ers.
- Inappropriate types of behavior or feelings under normal cir- cumstances.
- A general pervasive mood of unhappiness or depression.
- A tendency to develop physical symptoms or fears associated with personal or school prob- lems (Individuals with Disabili- ties Education Act, IDEA, 1997, CFR 300.7 (a) 9).

In addition, students with EBD may display these characteristics during aca- demic situations when teacher demands are consistently high and if they have a history of school failure (e.g., perform- ing below grade level).

choices during academic situations can promote increased levels of functional and prosocial student behavior. Here are some findings:

- Cosden et al. (1995) found that student accuracy and completion of academic tasks increased when the students were provided with opportunities to choose the task or reinforcer.
- Dunlap et al. (1994) found that the levels of task engagement increased while levels of disruptive behavior decreased when students were provided with opportunities to choose the academic task to complete.
- Jolivette et al. (2001b) found that student task engagement increased, as did the number and accuracy of attempted problems, when students were provided with opportunities to choose the order in which to complete three tasks (same concept but variable formats).

Case Study: Isaac

Isaac is a 7-year-old first-grader with EBD who attends a combined first/second-grade special education class for students with EBD. He had a full-scale IQ of 79 (verbal = 85 and performance = 74), according to the WISC-III. Isaac's teacher reports that he performs below grade level in mathematics and that he is noncompliant and off task during independent math seatwork activities.

Isaac performs at the grade equivalence of beginning kindergarten (K.0) on the Woodcock-Johnson Calculation, Applied Problems, and General Math subtests (Woodcock & Johnson, 1989). In addition, Isaac is rated in the clinical range for the areas of hyperactivity, aggression, conduct problems, and somatization on the Behavior Assessment System for Children (BASC).

Isaac commonly displays the following behaviors during 15-minute regularly scheduled independent math activities:

- Ripping up or throwing the math worksheet to the floor when prompted to begin to work.
- Verbally disrupting the peer next to him.
- Making black pencil marks over the surface of the worksheet instead of solving the problems.
- Asking a peer for assistance on the first few problems.

- Asking the teacher for access to various manipulative items for use with the worksheet and if given a negative verbal response, verbally threatening the teacher.
- Walking around the classroom when the expectation was for him to be at his desk.
- Questioning the teacher as to what he was going to do after math.

The teacher also reports that because of Isaac's inappropriate behaviors during math, Isaac was experiencing academic failure in math and was not meeting his individualized education program (IEP) math objectives.

To address Isaac's inappropriate behavior, the teacher removed privileges (e.g., free time), moved Isaac's desk away from the other desk pods, and re-taught basic math skills on a one-to-one basis during his free time. The teacher states, however, that Isaac's inappropriate behaviors have only escalated; and he continues to make little progress in math.

Strategies for Infusing Opportunities to Make Choices into Math

Given Isaac's behavior and lack of success in math, we suggest providing Isaac with opportunities to make choices during his regularly scheduled, independent math periods to increase his appropriate social and academic behaviors. Because the punitive consequences (loss of privileges and isolation) were ineffective, perhaps the teacher can try another approach: providing opportunities to make choices. This may be a more proactive plan in addressing Isaac's inappropriate behaviors and math failure, and perhaps it will encourage Isaac to display appropriate behavior and achieve success during math activities and tasks.

For this particular student, the focus for choice-making opportunities will be on academic activities related to math instruction and related IEP objectives. There are several ways to implement these opportunities into the existing curricula for Isaac, either before or during tasks, to provide environmental predictability and a sense of control for him. Note that the provision of choice does not alter the curricular objective for Isaac: accurately completing math worksheets.

Choices Before the Task Demand

To provide Isaac with predictability in his independent math seatwork period, Isaac's teacher may provide him with the opportunity to decide *when he will begin* his math worksheet. For example, many students are expected to perform a variety of tasks in the classroom that can be completed throughout the day. Such tasks may include watering the plants, returning library books, and picking up and returning lunch tickets. In Isaac's case, he was expected to straighten the workbook shelf and sharpen the pencils each day. His teacher could then state those two tasks along with the math task demand and provide Isaac with the choice of when to start his math: before he completes those two tasks or after completion of the two tasks. The choice of when to begin his worksheet may provide Isaac with a sense of predictability and a sense of control over his math routine and thus decrease his displays of inappropriate behaviors.

If Isaac were observed to request information regarding what events were scheduled for him after completing his math worksheets, it may indicate that the teacher was not following a consistent classroom routine or that Isaac's daily schedule was more complicated than he could effectively follow on his own. Providing Isaac with this information before or while giving him his task demand may influence his behavior based on whether the event is preferred (e.g., free time) or nonpreferred (e.g., spelling test).

Students may engage in inappropriate behavior to obtain a predictable response from the teacher.

To promote appropriate behavior, his teacher may provide an opportunity for Isaac to *choose the event that will occur immediately following* completion of his math task, even if it is just for a few minutes, before another regularly scheduled class activity. For example, Isaac may select between a computer-simulated math game, a math card game with a peer, or a math board game. Thus, Isaac is rewarded for task completion with a selected event.

If the observation data suggested that Isaac's inappropriate behavior (e.g., out of seat behavior, disruption) increased because of his frustration with the math task, it may be helpful for his teacher to provide Isaac with *the choice of terminating the task* for brief periods of time (e.g., 30 seconds) so as to provide him with a "cooling off" period. Teaching Isaac to better regulate his own behavior within the context of a choice-making opportunity provides a functional and lifelong skill that most people could use.

Having opportunities to make choices in academic tasks can provide the environmental predictability needed to minimiize inappropriate behaviors of students, while strengthening appropriate responses and increased levels of engagement.

As the task is presented to Isaac, his teacher may remind Isaac that he has the option to take "mini-breaks" while working on the worksheet. For example, his teacher may ask Isaac how many problems he will attempt before choosing to take a break. Isaac may select three problems. The teacher then would remind Isaac: "After you work out three problems, you may choose to take a 30-second break before starting on your worksheet again." These mini-breaks are controlled by Isaac and provide him with the ability to self-regulate his behavior while still working on the task and may decrease his subsequent inappropriate behaviors.

The teacher can also allow Isaac to *select items* he feels he will need to complete his math task successfully. For example, the teacher may present Isaac with the math task and prompt him to prepare his work area. In this case, the

teacher may ask him what type of writing utensil (e.g., pencil, pen, colored pencil), what kind of eraser (e.g., stuck on the pencil, hand-held eraser), and what color of scrap paper for his work (e.g., white, yellow, blue) he will need to complete his math task. By preparing his work area through choice-making opportunities, the teacher is minimizing Isaac's out-of-seat behavior—his selected supplies are at hand.

Choices During the Task Demand

To provide Isaac with predictability and consistency, as well as to give him perceived control *during* the task, his teacher may give him a variety of choice-making opportunities. For example, if Isaac is expected to complete more than one worksheet during the independent math period, his teacher may allow him to *select the order* in which to complete the worksheets. After presenting Isaac with all the worksheets he needs to complete, his teacher may ask him which worksheet he wants to complete first, second, and so on. Then the teacher (or Isaac) can write the numbers 1 and 2 on top of the worksheets to indicate his order preference.

To reinforce the order Isaac has chosen, the teacher may give Isaac one worksheet at a time and, on completion, give him the second or third worksheet while saying, "Good job! You are ready for the worksheet you chose to complete second."

Isaac may also have been observed to seek out assistance from his peers during independent math periods, thus affecting his peers' ability to complete their math tasks. No matter if Isaac is displaying these behaviors as a means to gain peer attention or to escape the math task–his teacher can manipulate the environment so that Isaac is appropriately interacting with his peers during this time. For instance, when the task is given to Isaac, he may be permitted to *select a peer with whom to work* on the task. Isaac may complete the even-numbered problems while his peer completes the odd-numbered problems, and then each can "check" the answers of the other. In this case, the task demand has not been changed; Isaac still needs to complete all the math problems (solving and check-

ing). Or Isaac may be permitted to *select the communication mode* with which to gain teacher attention (e.g., assistance). When the teacher gives Isaac a math task to work on at his desk, the teacher may prompt Isaac to select either raising his hand, holding up a red note card (provided by the teacher), or making a thumbs-up gesture to solicit assistance with the task. Such a choice provides Isaac with a means to appropriately gain teacher attention without disrupting his peers or leaving his seat.

In addition, Isaac may have been observed to wander around the room during seatwork periods, disrupting his peers who remain in their seats. While presenting Isaac with his math task, his teacher may provide him with an opportunity to *select where in the room* he wants to complete his math work-sheet(s). In many classrooms, empty desks or portions of large tables may be available as choices. If Isaac has a history of displaying increased levels of inappropriate behaviors when in close proximity to certain peers, then empty desks in that area would not be part of his choice. In that case, the teacher may limit the possible areas in the room that Isaac can select from.

When multiple math worksheets are not part of the task, nor are other choices involving peer partners or different locations feasible, Isaac's teacher may permit him to *choose the methods* in which he will complete the task. For example, Isaac could start at the bottom of the page and work to the top of the page, work from right to left, or randomly select the order of the problems from the worksheet. The teacher may also remind Isaac to be careful not to skip problems. Again, the task does not change, but how Isaac can complete the task has been manipulated.

In addition, Isaac may have occasionally asked his teacher for access to math manipulatives to use while he worked on his task. When appropriate, Isaac's teacher may provide him with opportunities to select the *type of manipulatives (materials)* he wants to use to complete the task. For example, he may select base-ten blocks, blocks, or beans. Or he may select a one-hundred chart, counting strip, or counting bracelet.

Benefits of Infusing Choice-Making Opportunities into the Classroom

Initial research in classrooms on the use of choice-making opportunities for students with EBD indicates that providing opportunities to make choices during ongoing academic activities is an effective, efficient classroom strategy (Cosden et al., 1995; Dunlap et al., 1994; Jolivette et al., 2001b). The following benefits may result:

- Providing a student with EBD an opportunity to choose among *already existing materials* may be a cost-effective-method to minimize some of the inappropriate behaviors typically displayed by these students during academic situations. Teachers can manipulate existing environmental conditions, materials, and natural consequences without using scarce time and money to create "new" instructional materials (e.g., where to sit in the room to complete a task, order of completion for existing tasks, methods to use to complete a given task).

- Providing choices may *promote more positive relations among all students, better teacher-student interactions, and a more focused classroom environment* (Shores et al., 1993). Providing opportunities to make choices can help teachers assign tasks in a more positive way, while providing predictability for the student in the current task situation.

For example, when a student selects to raise his or her hand to communicate "I need help," then the teacher reinforces the student's choice and comes over and offers assistance. And when the student completes the task with accuracy, the teacher provides the student a choice of what to do next (e.g., put a puzzle together, work on any home-work assignments, check out a book from the library).

- By providing the student with opportunities to make choices, *the teacher is relinquishing some of the decision-making power in the classroom*. Being able to make choices during academic tasks may provide students with skills needed

in other academically focused programs.

For example, a small group of students may have the task of creating a bulletin board as part of their report on the human body. Instead of the teacher telling the students that they will create a bulletin board on the digestive system and will highlight it with an interactive component, the teacher may allow the group to select the specific content for the bulletin board but provide parameters for their choice. These parameters may include (a) select one of the following body systems-nervous, digestive, circulatory; (b) provide a detailed visual with supporting information on the selected system; (c) incorporate an interactive activity; and (d) double check all information for accuracy and organization. Thus, the teacher has provided the small group with multiple opportunities to make choices while completing an academic task. This example would be appropriate for older students, but can be adapted for younger students like Isaac.

- The provision of choice-making opportunities may *simultaneously affect social and task-related behaviors of students with EBD*. Students with EBD seek opportunities to influence (control) their classroom environments; unfortunately they may do so by displaying inappropriate behaviors. Guess, Benson, and Siegel-Causey (1985) suggested that choice-making opportunities not only provide a student with the power to manipulate variables but the ability to exert control over environmental events through appropriate means. For students with EBD, this is significant given their use of inappropriate behavior as a means to create more preferred contexts. By adding the predictability to the tasks, as well as providing the student with "power" to manipulate those tasks through choices, the teacher may encourage students to display higher rates of appropriate social behavior while making academic improvement.

In Isaac's case, he was provided with opportunities to make choices within the context of his math tasks, which provided predictability in the math routine

and the ability to manipulate events within it.

Implications for Practice

When considering opportunities to infuse increased choice-making within the curriculum, consider the following issues:

1. Start small and think "manageable" in terms of successive steps. Instead of offering students with EBD opportunities to make choices throughout the entire school day, begin with one or two curricular areas or periods of time. A convenient place to start is during student free time or when students are finishing tasks on a varied schedule. For example, during free time, provide a student with EBD with three options from the classroom environment, such as access to the computer, a book from the teacher's bookshelf, or a puzzle with which to play. Once the student demonstrates the ability to make choices, combine choice-making opportunities. For instance, provide the student with choice options and, once an option is selected, allow the student a choice of where in the room to use the free-time option.

For students with EBD, predictability and control may be critical concepts and skills that are necessary for appropriately coping with the environment.

2. Begin infusing opportunities to make choices within the curricular area in which the student will gain the most. With Isaac, we suggested starting in math because he was experiencing high rates of both academic and social difficulties in that area, contributing to his school failure. When selecting the specific area, review existing student data (e.g., anecdotal records, grade summaries) to guide area selection.

3. View opportunities to make choices along a continuum. For example,

What Does the Literature Say About Choice-Making and Environmental Predictability and Control?

What are Choice-Making Opportunities? Providing students with EBD opportunities to make choices means that the student is provided with two or more options, is allowed to independently select an option, and is provided with the selected option. For example, before distributing a test, the teacher states that each student will complete 25 multiple-choice questions but may choose to either write two essay responses or five short-answer responses as the second part of the test. Each student is called to the teacher's desk to make a selection and is then provided with the selection and told to sit at his or her desk and complete the test. Once all students are at their desks, the teacher says, "When you finish the test, turn it in, take an enrichment folder, and follow the directions inside." This example highlights the provision of choice-making opportunities within naturally occurring classroom events and the connection between choice and environmental predictability.

What is Predictability? Predictability may be defined as a person's ability to accurately judge and interpret what environmental events precede or follow other specific environmental events. That is, the students are provided with an opportunity to make a choice, the choice option is honored, and the events after the test are known. Positive effects of choice-making opportunities may be due, in part, to this predictability once a choice is made (Brown, Belz, Corsi, & Wenig, 1993).

The ability to predict environmental relationships through choice-making opportunities provides the student with an opportunity to act in a manner that helps assure the occurrence of expected environmental events, such as positive interactions with others, cessation of tasks, or reinforcement for a behavior. In the test-taking *with choices*, the students knew what they were expected to do (make a choice and complete the test) and what event was going to occur after the test (work on tasks in enrichment folder). It is common, however, for students with EBD to have difficulty regulating their behaviors when environmental events are perceived to be unpredictable.

In the test-taking example, if the student selected the five short-answer responses but the teacher gave him or her the two essay questions instead, that would create unpredictability. In the student's search for a known or predictable environmental event, the student may consequently display high rates of inappropriate behaviors because he or she knows what the consequences of these behaviors will be. Although potentially undesirable, the consequences are, nevertheless, predictable. For example, a student may act out to gain teacher attention during independent seatwork if teacher attention does not occur when the student displays appropriate behavior and is consistently provided for inappropriate behavior during seatwork times. A student with EBD, however, with the skill to predict potential consequences of his or her own behavior, may display higher rates of appropriate behavior to help ensure the desired teacher attention.

The need for predictability may influence students' behavior even when the ability to exert control over the environment is unavailable (Gunter, Shores, Jack, Denny, & DePaepe, 1994). Given this need for predictability, it is important to assess and modify environments proactively to assist students in making positive choices that will result in both predictable and desirable outcomes (Brown et al., 1993).

How are Predictability and Inappropriate Behavior Linked? Current research in classrooms for students with behavior problems suggests that, unfortunately, predictability most often comes as the result of inappropriate behavior. For example, Van Acker, Grant, and Henry (1996) investigated the interactions that occurred between teachers and students at risk for EBD by conducting a study of 25 teachers and 206 students with mild levels of behavioral problems or higher levels of behavioral problems. These researchers found that most predictable teacher and student interaction patterns were that of teacher demand (academic or social)-to-student noncompliance behavior-to-teacher reprimand-to-student noncompliance behavior. When students engaged in appropriate behavior, however, there was less consistency in teacher responses to the student. Therefore, not surprisingly, if predictability in interactions were important, *students might engage in inappropriate behavior to obtain a predictable response from the teacher.*

The simultaneous effects of choice-making opportunities on both academic and social behaviors is an area that has been underexplored (Powell & Nelson, 1997) and will be an important area for future research and application of choice in the classroom for students with EBD.

How Do We Break the Cycle of Negative Responses? Providing opportunities for students with EBD to make choices related to academic tasks may disrupt the negative cycle of teacher-student interactions described by Van Acker et al. (1996), as well as provide consistency and predictability to academic contexts. For students with EBD, predictability and control may be critical concepts and skills that are necessary and required for appropriately interpreting and coping with the environment, as well as practicing new prosocial skills. When students with EBD perceive their environments to be less threatening and perceive themselves as able to predict and control events, they may increase appropriate kinds of behavior.

For example, in the test-taking scenario *with choices*, the test became more predictable through teacher direction and known events after completion of the test, and the students were able to control the type of written responses required—short answer or essay. Thus, the use of choice-making opportunities can provide the environmental predictability needed to minimize the characteristically inappropriate behaviors exhibited by students with EBD during task situations, while strengthening appropriate responses and increased levels of engagement.

the choices provided to Isaac were basic and concrete. That is, those choices were not significant to decisions he will need to make in the future (e.g., such as what job to train for) but still provided practice in choice-making critical to his proficiency and success in making more important choices.

4. Be consistent in both the presentation and follow-through with choice-making opportunities. For example, offer the same number of choice-making opportunities for the targeted area; and when a student makes a choice, reinforce the selection by providing him or her with the selected item.

By considering these four issues before infusing opportunities to make choices into the curricula for students with EBD, you may provide the appropriate environmental context for both student and teacher success.

Final Thoughts

Overall, research on classroom environments for students with EBD has suggested that punishing students (e.g., withholding rewards, denying choices) for inappropriate behavior only promotes negative and inconsistent interactions between teachers and students (Steinberg & Knitzer, 1992; Van Acker et al., 1996). These findings support the classroom components cited by Reitz (1994) as necessary for students with EBD to experience school success (e.g., high rates of social reinforcement and student academic involvement and achievement).

The provision of choice-making opportunities for students with EBD is a viable curricular modification that links student involvement with student decision making for social and academic suc-cess (Mathur, Nelson, & Rutherford, 1998).

References

Brown, F., Belz, P., Corsi, L., & Wenig, B. (1993). Choice diversity for people with severe disabilities. *Education and Training in Mental Retardation, 28,* 318–326.

Cosden, M., Gannon, C., & Haring, T. G. (1995). Teacher-control versus student-control over choice of task and reinforcement for students with severe behavior problems. *Journal of Behavioral Education, 5,* 11–27.

Dunlap, G., DePerczel, M., Clarke, S., Wilson, D., Wright, S., White, R., & Gomez, A. (1994). Choice making to promote adaptive behavior for students with emotional and behavioral challenges. *Journal of Applied Behavior Analysis, 27,* 505–518.

Guess, D., Benson, H. A., & Siegel-Causey, E. (1985). Concepts and issues related to choice making and autonomy among persons with severe disabilities. *Journal of the Association of Persons with Severe Handicaps, 10,* 79–86.

Gunter, P. L., Shores, R. E., Jack, S. L., Denny, R. K., & DePaepe, P. (1994). A case study of the effects of altering instructional interactions on the disruptive behavior of a child identified with severe behavior disorders. *Education and Treatment of Children, 17,* 435–444.

Individuals with Disabilities Education Act Amendments of 1997, P. L. 105–17. 105th Congress, 1st Session.

Jolivette, K., Stichter, J., Sibilsky, S., Scott, T. M., & Ridgely, R. (2001a). *Naturally occurring opportunities for preschool children with and at-risk for disabilities to make choices.* Submitted for publication.

Jolivette, K., Wehby, J. H., Canale, J., & Massey, N. G. (2001b). Effects of choice making opportunities on the behavior of students with emotional and behavioral disorders. *Behavioral Disorders, 26,* 131–145.

Mathur, S. R., Nelson, J. R., & Rutherford, R. B. (1998). Translating the IEP into practice: Curricular and instructional accommodations. In L. M. Bullock & R. A. Gable (Eds.), *Implementing the 1997 IDEA: New challenges and opportunities for serving students with emotional/be-havioral disorders.* Reston, VA: Council for Exceptional Children.*

Munk, D. D., & Repp, A. C. (1994). The relationship between instructional variables and problem behavior: A review. *Exceptional Children, 60,* 390–401.

Powell, S., & Nelson, B. (1997). Effects of choosing academic assignments on a student with attention deficit hyperactivity disorder. Journal of *Applied Behavior Analysis, 30,* 181–183.

Reitz, A. L. (1994). Implementing comprehensive classroom-based programs for students with emotional and behavioral problems. *Education and Treatment of Children, 17,* 312–331.

Shores, R. E., Jack, S. L., Gunter, P. L., Ellis, D. N., DeBriere, T. J., & Wehby, J. H. (1993). Classroom interactions of children with behavior disorders. *Journal of Emotional and Behavioral Disorders, 1,* 27–39.

Steinberg, Z., & Knitzer, J. (1992). Classrooms for emotionally and behaviorally disturbed students: Facing the challenge. *Behavioral Disorders, 17,* 145–156.

Van Acker, R., Grant, S. H., & Henry, D. (1996). Teacher and student behavior as a function of risk for aggression. *Education and Treatment for Children, 19,* 316–334.

Woodcock, R. W., & Johnson, M. B. (1989). *Woodcock-Johnson Psycho-Educational Battery-Revised.* Allen, TX: DLM.

Kristine Jolivette, *Assistant Professor, Department of Special Education and Rehabilitation Counseling, University of Kentucky, Lexington.* **Janine Peck Stichter** (*CEC Chapter #27), Associate Professor, Department of Special Education, Central Michigan University, Mt. Pleasant.* **Katherine M. McCormick** (*CEC Chapter #180), Assistant Professor, Department of Special Education and Rehabilitation Counseling, University of Kentucky, Lexington.*

Address correspondence to Kristine Jolivette, Department of Special Education and Rehabilitation Counseling, University of Kentucky, 119 Taylor Education Building, Lexington, KY 40506-0001 (e-mail: kjolive@uky.edu).

Homeless Youth in the United States

By Jacqueline Smollar, Ph.D.

Homeless youth in the United States are defined as individuals age twenty-one or younger who meet at least one of the following criteria:

- They have run away from their homes or from their alternative care placements and remained away for a long period of time with little or no connection with their families or caretakers.
- They have been pushed out of their homes or foster care placements, have been abandoned by their parents, or have left home for the streets with their parents' knowledge and consent.
- They have no stable place of residence; lack adult supervision, guidance, and care; and have little likelihood of reunification with parents.

The current number of homeless youth in the United States is not known and estimates are dated. In 1991 the National Network for Youth estimated the number of homeless youth ranged from 100,000 to 500,000. Although estimates of one to two million have appeared in the literature, these larger estimates include youth who run away from home and return fairly quickly, usually within a few days.

History of Homeless Youth

Homeless youth have been a part of U.S. society since its early history. During the settlement of the thirteen colonies and the ensuing westward expansion, many adolescents left home to seek adventure and economic opportunity. Homeless youth were also prevalent in the 1800s, but they were perceived as criminals constituting a significant social problem. In the early 1900s, many youth became homeless during the Great Depression. However, because large segments of the population were homeless during the era, the specific problem of youth homelessness was generally ignored.

In the 1960s, a new group of homeless youth, referred to as "runaways," began to be perceived as a significant social problem. Unlike earlier homeless youth, these adolescents left middle- and upper-class homes and forfeited the educational advantages and future professional prospects available to them as part of their families' socio-economic status. Congress enacted the Runaway Youth Act of 1974, which provided funds for establishing shelters to temporarily house the youth and reunite them with their parents. Shelter staff were required to inform parents or legal guardians of a youth's presence within forty-eight hours of arrival.

The Runaway Youth Act was revised in 1977 and renamed the Runaway and Homeless Youth Act. This revision was in response to reports from youth shelter personnel that they were seeing many youth who had not run away from home but had been pushed out of their homes, been abandoned by parents, or left home for life on the street with their parents' knowledge and consent. Although the 1977 act continued to stress family reunification, it acknowledged that both youth and their families needed extensive services for reunifications to be successfully accomplished.

> *Many youth had not run away from home but had been pushed out of their homes, been abandoned by parents, or left home for life on the street with their parents' knowledge and consent.*

The number of teens seen by the shelter system who had not run away from home but had been pushed out, abandoned, or remained away with parental consent continued to increase during the 1980s. Shelter personnel reported that these youth exhibited multiple psychological and behavioral problems and came from families characterized by parental substance abuse, family violence, child maltreatment, long-term family conflict, and dysfunctional parents (many of whom had severe psychological and behavioral problems of their own).

In the 1990s, family dysfunction continued to be a primary cause of youth homelessness, although poverty once again emerged as a potential contributing factor. The 1990s also saw an increase in the numbers of youth who were homeless as a result of their families' homelessness.

Today's Homeless Youth

Accurate knowledge about homeless adolescents is limited by the fact that most studies focus on young people who are seen by the shelter system, which is only a small percentage of the total number of homeless youth. A report by the Office of the Inspector General estimated that only one in twelve homeless youth ever comes into contact with the shelter system. Despite the limitations, there is sufficient research to draw some general conclusions about the causes of youth homelessness, the characteristics of homeless youth, and the nature of life on the streets.

The primary cause of youth homelessness is family dysfunction, specifically parental neglect, physical or sexual abuse, family substance abuse, and family violence. Furthermore, these family problems have been found to be long-standing ones, rather than single episodes occurring shortly before youth leave home.

Homeless youth lead unstable and hazardous lives. They rarely reside in one location for long, and many have been found to live in four or more places over a six-month period. Homeless youth are at high risk for health problems, particularly hepatitis, respiratory problems (asthma and pneumonia), scabies, and trauma. They exhibit high levels of depression, suicidal tendencies, and suicide attempts, although one study reported that the incidence of suicide attempts was higher prior to leaving home than after leaving. Homeless youth also exhibit poor mental health, high use of alcohol and other drugs, and high risk factors for contracting HIV.

Accurate knowledge about homeless adolescents is limited by the fact that most studies focus on young people who are seen by the shelter system.

Lesbian and gay homeless youth have been found to have a greater and more severe incidence of problems such as depression and suicide than other homeless youth. In one study of homeless street youth, 53% of lesbian and gay adolescents had attempted suicide, compared to 32% of a cohort that did not differentiate individuals by sexual orientation.

Although the developmental implications of youth homelessness in the United States have not been examined directly, the research on developmental processes during adolescence may be used to understand the consequences of youth homelessness. The results of this research and their implications for developmental outcomes among homeless youth may serve to guide future program, research, and policy initiatives directed toward this population.

Adolescent Development

Development is a process that occurs through reciprocal and dynamic interactions that take place between individuals and various aspects of their environment, with the person and the environment simultaneously influencing one another. Through examining the individual and environmental characteristics that foster positive development among adolescents, it is possible to draw inferences about the developmental prospects for homeless youth.

Four specific characteristics that foster positive developmental pathways from childhood to adulthood have been identified:

- A sense of industry and competency,
- A feeling of connectedness to others and to society,
- A sense of control over one's fate in life, and
- A stable sense of identity.

A Sense of Industry and Competency. Individuals who are confident in their own abilities develop a sense of industry and competency. Being involved in productive activities in school, at home, or in the community, and winning recognition for their productivity, nurtures this sense of industry and competency in children. This in turn fosters the development of a stable identity during adolescence and the perception of oneself as a potentially productive member of society.

Youth who become homeless do not appear to have the opportunity to engage in interactions and activities that foster the development of a sense of industry or competency in their school environments. Homeless youth have been found to have a history of school failure that often dates back to their early school years. One study found that only 44% of homeless youth had attended school regularly before leaving home, 43% had failed or repeated a grade in school, and 11% had failed more than once.

The home environments of homeless youth also do not appear to provide many opportunities for developing a sense of industry or competency. While living at home these youth reported that their parents or caretakers constantly denigrated them, frequently expressed dissatisfaction with them, and spent very little time with them. Once they are homeless, many youth have the opportunity to experience a sense of industry and competency, often for the first time in their lives. Youth who develop the survival skills necessary for life on the streets are able to win recognition from other homeless individuals in the street culture who value those skills. However, because these skills often include shoplifting, stealing, swindling, pickpocketing,

CASE STUDY—NINA

Eighteen, pale, petite and dressed in black, Nina's ears, nose and fingers are studded with rings and her black hair is teased into a new-wave frizz. She is an alternative kid in a non-alternative town, and she knows how very different she is. A lesbian, she left for California when she was only 16. Though she was seeking greater acceptance, what she found was life on the streets. After a few months she hitched her way back to Maine. She found an apartment with a bunch of other kids, but recognizes now that none of them knew what they were doing. Life there was chaos. She worked nights, and often couldn't rouse herself in the morning to go to school. "I wanted to stay in school," she says now, looking back. "I wanted to get my diploma, even go to college. But things change when life becomes more real. When you're living on your own, you work the third shift, you got to get up at six in the morning and walk to school? It's like, it's way too much of an inconvenience to worry about, so you end up not going." When she did go, she found that she was so far behind that she was chalking up F's instead of her usual A's. "Nobody ever asked me why," she says. She ended up dropping out and going for a GED instead.

From M. Wilson & A. Houghton (1999). *A Different Kind of Smart: A Study of the Educational Obstacles Confronting Homeless Youth in New England.* New England Network for Child, Youth & Family Services. Reprinted with permission.

prostitution, and begging, they are not consistent with skills valued by mainstream society. Consequently, the sense of competency developed in the context of the street culture may further impede the potential of these youth for becoming integrated into mainstream society. In fact, youth services professionals have reported that the most difficult youth to reach are often those who have achieved the greatest success in adapting to street life.

A Feeling of Connectedness to Others. Interactions that promote development of a sense of connectedness to other people are those in which adults provide social and emotional support to adolescents while permitting them psychological and emotional independence. Interactions in which adults attempt to control adolescents' behaviors by monitoring their activities and applying sanctions in a consistent and caring manner also promote the development of a sense of connectedness because they signal to adolescents that adults care about them and are willing to become involved in their lives.

Research on the family lives of homeless youth prior to leaving home suggests that they have few opportunities to develop a sense of connectedness to parents. Most homeless teens are leaving homes in which they were abused or neglected rather than supported or encouraged. In one study, it was found that 60% of youth in shelters nationwide were physically or sex-

ually abused by parents. Furthermore, the parents of homeless youth, rather than monitoring them in a caring and consistent manner, were found to be excessively strict, use excessive punishment, or be highly neglectful.

The lack of connectedness between homeless youth and their families is evident in the fact that parents often knew that their children were leaving home and informed shelter personnel that they did not want their children to return.

Some researchers have suggested that one of the reasons many of these children leave home is to find the connectedness that is missing in their lives—the love and support they did not get at home. In fact, many homeless youth report that they were able to find adults who cared about them while living on the streets. Unfortunately, these adults often exploited them and involved them in criminal activities.

Homeless youth lead unstable and hazardous lives.

While on the streets, homeless youth also appear to develop a strong sense of connectedness to one another, which offers them a semblance of security and comfort. Street companions often provide the friendship, acceptance, and understanding previously lacking at home or in foster care placements. As difficult as life is on the streets, many homeless youth prefer it to the homes they left.

Although homeless youth may be able to develop a sense of connectedness to other persons, they are not developing a sense of connectedness to society. As a result of years of victimization by parents or other caretakers, homeless youth are mistrustful and fearful of society's institutions and do not believe that these institutions are concerned about their welfare. For that reason, homeless youth typically have not made use of traditional services and community resources. Shelter personnel frequently report that the most difficult task in working with street youth is gaining their trust.

Sense of Control Over One's Fate in Life. Adolescents who have a sense of control over their fate believe that they have some influence over what happens to them. When adults consistently respond to prosocial behaviors with positive sanctions and to misbehaviors with negative sanctions, children learn that their behaviors are related to particular responses. The dysfunctional families of many homeless youth do not provide these kind of responses. Parental substance abuse and family violence often result in parent-child interactions characterized by random responses to children's behaviors. Consequently, children in these families are likely to develop a sense of helplessness rather than control. For many of these youth, leaving home may be a means of trying to gain some control over their fate in life. However, life on the streets does not appear to provide these youth with many opportunities to engage in interactions that foster the development of a sense of control over their lives.

Youth services professionals have reported that the most difficult youth to reach are often those who have achieved the greatest success in adopting to street life.

Sense of Identity. Development of a stable identity has been found to be associated with positive interpersonal relationships, psychological and behavioral stability, and productive adulthood. The development of a stable identity is derived from an adolescent's sense of competency, connectedness to others and to the larger society, and control. Homeless youth are unlikely to have opportunities to engage in interactions that foster the development of these characteristics prior to leaving their homes. Consequently, they are unlikely to have formed the basis for a stable identity before becoming homeless.

The fact that some homeless youth are able to develop a sense of competency with respect to survival skills on the streets and connectedness to others in their street communities may provide a basis for identity development. However, the identity that develops out of this process is likely to reflect alienation from society and identification with the street culture.

Implications for Social Policies and Services

Because homeless youth in the United States tend to come from severely dysfunctional families, they are already at risk for negative development outcomes prior to running away. Although leaving home may be an adaptive response to a threatening situation, those who leave to escape serious family problems often face equally threatening problems on the street.

The prospects for homeless youth making a successful transition from childhood to adulthood are not positive. These youth do not have families that offer guidance, structure, and encouragement; they are isolated from the institutions of society; and although they often develop a sense of connectedness to the street community, that community generally does not pro-

vide the assistance and support necessary to foster positive developmental pathways.

One implication for social policies and services is that homeless youth need not only safe places to live, access to education and job training, and physical and mental health services, but also environments in which they can engage in interactions with adults and peers that are productive of positive developmental pathways. Although the youth shelter system offers these kinds of environmental opportunities, the efforts of this system are often impeded by the short time period in which youth can remain in the shelter and by the scarcity of long-term care options for youth. The focus on reunification with families needs to be rethought in the light of the evidence that many of these youth do not have families to which they can turn, and many of the families they could return to are likely to be highly dysfunctional.

Altering the developmental pathways or outcomes of homeless youth is not an easy task. A major challenge is that only a small percentage of homeless youth seek assistance from the community agencies that have been established to help them. This suggests that more outreach is needed to contact these youth and provide the services that they need.

Another challenge to helping homeless youth develop along more positive pathways is the absence of advocacy efforts for youth among professional organizations. Developmentalists, long active in advocating services for young children, have not made the same effort on behalf of adolescents. Increased advocacy, as well as increased research efforts by professionals and their organizations, would foster services to help homeless youth develop along more positive pathways.

This article is condensed from J. Smollar (1999). Homeless Youth in the United States: Description and Developmental Issues. *New Directions for Child and Adolescent Development*, 85, 47–58. Copyright 1999 by Jossey-Bass Publishers. Used with permission. References are available on the web site (www.TPRonline.org) or in the original article.

Jacqueline Smollar, Ph.D. is a Senior Research Associate with James Bell Associates in Arlington, Virginia.

UNIT 7

Vision and Hearing Impairments

Unit Selections

Key Points to Consider

- Are schools for the visually disabled dinosaurs or mainstays? Defend your answer.

- What important lessons can teachers and students with good vision learn from a student who is blind and participating in an inclusive classroom?

- How can visual materials be used to enhance learning environments?

 **Links: www.dushkin.com/online/**
These sites are annotated in the World Wide Web pages.

Info to Go: Laurent Clerc National Deaf Education Center
http://clerccenter.gallaudet.edu/InfoToGo/index.html

The New York Institute for Special Education
http://www.nyise.org/index.html

Earlier, more adequate prenatal care, preventive medicine, health maintenance, and medical technology have reduced the number of children born either blind or deaf. In the future, with knowledge of the human genome and with the possibility of genetic manipulation, all genetic causes of blindness and deafness may be eliminated. Now and in the future, however, environmental factors will probably still leave many children with vision and hearing impairments.

Children with visual disabilities that cannot be corrected are the smallest group of children who qualify for special educational services through the Individuals with Disabilities Education Act (IDEA). Legally, a child is considered to have low vision if acuity in the best eye, after correction, is between 20/70 and 20/180 and if the visual field extends from 20 to 180 degrees. Legally, a child is considered blind if visual acuity in the best eye, after correction, is 20/200 or less or if the field of vision is restricted to an area of less than 20 degrees (tunnel vision). These terms do not accurately reflect a child's ability to see or read print.

The educational definition of visual impairment focuses on what experiences a child needs in order to be able to learn. One must consider the amount of visual acuity in the worst eye, the perception of light and movement, the field of vision (a person "blinded" by tunnel vision may have good visual acuity in only a very small field of vision), and the efficiency with which a person uses any residual vision.

Public Law 99-457, fully enacted by 1991, mandated early education for children with disabilities between ages 3 and 5 in the least restrictive environment. This has been reauthorized as PL102-119. It requires individualized family service plans outlining what services will be provided for parents and children, by whom, and where. These family service plans (IFSPs) are updated every 6 months. This early childhood extension of IDEA has been especially important for babies born with low vision or blindness.

In infancy and early childhood, many children with low vision or blindness are given instruction in using the long cane as soon as they become mobile. Although controversial for many years, the long cane is increasingly being accepted. A long cane improves orientation and mobility and alerts persons with visual acuity that the user has a visual disability. This warning is very important for the protection of persons with blindness/low vision.

Children with visual impairments that prevent them from reading print are usually taught to read braille. Braille is a form of writing using raised dots that are "read" with the fingers. In addition to braille, children who are blind are usually taught with Optacon scanners, talking books, talking handheld calculators, closed-circuit televisions, typewriters, and special computer software.

Hearing impairments are rare, and the extreme form, legal deafness, is rarer still. A child is assessed as hard-of-hearing for purposes of receiving special educational services if he or she needs some form of sound amplification to comprehend oral language. A child is assessed as deaf if he or she cannot benefit from amplification. Children who are deaf are dependent on vision for language and communication.

When children are born with impaired auditory sensations, they are put into a classification of children with congenital (at or dating from birth) hearing impairments. When children acquire problems with their hearing after birth, they are put into a classification of children with adventitious hearing impairments. If the loss of hearing occurs before the child has learned speech and language, it is called a prelinguistic hearing impairment. If the loss occurs after the child has learned language, it is called a postlinguistic hearing impairment.

Children whose hearing losses involve the outer or middle ear structures are said to have conductive hearing losses. Conductive losses involve defects or impairments of the external auditory canal, the tympanic membrane, or the ossicles. Children whose hearing losses involve the inner ear are said to have sensorineural hearing impairments.

In 1999 The Newborn and Infant Hearing Screening and Intervention Act in the United States provided incentives for states to test the hearing of newborns before hospital discharge. Thirty-four states now offer this test for a small fee. When an infant is diagnosed with deafness or hearing loss, an appropriate early education can begin immediately under the auspices of IDEA.

Students with vision or hearing impairments whose disabilities can be ameliorated with assistive devices can usually have their individualized needs met appropriately in inclusive classrooms. Students with visual or hearing disorders whose problems cannot be resolved with technological aids, however, need the procedural protections afforded by law. They should receive special services from age of diagnosis through age 21, in the least restrictive environment, free of charge, with semiannually updated individualized family service plans (IFSPs) until age 3 and annually updated individualized education plans (IEPs) and eventually individualized transition plans (ITPs) through age 21. The numbers of children and youth who qualify for these intensive specialized educational programs are small.

Many professionals working with individuals who are deaf feel that a community of others who are deaf and who use sign language is less restrictive than a community of people who hear and who use oral speech. The debate about what has come to be known as the deaf culture has not been resolved.

The first article in this unit deals with the pros and cons of inclusion in general education classes for students with visual disabilities. In this informative article the author argues that special schools or special classes may be less restrictive for children with severe visual disorders. Public schools with regular classroom placements can be prohibitive.

The second article is the story of a girl, blind from infancy, who was warmly welcomed in an inclusive classroom. Gathary gave lessons on hope and wonder as she received lessons in academics. Two support staff aides helped her classroom teacher, and some modifications of the classroom were necessary, but the efforts were small compared to the enormous benefits experienced by all.

The unit's third selection is concerned with the education of students who are deaf or hearing impaired. The promise of the authors is that communication and instruction are best enhanced with visually stimulating environments. The article describes how to use visual strategies as graphic organizers of information.

Schools for the Visually Disabled: Dinosaurs or Mainstays?

In an age of inclusion, specialized schools for the visually disabled play an integral part of the continuum of placements offered for students with disabilities.

Michael J. Bina

Schools for blind or visually disabled children have existed in the United States for more than 169 years. Some ask, Why have they survived this long? Has not inclusion made these placement options obsolete? If federal and state laws mandate education in the least restrictive environment, why do local school districts still send children to segregated settings? Are the high per capita costs justifiable? Should not the resources for these schools be redirected to local education agencies to improve services in students' home communities?

These are fair and not uncommon questions asked by the general public, legislators, and even many educators. For answers, we must listen carefully to current students, former students, local school leaders, and parents whose children attend or have attended these schools. Schools

for blind children may seem an outdated service delivery model, but as Jim Durst, principal of the Indiana School for the Blind, recognizes, the educational outcomes of students prove that these placement options are justifiable, legitimate, and critically essential "for some children all of the time and for all children some of the time."

Obsolete and Unnecessary?

The inclusion movement has not eliminated the need for specialized schools for blind children. In fact, to a large extent it has increased the need for specialized services to enable children with visual disabilities to succeed in regular classrooms.

For students with visual disabilities to be meaningfully and successfully included in regular programs and to keep up with their classmates, they must have educational support

services, reading and writing skills, and materials in accessible formats. To expect a child without skills to be successful in a regular education setting without supports would be as ill-advised as immersing a nonswimmer in the deep end of a pool with a sink-or-swim expectation. Although students might survive the experience, they certainly wouldn't enjoy it or thrive to their full potential.

Today, local directors of special education schools refer blind children to schools for the blind to help them thrive rather than just survive—so that they can better integrate themselves into their local schools. Often, these referrals are for short-term placements in the school's on-campus program, summer school enrichment or compensatory skill training, or consultative outreach services that support children remaining in their local districts.

In 1900, the blindness field was the first disability group to integrate or mainstream students in public schools. Even before the advent of the Education for All Handicapped Children Act, approximately 93 percent of students with visual disabilities were already placed in their local school districts, with 7 percent in specialized schools. Although this ratio has remained the same, many specialized schools report increasing referrals for outreach services and summer and regular on-campus enrollment. The U.S. trend shows not a diminishing need but rather a legitimate placement option in response to the steadily increasing demands from local districts. Schools for the blind are not a substitute for public school programs but are an important complementary option.

Least Restrictive Environment

Educators in local schools are committed to fulfilling the spirit and letter of the federal and state legislation that mandates that all children with disabilities be educated with their nondisabled peers to the maximum extent possible. However, some school districts find its implementation impossible owing to circumstances over which they have no control.

For example, Mr. Adams, a rural area director of special education, has been unable for the past five years to recruit qualified staff to meet the needs of visually disabled students in his district because of a national specialized-teacher shortage. Only 33 U.S. universities offer preservice training programs for teachers of the visually disabled. Unfortunately, these 33 programs graduate fewer than 200 students each year. The demand throughout the United States far outweighs the supply of graduates from each program. This is compounded by the very high yearly attrition rate of specialists. Mr. Adams, therefore, must refer many of his district's visually disabled students to the school for blind children.

In another scenario, Mr. Sands, a director of special education in a large Indiana community, is fortunate to have recruited and retained qualified teachers for visually disabled students. Even though his district has qualified staff, he makes occasional referrals for placements to the school for blind children. He refers students who have difficulty achieving academically in the regular classroom and who need more intensive and individualized instruction than what is locally available. In these cases, the individualized education program team has determined that a school for blind children is the least restrictive environment—or the most productive setting. Many students benefit from immersion in a learning environment where all the staff in every class and dormitory can instruct and reinforce critical blindness-specific skills, such as Braille reading and writing, orientation and mobility (independent travel) and daily-living skills.

Rebecca, a high school sophomore from Mr. Sands's district, attended her first five grades at a school for the blind, returning to her neighborhood school for junior high. Her family, Mr. Sands, and his staff determined that Rebecca would benefit from returning to the school for the blind for at least the first two years of high school. Rebecca, who also attends a nearby local high school part-time, has taken advantage of the school's revolving door policy, in which students can come and go depending on their changing needs. Rebecca's parents and the staff from both schools agree that placement cannot be a one-size-fits-all solution: The question is not which option is best—they both are.

In another situation, Ms. Dare, a director of special education in the state's largest city, utilizes a school for the blind on a daily basis for students in her district who are having difficulty in large school settings. Often, these students can attend both schools, taking academic courses at the school for the blind, for example, and vocational courses at the local high school. These children can go home every evening, but frequently they stay overnight in the dormitory to take advantage of recreational programs, such as swimming, dances, Boy Scouts or Girl Scouts, or Special Olympics; on- or off-campus jobs; extracurricular competitive sports, such as track and field, swimming, or wrestling; or band, choral, speech, or debate activities.

Real-World Connections

Shawn, who was born blind, has a twin sister who is fully sighted. Although he attended a school for the blind for his entire school career, he was able to have the best of both worlds by attending a nearby local high school part-time. Now an alumnus of the school, Shawn told me,

> I knew when I was in high school that I was getting a good education because I could compare it to what my twin sister was getting from our public school. But until I got to college, I really didn't recognize how very well prepared I was.

Shawn described how the premed students in his fraternity house frequently sought his assistance with English themes, research papers, and math assignments. He knew that his abilities to match subjects with verbs, to organize his thoughts on paper, and to calculate numbers were superior in many cases to his fraternity brothers' abilities. He also felt more mature than his fraternity brothers because of his early dormitory experience dealing with, and adapting to, others.

Shawn's dormitory experience also helped him work independently. When he went home on weekends, he taught his parents, who tended to be overprotective, how he could do things for himself and why they needed to let him. His parents struggled with his living away from home, particularly in the early grades. However, when they saw his progress—his strong "can do" attitude, his confidence, his happiness, and his many friends—they realized that this sacrifice was necessary for his current and future independence and success.

Shawn just earned his college degree and is currently employed as a social worker. He lives in an apartment and does his own cooking, shopping, and other household chores. He travels in the community independently, using skills he learned in orientation and mobility, a related service that was not available in his home school.

Not all students are exactly like Shawn. Blind and developmentally delayed, Megan just graduated from a school for the blind. Unlike Shawn, she will not go to college or live independently in an apartment. But with the assistance of a job coach, she is employed, and she lives in a supervised group home. Megan, too, was not sheltered from "real world" realities or segregated from the community.

Shawn's and Megan's career experiences began in their early grades, and later both had on- and off-campus jobs. Shawn attended the local high school for academic enrichment and social experiences; Megan went off campus to gain experience working in a community adult workshop. Both Shawn and Megan moved from their dormitories into three-bedroom houses while in high school, and both were expected to shop for groceries, prepare food, clean the house, and meet other responsibilities. Shawn lived in one of the school's independent living houses without a live-in supervisor; Megan lived in a semi-independent living program with ongoing staff supervision. Shawn earned a pass to travel off campus independently to any location; Megan went many places in the community with adult supervision. Megan was required to open and maintain a checking account at a local bank where she deposited her check each week and conducted financial transactions.

Both Shawn and Megan also distinguished themselves in extracurricular activities. Shawn was a wrestler, competing with other blind athletes on the national level and with public school opponents in state competitions. He also developed powerful speaking skills, which led to participation in state and national oratory contests, and had challenging roles in school plays. His parents, proud of his extensive involvement, often asked Shawn if he ever had time to sleep! Megan was widely recognized for her singing. Twice she sang the national anthem at the state Special Olympics competition, and she sang in the school's chorus that traveled around the state and country.

The Cost of Value

These are impressive achievements. A state government official, after attending graduation at a school for the blind, commented on how well prepared the graduates appeared and how much progress they had made at the school. A school administrator replied, "Yes, but you are well aware of the criticism our school receives for the high per pupil cost and perceived 'expensiveness.'" The state official responded,

> How can they place a value on what these children were provided, what they have clearly gained, and what we know they are going to accomplish because of our investment in them? Look at the value rather than the cost.

In a similar conversation, Mrs. Botkin, whose teenage son is visually disabled and autistic, said,

> They can either pay now to make my son independent or *he* will pay in the future if he does not get the services he needs. We must decide whether we are going to socialize our children in less expensive programs that do not have all the essential services or we are going to instruct them and make sure they get skills. My son's success is only possible in a program that costs more.

The per capita cost statistics are often misleading. If all the services provided at a school for the blind could be replicated in the local district, the cost per capita would be the same in both settings. However, because blindness is a low-incidence condition and each district does not have large numbers of visually disabled students, the local services would likely be less economical than those in a centralized setting where the ratio of staff to students is higher and therefore the cost is less per pupil.

A colleague employed in a large Illinois public school reported that the per capita costs of students in her district were comparable to the instructional costs at a school for blind children. She indicated that because her district provided comprehensive and intensive full services, costs were higher than those in a local district that provided only the bare essentials, such as an itinerant teacher working with a student only one or two times a month. She defined full services as highly adapted technology; a full complement of specialized itinerant and resource teachers; and such related services as orientation and mobility, physical and occupational therapy, and special transportation. In her district, transportation costs were high because of the need to bus children extensively throughout the large metropolitan area.

Another factor is that the specialized school's costs include not only the educational expenses but also the provisions for food, housing, supervision, utilities, and other expenses over a 24-hour day. These costs are not included in public school expenditure figures. When comparing costs in both settings, we must match services for services. To say that one option with fewer services is less expensive is unfair. The more expensive options provide more services.

But shouldn't the resources be redirected to local education agencies to improve services in students' home communities? This appears to be a logical strategy given the least restrictive language in the law. However, because qualified specialists are typically not available, local districts are not likely to fill all the positions needed and would have to regionalize programs to consolidate services. Therefore, students would still be unable to attend their neighborhood schools, and some students would end up without any services. Specialized services would lose their effectiveness if they were scattered throughout the state. The state would also lose a major resource center and would no longer be able to provide outreach services.

Least Restrictive or Most Productive?

Are schools for the visually disabled dinosaurs on the verge of extinction or credible placements of distinction? Consider the impact that blindness has on learning for such students as Megan and Shawn, the role that specialized schools play in overcoming their potentially devastating disabilities, and the ever-increasing demands for these services from local districts.

All these examples illustrate the value and necessity of providing a continuum of service options when students need alternatives to their local school programs. Schools for visually disabled students are an integral part of this continuum of options. A district may call upon the specialized school when it is unable to recruit specialized staff and provide services locally. Whenever a particular student is not achieving to his or her potential, school leaders can turn to this "more restrictive"—or potentially more productive—setting.

Michael J. Bina is Superintendent of the Indiana School for the Blind, 7725 N. College Ave., Indianapolis, IN 46240 (e-mail: binami@speced.doe.state.in.us).

Seeking the Light:
Welcoming a Visually Impaired Student

Anita Meyer Meinbach

Every once in a while, if you are lucky, you will have a student in your classroom who reaches into your heart, touches your soul, and stays with you a lifetime. Once in a while, if you are lucky, you will have a student whose wisdom and *joie de vivre* are a constant reminder of the choices we have to make every day, the perspectives we choose to take, and how we choose to see the proverbial glass. I was one of the lucky ones—a teacher with a very special student whose determination, outlook, and indomitable spirit provided special lessons in living. Gathary sees the beauty in what is invisible to the eye. She takes delight in everything around her and celebrates life. Her mind is filled with images; her heart is filled with joy. Those of us fortunate enough to know Gathary have gained in countless ways. She has forced us to reassess what we perceive to be our own limitations and has made us aware that each of us is responsible for determining what limits we reach. Gathary is blind, and has been from infancy; but, in a sense, Gathary has opened our eyes by sharing her visions of hope and wonder.

Gathary joined our sixth grade class, a language arts and geography block, in January 1997. For most of us, it was our first opportunity to interact with someone who is blind. While every day did not go smoothly, the journey was worth every bump; and in the end, we all gained in kindness, understanding, and empathy. What follows is based on a conversation that took place at the end of the school year. Gathary, her mother Leslie (an art teacher at our school), Beth Gordon (the visual itinerant teacher), three friends, and I met to discuss many issues that affected Gathary, her classmates, and teachers and to evaluate the ways in which the classroom atmosphere and curriculum met the needs of the visually impaired. As the classroom teacher, I was especially anxious to know what changes and adaptation were most worthwhile and what I might have done differently to contribute to an even more successful experience.

With the growing popularity of inclusion, more and more teachers will be concerned with mainstreaming and its ramifications. Teaching middle school adds to the challenge simply because of the very nature of middle school students who are experiencing dramatic physical, social, and emotional changes. It is sometimes difficult for middle school students, who are coping with their own lives, to empathize and reach out to others. Often, their own lack of confidence and lowered self-esteem cause them to appear heartless and unfeeling. Their need for peer-acceptance makes inclusion not only difficult for the special needs students who so desperately want to fit in, but also for the regular classroom students who desire conformity and wish to find their own place in which to fit.

Since the conversation shed light on many important issues affecting the visually impaired in the mainstreamed setting of a middle school, a synthesis of the responses to specific questions pertinent to teachers are being shared in the hope that it will provide ideas and inspiration for those working with middle school students who face special challenges.

> **Gathary has made wonderful friends this year; and, according to Gathary, these are the first strong friendships she has made with peers who are sighted.**

Issue: Mainstreaming

Question: What considerations were most important in determining whether or not to fully mainstream Gathary into Southwood Middle School?

A close working relationship among the teachers in a school is critical for a blind student. Since Southwood Middle has an extremely close knit faculty, both Gathry's parents and the support staff, provided by Dade County schools, who have worked with Gathary over the years, believed this would be the best setting to allow Gathary to "spread her wings." Gathary was first mainstreamed in the second grade, but it was a more sheltered atmosphere, which was appropriate at the time. For part of the day she was in a class with eight other visually impaired students (K–4), all functioning at different levels. She was only mainstreamed for a short time each day (45 minutes, two times a day). This was not enough time to develop friendships. It also made it hard for her to gain a perspective on peers. This year, except for math class, Gathary has been completely mainstreamed. She has learned how to cope and deal with situations she probably would not confront in a more protective environment. She also has been more challenged academically and has risen to this challenge. Gathary has made wonderful friends this year; and, according to Gathary, these are the first strong friendships she has made with peers who are sighted.

Question: What qualities are most important for teachers with students who have special needs?

Perhaps the most important quality for teachers working with special needs students is attitude. There needs to be a willingness to work with the itinerant vision teacher and other members of the support staff. Teachers working with special students must realize that they are part of a team. While the support staff tries not to pull Gathary out of content area classes, there have been times when this was necessary, and it was important that the classroom teacher make allowances. While every teacher tends to believe that his or her subject is the most important and can not be missed, in reality there are other important skills such as assistive technology and life skills instruction that students like Gathary must master. Therefore, there are times that the training for this must take precedence over subject matter curriculum. The support of mainstream teachers is imperative.

Additionally, because there is a need for special equipment and materials, teachers have to be quite flexible and adapt these materials into lessons. The flip side is also true; sometimes there may not be materials in braille, for example, to support the lesson. The teacher must then attempt to find ways in which the material can best be taught. In science lab, for example, much of the learning is empirical. In Gathary's case, the teacher found ways for Gathary to become involved through the use of senses other than sight.

Finally, teachers of students with special needs must be especially organized and able to plan well in advance. Supplementary materials and resources need to be gathered and there needs to be sufficient time for worksheets, notes, and tests to be transcribed in braille and available in time for the lessons.

Issue: Use of paraprofessionals

Question: Often students with physical disabilities are provided with a paraprofessional. Did Gathary have this option?

In some situations, the use of a paraprofessional is advisable to aid the visually impaired with mobility and assist with classroom adaptations. However, in Gathary's case, her itinerant vision teacher felt it was not necessary. She seems to be functioning well under the guidance of two support staff members who work directly with Gathary and indirectly with the classroom teacher. The two support staff members include Beth, the itinerant vision teacher, and an orientation and mobility (O&M) instructor. Acting as a liaison with her classroom teachers, Beth sees Gathary on a daily basis to provide instruction in the use of her assistive technology compensatory academic skills including Nemeth code (mathematical braille code), social interaction skills, and other life skills. This curriculum is provided to facilitate her full integration into the mainstream classroom environment.

At the beginning of each school year, a team meeting is set up with all of Gathary's teachers. The support staff is introduced and suggestions are offered to help the classroom teachers fully integrate her into their class routines.

Another factor in deciding against the use of a paraprofessional was the fact that Gathary needed to be more independent. Knowing how middle school students are beginning to assert their independence from adults, we were confident that she would have more of an opportunity to make friends without a paraprofessional by her side. Additionally, as Leslie explained, "If there were a paraprofessional, I was concerned that there might not be the direct relationship between student and teacher, but rather between the teacher and paraprofessional." As it was, there were many opportunities to discuss Gathary's progress with support staff and to ask questions and get advice on materials and techniques to help Gathary become successful in learning specific subject matter. Sometimes, we met during a planning period, other times during lunch, or sometimes in the few minutes between classes.

Question: How was Gathary able to maneuver about the school; what special training did she receive?

Before Gathary goes to a new school, she is usually given extensive mobility training. In addition, the O&M

instructor works with Gathary for thirty minutes, two times a week. This instruction is ongoing, throughout the school year, and will be maintained each year she is in mainstreamed situations.

Figure 1

Organizations

American Foundation for the Blind
15 W. 16th St. NY, NY 10011
(212)620-2000 (800)232-5463

American Printing House for the Blind
1839 Frankfort Ave., Louisville, KY 40206
(502)895-2405

Association for Education and Rehabilitation of the Blind and Visually Impaired (AER)
206 N. Washington St., Suite 320
Alexandria, VA 22314-2528 (703)548-1884

Council for Exceptional Children, Division for the Visually Handicapped
1920 Association Dr., Reston, VA 22091 (703)620-3660

Howe Press of the Perkins Schools for the Blind
175 North Beacon St., Watertown, MA 02171
(617)924-3400

Library of Congress National Library Service for the Blind and Physically Handicapped/Talking Book Library
1291 Taylor St., NW, Washington, DC 20542
(202)707-5100 (800)424-9100
www.loc.gov/nls/nls.html

National Braille Press
88 St. Stephen Street, Boston, MA 02115 (800)548-7323

National Federation of the Blind
1800 Johnson St., Baltimore, MD 21230 (410)659-9314
http://www.nfb.org

Recording for the Blind and Dyslexic
20 Roszel Road, Princeton, NJ 08540 (609)452-0606
http://www.rfbd.org/

Seedlings Braille Books for Children
P.O. Box 51924, Livonia, MI 48151-5924 (800)777-8552

Before Gathary would attempt to maneuver the halls of Southwood Middle, the O&M instructor first created a three dimensional layout of the school for Gathary to study. This layout is like a raised map that allowed Gathary to mentally conceptualize the space. The second part of the instruction involved mobility skills so that Gathary could move about the space safely.

Gathary also learned about sighted guide techniques (how to safely use a sighted person as a guide), how to use auditory clues to maneuver and find her way, and how to use her cane. I selected several students to assist Gathary when she needed help. These students walked to class with Gathary to make sure she arrived safely and Gathary taught them the correct way for guiding her. While this was successful the majority of the time, Gathary often felt the need for more independence. Her guides, however, were afraid to let go, afraid Gathary would fall. Gathary, however, anticipated the falls, knowing they were necessary if she were to become more self sufficient.

Question: What special training is usually given to teachers?

Generally, at the beginning of each school year, a team meeting is set up with all of Gathary's teachers. At this time, the support staff is introduced and suggestions are offered to help the classroom teachers fully integrate her into their class routines. Additionally, a full day, county-wide inservice is provided in the fall for classroom teachers and administrators to provide more comprehensive curriculum and background information on mainstreaming our visually impaired students.

While it is important that teachers be prepared and trained to work with special needs students, teachers must also be prepared to deal with the attitudes of a classroom of students—each with their own problems who do not always empathize or even attempt to understand the specific needs, problems, or concerns of those around them. If mainstreaming is to be successful, students and teachers must work together as a team.

Gathary came to our school in the middle of the school year, and unfortunately, none of her teachers were given the chance to take advantage of this special training opportunity. However, teachers working with special needs students should be well versed in the exceptionality and explore the different classroom dynamics that may occur as the result of mainstreaming.

Issue: Classroom curriculum and classroom modifications

Questions: What modifications needed to be made in the classroom to accommodate Gathary?

Gathary needed to be seated in a desk that facilitated her entering and leaving the classroom easily. Her work area also needed to be situated close to the shelves in which the braille books were stored so that she could reach them independently.

Because it is important that the visually impaired be able to safely move around the room and feel comfortable doing so, students in the class had to be very aware of where they put their own materials such as bookbags and lunch boxes so that Gathary would not trip over anything. Care was given to ensure that cabinet doors were closed. Special procedures for fire drills and other emergencies had to be established to ensure Gathary's safety and specific students were selected to guide Gathary in the event of an emergency. However, regarding emergencies, some authorities suggest that the blind child "be instructed to take hold of the nearest moving child or adult and quickly and quietly follow others" (Torres & Corn, 1990, p. 25).

The other students resented her going to lunch early and felt that Gathary got special treatment.

Another area of concern is in the use of the restroom. It is extremely important that blind students have someone of the same sex accompany them to the restroom so stalls can be checked to make sure that they are reasonably sanitary and to ensure that no one is hiding in one. Additionally, several students were selected to take turns being Gathary's sighted guide on the way to lunch and other classes. Southwood Middle is two stories high and even for a sighted person the stairways are not always easily maneuvered. Consequently, we allowed Gathary and one other student to leave class five minutes before the bell so that she could get to her next class without having to "fight" the crowds. We also allowed her to leave for lunch a few minutes earlier so that she could get through the line more easily. The other students, however, resented this and felt that Gathary got special treatment. To them, Gathary is lucky—she gets to go to lunch early. "Why should she get special privileges?" they asked. This problem reflects the importance of involving students, especially at the middle school level, in sensitivity training which is paramount to a successful mainstreaming effort.

During a biography unit, we read about Louis Braille. This gave Gathary the springboard for talking about her experiences learning braille.

Another area of modification is in the realm of discipline. Children with special needs must be held accountable to the same code of conduct as the other students in the classroom. I sometimes bent the rules for Gathary and this actually was a tremendous disservice to her. It angered the other students who tended to see issues only in black and white, not shades of gray. This characteristic of the middle school students leads to their strong sense of justice and they were incapable of understanding why I would allow Gathary to do something they were not allowed to do.

Finally, as with all students, special students need positive feedback and acknowledgment that they have done a good job. It is important that the teacher remember that non-verbal communication—a smile, body language, etc. needs to be transformed for the visually impaired into a pat on the back or a quiet, "Good job."

Question: What modifications needed to be made in the curriculum to accommodate Gathary?

Opportunities for tactual and auditory learning need to be considered. In some cases, for example, Gathary was "walked" through an activity area to get a feeling for the environment before the class participated in a specific activity. It is also important to provide concrete experiences and suggest ways that parents can supplement these at home.

Curriculum should include issues that related to the visually handicapped. For example, during a biography unit, we read about Louis Braille. This gave Gathary the springboard for talking about her experiences learning braille. It is, however, important to remember that these modifications to the curriculum be subtle.

During class, I involve students in a great deal of oral reading, writing, discussion, and cooperative learning. Gathary was not only able to take part in these, but students were consistently amazed at her fluency in reading braille. I did find that I minimized my use of the chalkboard and overhead transparencies, although there were times I needed to use these to illustrate a point or to model writing. If teachers find, however, that the modifications for a specific activity are so great that they significantly change the focus or objective of the activity, than perhaps a parallel activity designed for the special needs student should be considered. While the goal of mainstreaming is to make adaptations so that all students can be involved, this may occasionally prove difficult. In some content areas, for some lessons, alternative teaching methods should be considered.

Specific materials for the visually impaired can help advance the lessons. Special measurement tools are available to teach math skills such as braille clocks and rulers. Special maps with raised borders can be ordered to augment geography lessons. A variety of trade books and text books are available on audio tape as well as in braille (see Figure 1). When our class read specific literary works, Gathary not only had a copy of the book in braille, but also listened to the words read aloud on auditory tapes. The best lessons, I discovered, included the use of both braille text and audio tapes. The braille allows the student to better understand the structure of language and revisit certain sections.

According to Beth, "The most successful of the blind are those who have been readers of braille." Many textbooks are available in braille but usually have to be ordered well in advance, in June if possible. We are able to get most of our textbooks on loan from the Florida Instructional Materials Center.

The key, as with working with any student, is to find and encourage the strengths and talents that will allow the student to "shine" in any type of learning environment.

In order to make communication between the classroom teachers and the support staff more efficient, a special mailbox in the teacher's workroom was set aside. Any worksheets, class notes, tests, or other instructional materials that needed to be written in braille were placed in this box. Beth then either transcribed the material herself, or if time allowed, sent the material to a transcriber in the county office. The transcribed braille worksheets were placed in another specially labeled box and a note was placed in our mailbox to advise us that the material was ready. The mailbox also afforded us an opportunity to ask questions, present concerns, and make special requests for help.

Question: How was Gathary provided with specific information that could not be put into braille?

This question was at the heart of my biggest concern when I learned Gathary was joining our class. It is not uncommon for me, as I am sure it is for most teachers, to change my lesson plans at the last minute. When it was impossible to have the material I needed for a revised lesson transcribed into braille, Gathary worked with another student who read the material aloud. Often, Gathary took a copy of the material home so that she could "reread" it with her family. Each week, for example, our class received a copy of a special current events magazine. Students took turns describing different pictures and features in the magazine and others read articles aloud. When videos were shown, a student was selected to sit next to Gathary and quietly describe what Gathary could not see. I realized that not only was this helpful to Gathary, but it was also extremely beneficial to the other students because they became aware of the power of words to bring pictures to life and create mental images. In their own way, they enabled Gathary to "see." Descriptive videos are available in which a narrator describes much of the action. Companies such as Descriptive Video Service (DVS) provide narration for certain shows that air on public television as well as commercially produced vid-

eos. The videos are excellent and rich in language and vocabulary. They are also the perfect tool for training students in this type of narration.

Question: What group configurations worked best?

While Gathary worked well independently, she seemed to truly enjoy working in a cooperative group. Gathary brought many talents to group settings. Her group project on the pyramids of Egypt resulted in the creation of a video in which Gathary used her ear for languages and accents to play the part of an English archaeologist. On a mythology project, she and her team created a mythological crossword puzzle using special tiles with raised letters that could be felt. Having her work with others in her group not only helped them create unique products but also allowed other members of the group to know Gathary in a new context. This, in turn, led to tremendous social growth and friendships.

The key, as with working with any student, is to find and encourage the strengths and talents that will allow the student to "shine" in any type of learning environment. As students such as Gathary become acknowledged for their abilities, they become more confident, more secure of their place in the classroom, more accepted, and more accepting.

Issue: Technology equipment

Question: What special equipment is needed to help the visually impaired progress successfully?

One of the biggest concerns facing a parent of a special needs student in the mainstreamed environment is that their child be able to compete academically in the classroom. In addition, Gathary's parents were especially determined that Gathary "not be a burden to the classroom teacher." As a consequence, Gathary's parents made every effort to equip Gathary with special equipment that would enable her to function more independently and more efficiently in the classroom. Some of the equipment was provided by the county but certain other devices were purchased by her parents. Gathary uses a Braille Lite which is a computerized braille note taker. It is quite small and easy to manipulate. Her Braille Lite fits into her book bag and takes up little room on her desk. It has many of the features of a computer which allow her to edit her work and then print it on a printer or emboss it for her own use. Additionally, it has a raised braille display so that Gathary can tactually read what she has typed in. Before she received her Braille Lite, everything Gathary brailled had to be transcribed. Now, she can plug the Braille Lite into a regular printer and a printed copy is generated for the sighted teacher. As a result, she is much less dependent on a sighted transcriber to complete assignments. This equipment enabled Gathary to take almost the same exams and tests as did her classmates, typing the answers into her Braille Lite and then printing them so they could be graded. Once in a while, certain questions were eliminated from a test when it was not possible to create an appropriate tactual equivalent. For example, some questions used maps and graphs which could not easily be transcribed into braille.

Question: Did the special equipment needed ever present a problem?

The students in the class were naturally very curious about the equipment and wanted to experiment with it. Since Gathary's equipment allows her to function more self-sufficiently and experience added success and independence, she is extremely protective of her things. During the year, she was quite apprehensive that something would be broken and, in a sense, cut her connection to the visual world—a very frightening and real possibility. As a result, it is vital that students be taught to understand the importance of these devices and how they assist Gathary. When Gathary first entered Southwood, Beth Gordon came to the classroom and, with Gathary's assistance, demonstrated the use of each piece of equipment. Students were especially impressed with the fluency with which Gathary read braille when they could not even "feel" the raised dots. However, while a majority of students understood the need to respect Gathary's equipment, there was still a handful of students, who despite the repeated demonstrations and explanations, continued to "tease" Gathary by touching her equipment—another reminder of the importance of sensitivity training. Others continued to touch the equipment out of curiosity. "The challenge," as Leslie aptly put it, "is to make the equipment interesting to others but, at the same time, make sure they understand its importance to Gathary and learn to respect it."

Question: What equipment is most important for the visually impaired to have in the classroom?

There were two different perspectives in regard to this question. According to Gathary," As far as academics are concerned, the computer (Braille Lite) is most important to me. As far as mobility, my cane is the most important." Beth, however says that, "Actually, it's not the equipment but rather the braille proficiency and listening skills that our visually impaired students have learned that allow them to be successful in the classroom. However, the braille note takers have certainly enhanced our students' abilities to be competitive with their mainstream peers."

Issue: Socialization

Question: In terms of friendships, what has Gathary experienced at Southwood?

When asked this question, Gathary's face lights up— and so does her mom's! "I've made great friends—for the first time!" Gathary explained. Her mom added, "This is the first time Gathary has fostered strong friendships with sighted peers. It's the first time she's been to 'slee- povers' at someone's home other than a relative." On Mondays, Gathary would come to class regaling us with all the new and wonderful experiences she had had over the weekend with her friends.

Question: From the first time you met Gathary, how has your impression changed?

It did not take any of us long to change any preconceptions we might have had about the blind. We soon realized that Gathary is much more like the other students than she is different. We began to see her simply as someone who must do some things a bit differently. Her friends both responded similarly, saying," We see her as a person, just like us. She just doesn't have the ability to see. She uses her hands to read."

However, while mainstreaming has taken away the veil of mystery surrounding the blind, it has changed Gathary's perception of herself. Leslie explained, "For the first time in her life, Gathary is beginning to realize that she doesn't have something others have." Yet, she is dealing with this and makes the most of the gifts she does have—a lesson all of us need to learn.

Question: While Gathary made many friends at Southwood, she also seemed to have difficulty with some students. What problems occurred and what do you think could be done to improve the situation?

"Sometimes students poked me and screamed in my ear. They frightened me," Gathary explained. One of her friends responded to this, "being blind is hard. I wish they could understand what it's like. I get frustrated seeing others tease her. It almost makes me cry inside."

I am terribly troubled when I reflect on the way in which some of my students treated Gathary. While so many were kind, caring, and went out of their way to help Gathary whenever possible, there were others who went out of their way to inflict added pain. I found that just talking to students about this issue was not always sufficient. Many could not see beyond their own problems and did not have the capacity to empathize. "Most who tease Gathary," Leslie acknowledged, "never gave much thought to what it would be like to suddenly approach a person who is in darkness."

Leslie, however, expressed optimism in terms of our ability to affect the way in which students react to one another, "I think sensitivity can be developed—maybe not to the same level in each person, however. People need to become sensitive not only to the challenges a blind person must face, but also sensitive to the issue of how hard a blind person must work to make accomplishments appear effortless." Again, the need for sensitivity training is evident.

Figure 2

Print Resources for Teachers

Hazekamp, J. and Huebner, K.M. (Eds.). (1989). *Program planning and evaluation for the blind and visually impaired students: National guidelines for educational excellence.* New York: American Foundation for the Blind.

Mangold, S.S. (Ed.). (1982). *A teacher's guide to the special educational needs of blind and visually handicapped children.* New York: American Foundation for the Blind.

Torres, I. and Corn, A.L. (1990). *When you have a visually handicapped child in your classroom: Suggestions for teachers.* New York: American Foundation for the Blind.

Unfortunately, as mentioned earlier, because Gathary entered our school in the middle of the year, our students did not receive any type of sensitivity training. "In the past though," Beth explained, "we had a workshop for teachers and put devices on their eyes to simulate different eye problems. This was very successful and helped teachers gain an appreciation for what visually impaired students experience. I believe this type of simulation could benefit not only teachers but students as well. However, because of the seriousness of this exercise, students should be exposed to the situations in small group counseling situations with a counselor to follow up the simulation with discussion that allows students to freely discuss their experience and how it will determine or affect their behavior.

Question: Why is it important that students with disabilities be in the regular classroom?

We have all seen tremendous growth in Gathary not only academically but socially. As Leslie explained, "I know how much better she's doing and how much more 'normal' she's acting in social situations outside of school. This is critical so that she can function in the world as an adult. The things she's grappling with now are things all of us deal with. Frustrations are part of the growth pattern."

Being in this school and being successful have given Gathary the confidence she needs to deal with new situations. Students with disabilities need to have the opportunities to interact with all kinds of children. This promotes their social and emotional growth and affords the other students an opportunity to see how proficient students with disabilities can be.

However, mainstreaming does not just benefit the special needs student. It benefits us all, as the responses to the final questions suggest. Because of the nature of these questions, I would like the reader to "hear" the answers just as they were spoken—from the heart:

Question: How has knowing Gathary changed you?

Lauren: I think I've become a better person. She helps me know how to treat all people better.

Amanda F: She's taught me that I can help others and she's shown me how. I respect what Gathary does for herself and I have also become more sensitive.

Amanda A: Having her as a friend makes me look at life from a different point of view. I learned what it means to have a true friend, how to treat friends, and what it's like to be blind. Knowing Gathary has made me respect people more, those with other problems, not just the blind.

Question: In 10 years, where do you see Gathary?

Beth: I can't wait to see where Gathary is in years to come. I see her as a journalist, traveling the world. She has a zest for life, an ability with languages, and she has a way with people and with words.

Leslie: I anticipate she'll have a full education and travel. I see opportunities for her to use her love for different cultures, especially the Hispanic culture. She becomes completely absorbed in every culture she is introduced to.

Gathary: I would like to be a translator. I want to speak to people in their language

Question: What is one word that best describes Gathary?

Lauren R and Amanda F: Amazing

Amanda A: *So* amazing there's no word

Anita: Joyful

Beth: A gift

A Final Note

The 1997–98 school year was one of tremendous growth and awareness of the various considerations and adaptations that must be addressed to insure successful mainstreaming of the visually impaired in the middle school. But beyond that, and far more critical, is the way Gathary helped illuminate that which is important. From her we all gained a deeper appreciation for life, and a sense that "nothing is impossible." These were the lessons Gathary taught us—her gifts to those lucky enough to embrace them. As teachers we must remember that all our students are gifts. We must remember to nurture their dreams and encourage their visions for tomorrow. And if we are smart, the lessons we learn from students such as Gathary will become part of us as we consistently seek the light of understanding.

Anita Meyer Meinbach is a teacher at Southwood Middle School, Miami, Florida.

Visual Teaching Strategies for Students Who Are Deaf or Hard of Hearing

John Luckner • **Sandra Bowen** •**Kathy Carter**

How do we enhance communication and instruction with students who are deaf or hard of hearing? Many educators and researchers suggest that we establish visually rich learning environments. In such environments, teachers would use the following instructional aids:

- Sign, fingerspelling, and speech reading.
- Equipment such as overhead projectors, bulletin boards, computers, and televisions.
- Materials including pictures, illustrations, artifacts, slides, computer graphics, and films with captions.

Why use these methods and materials? Given the auditory limitations that accompany a hearing loss, most students who are deaf are primarily visual learners (e.g., Nover & Andrews, 1998; Reeves, Wollenhaupt & Caccamise, 1995). Lane, Hoffmeister, and Bahan (1996) used the term "visual people" to describe the deaf population (p. 116).

In recent years, we have witnessed a strong push for greater use of sign and American Sign Language (ASL) features in educational settings (e.g., Mahshie, 1995). Though using sign for communication and instruction has many benefits for students, signing, like speech, provides a *transient* signal. The signal moves—it is there, and then it is gone. Consequently, we need to find more visual strategies to help students focus on important information, see how concepts are connected, and integrate prior knowledge with new knowledge.

PEOPLE WHO ARE DEAF OR HARD OF HEARING ARE
"VISUAL PEOPLE."

This article describes some general visual teaching strategies, discusses how to develop and use graphic organizers, provides a sample unit and lesson using graphic organizers, and furnishes many examples of visual materials to use with *all* students.

VARIETY IS IMPORTANT: USE WRITTEN WORDS, LINE DRAWING PICTURES, DETAILED DRAWINGS, COMPUTER-GENERATED PICTURES, PHOTOGRAPHS, PHOTOCOPIED PICTURES, CUTOUTS FROM MAGAZINES, ACTUAL LABELS AND WRAPPERS, SIGNS AND LOGOS, AND COUPONS AND REAL OBJECTS.

General Visual Teaching Techniques

We have found it essential to adapt learning environments and use teaching strategies that help students maximize their learning time—essential, that is, if we want students who are deaf or hard of hearing to succeed in school. Here are some general suggestions for choosing visual materials (Hodgdon, 1995):

- Choose visuals students will easily recognize.
- Use larger-size pictures or photographs (5 x 7 or 8 x 10 inches) with younger students.
- Use a variety of visual materials, including written words, line drawing pictures, detailed drawings, computer-generated pictures, photographs, photo-copied pictures, cutouts from magazines, actual labels and wrappers, signs and logos, and coupons and real objects.

Table 1: Examples of Web Sites and Addresses with Valuable Visual Information

Site Name	Address
National Geographic	http://www.nationalgeographic.com
The Smithsonian Institute	http://www.si.edu
The History Channel	http://www.historychannel.com
Nova Online	http://www.pbs.org/wgbh/nova
American Museum of Natural History	http://www.amnh.org
Windows to the Universe	http://www.windows.umich.edu
Archiving Early America	http://www.earlyamerica.com
Britannica Online	http://www.eb.com
Science A Gogo	http://www.scienceagogo.com
How Stuff Works	http://www.howstuffworks.com
National Air and Space Museum	http://www.nasm.si.edu

Combinations of words and some form of graphics is usually the best choice. Learn to draw simple pictures yourself—uncomplicated shapes and stick figures can be helpful.

Examples of visual aids that teachers can use in the classroom to enhance the communication and learning process include the use of a classroom rules chart, job and choice menus, transition time cards and charts, task organizers, daily schedules, and the Internet.

Classroom Rules Chart

An important element of effective classroom management is establishing, teaching, and enforcing classroom rules. Rules that are posted and referred to often help students function in the complex social and emotional environment of the classroom and provide a framework for the teacher to reinforce appropriate behaviors. You can develop a chart with classroom rules, and pictures, photographs, or clip art can accompany the written rules on the chart to help students learn to manage themselves more independently. Whenever possible, students should assist in developing the rules. Examples of rules for elementary age students might include:

- Always try your best.
- Raise your hand when you need help.
- Keep your work and work area neat.
- Respect one another.
- Pay attention when others are communicating.

Job and Choice Menus

Involve students in the daily chores of making a classroom an organized and comfortable environment for learning and socializing. For the teacher, student participation reduces the number of tasks that you need to complete each day. Students experience personal responsibility, decision making, and contributing to a common cause. Classroom jobs can be posted with words and pictures or photographs, and the person responsible for completing the task can be rotated on a daily or weekly basis. Choice menus can be established using words, photographs, pictures, or logos for things such as the areas of the room to work in, who to work or play with, activities to do when work is finished, enrichment activities to be completed, or books that can be read related to the unit of study.

Transition Time Cards/Charts

Transition time refers to the time it takes to change from one activity to another. You and your students can develop a set of cards or a chart with the specific tasks that need to be accomplished during transition times. Use written words and accompanying pictures or photographs. Examples include: Put your materials away, get your lunch, line up, and walk to the cafeteria quietly.

Table 2. Creation and Use of Graphic Organizers

Created by	When Created	Purpose of Creation
Teacher	Before students read the materials in the textbook	To preview reading material, assess prior knowledge, and to provide an advanced organizer for content.
Teacher	After students have read the material in the textbook	To review the reading material, highlighting key points from the chapter. To use as a review or for assessment.
Teacher and students	During reading of the material	To highlight main ideas. To provide assistance for difficult reading passages or concepts.
Teacher and students	After students have read the material in the textbook.	To assess comprehension and to outline key points. To use as a review or for assessment.
Students	After students have read the material in the textbook.	To enhance or assess reading comprehension and content information or to review for an examination.

Task Organizers

Some students experience difficulty completing an activity or job because they are distracted easily or they can't remember the order of steps needed for completion. Such students would benefit from a set of pictures in a pocket-size photo album or a chart that lists all the steps to be done with accompanying pictures or photographs. Examples include listing the steps for starting the computer, completing a science experiment, reader and writer workshops, or taking care of a class pet.

Daily Schedules

The daily schedule can be used as a guide for structuring the classroom environment, as well as a way to stimulate conversation and language development. Hodgdon (1995) suggested the following steps for creating and using a daily schedule:

- Divide the day into segments reflecting the major activities of the day.
- Give each segment a name that you will refer to consistently.
- Choose a representation system, such as words and pictures or words and photographs, that will be understood easily.
- Determine what the schedule will look like—size and location—and whether it will be a chart, written on the blackboard, or photocopied and given to students individually.
- Decide how the students will use the schedule at the beginning of the day.
- Decide how the schedule will be referred to throughout the day.
- Establish ways to use the schedule to communicate with other professionals and family members.

The Internet

The technology of the World Wide Web (WWW) can be used to access an enormous electronic library of pictures, photographs, graphics, and videos. These resources can be integrated across the curriculum to help develop background knowledge, to provide specific examples, or to develop media-rich lessons. Table 1 lists examples of Web sites that have valuable visual information.

Using Graphic Organizers

Visual representations of knowledge are referred to by a variety of names including semantic maps, webs, semantic organizers, story maps, or Venn diagrams. We use the general term *graphic organizers* to refer to representations used to assist in making organizational patterns of text visual (Bromley, Irwin-DeVitis, & Modlo, 1995). When used with students, graphic organizers provide a framework to make thought and organization processes visible (Tarquin & Walker, 1997). This framework provides

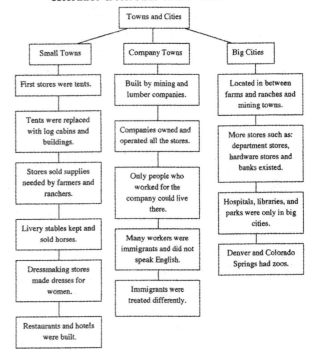

Figure 1. Example of a Hierarchical Graphic Organizer from *Colorado: Crossroads of the West*

Figure 2. Example of a Conceptual Graphic Organizer from the First Chapter of *Bridge to Terabithia*

a foundation for learning by linking background knowledge with the major concepts and facts of new learning.

A TEACHER AND STUDENTS CAN USE DIALOGUE AND GRAPHIC ORGANIZERS TO REVIEW TEXT MATERIAL.

Figure 3. Example of a Sequential Graphic Organizer Using the Events of *The Very Hungry Caterpillar*

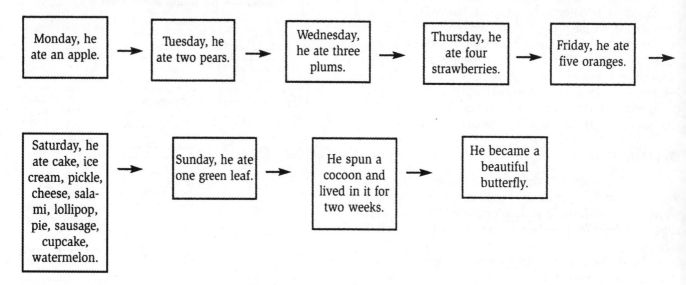

Graphic organizers allow teachers to omit extraneous information while emphasizing important concepts and demonstrating their connection to each other. This visual representation of information is easier for students to remember than extended text (Bromley et al., 1995; Dye, 2000). Most important, the use of graphic organizers allows students to be actively involved in the processes of listening, speaking, signing, reading, writing, and thinking. And, as Table 2 summarizes, teachers can create graphic organizers and use them in a variety of ways. A valuable software program that can be used for developing graphic organizers has been created by Inspiration Software, Inc. They allow you to try the software for a 30-day trial period by accessing their Web site: http://www.inspiration.com.

The following are examples of four basic patterns of graphic organizers, identify by Bromley et al. (1995). Each graphic organizer can be simplified or made more complex by deleting or adding "branches." This flexibility allows students with different levels of knowledge and skill to participate in the same activity.

Hierarchical Patterns

If information includes a main concept and subconcepts, you can organize it in a linear manner, using a hierarchical pattern. Figure 1 shows a hierarchical pattern that provides an outline of the material found in a chapter from *Colorado: Crossroads of the West* (Downey & Metcalf, 1999, Chapter 11, pp. 161–178). This chapter describes the history of towns and cities in the state of Colorado.

Conceptual Patterns

If information has a central idea, category, or class with supporting facts such as characteristics, examples, or descriptors, you can use a conceptual pattern. Figure 2

Figure 4. Example of a Cyclical Graphic Organizer from *Biology: An Everyday Experience*

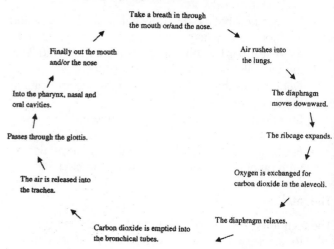

shows the use of a complex conceptual pattern to organize the events that occurred in Chapter 1 of the book *A Bridge to Terabithia* (Paterson, 1977). This chapter centers around the main character, Jesse Oliver Adams, Jr., and his family.

Sequential Patterns

Displaying the chronological order of events, particularly those having a specific beginning and an end, can be done by using a sequential pattern. The most common sequential pattern is a timeline. These patterns also can be used to represent cause/effect, process/product, or problem/solution-type situations. Figure 3 shows a simple sequential pattern used to identify the specific events that happen to the caterpillar in *The Very Hungry Caterpillar* (Carle, 1969). The caterpillar spends 1 week eating more and more food

Figure 5. Graphic Organizer of *America's Past and Promise* Created with Students

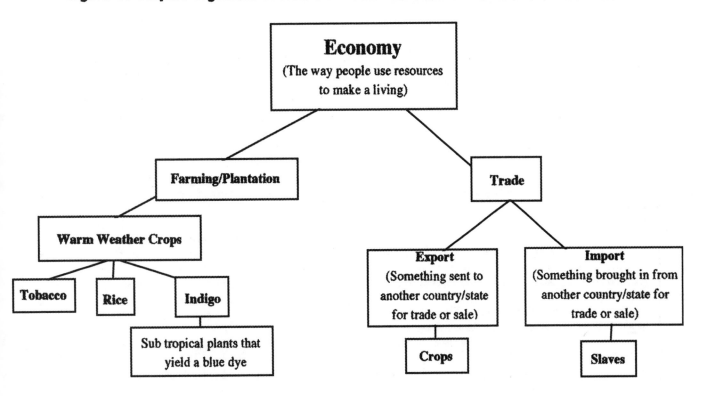

until finally he becomes a fat caterpillar and builds a cocoon. By ordering each event, a student can easily understand the process of how a caterpillar transforms into a beautiful butterfly.

Cyclical Patterns

You can use a circular formation to display a series of events that occur within a process. There is no beginning or end, just a continuous sequence of events. Figure 4 shows a cyclical pattern that could be used to summarize the cycle of respiration that has been presented in *Biology: An Everyday Experience* (Kaskel, Hummer, & Daniel, 1992, Chapter 13, pp. 267–277).

Sample Unit and Lesson Using A Graphic Organizer

Here we have provided an outline of a sample unit of study that uses a variety of graphic organizers. We prepared this unit for middle school students, Grades 6–8. We took the content material for this unit from *America's Past and Promise* (Mason, Garcia, Powell, & Risinger, 1998, Unit 1, Chapter 7, Section 2, pp. 132–135). The main concepts discussed in this section are the economy and culture of the southern colonies of the United States. The teacher and students will create the graphic organizer, shown in Figure 5, after the students have read the assigned section. Figure

6 provides an example of the dialogue that may occur as the teacher and students create the graphic organizer.

VISUAL AIDS INCLUDE CLASSROOM RULES CHART, JOB AND CHOICE MENUS, TRANSITION TIME CARDS AND CHARTS, TASKS ORGANIZERS DAILY SCHEDULES, AND THE INTERNET.

Figures 5 and 6 show how a teacher and students can use dialogue and graphic organizers to review text material. The graphic organizer shown in Figure 7 may also be created in a similar manner.

Final Thoughts

Teaching students how to access the information provided on visual supports can improve student participation and understanding, as well as prepare them to better use the visual supports found in our daily lives, such as packages, menus, logos, maps, and assembly instructions. In addition, teachers and students can use visual strategies to illustrate the organization of ideas and information and provide background information for topics of study or discussion. Visual teaching strategies provide nontransient signals that can be used for prereading, postreading, writing, content subjects, assessment, improving social interactions, and

Figure 6. Example of a Lesson for Teaching with a Graphic Organizer

Create graphic organizer (Figure 5) with the students as they answer questions and discuss economy, from the chapter in the book.

Teacher (T): Yesterday we read section 2 from the social studies book. Let's review what you read. (Call on individual students to review main topics and ideas from the reading.)

Student (S): Slavery.

T: Yes. What is slavery?

S: When white people owned black people to help them work on their farms.

T: What were the large farms called?

S: Plantations.

T: Were the plantations important to the southern colonies?

S: Yes

T: Why?

S: That's how they earned money.

T: That's right. The term used to discuss how people earn money to live in an area is called the economy. Let's write a definition for economy on the map. (Write economy and a definition on the map. Definition: The way people use resources to make a living).

T: Great. Let's take a look at the plantations in the southern colonies and figure out why the plantation owners needed slaves. You have already mentioned that farming and plantations as part of the southern colonies so let's add that to the map too. (Write in farming and plantations.)
What was special about the land of the southern colonies that helped the economy?

S: The soil was good for growing crops.

T: That's right. The southern colonies were able to grow specific crops that the other regions of the states could not grow. One of the reasons was the soil. What was another reason they could grow the crops?

S: The warm weather.

T: Exactly. What crops did they grow?

S: Tobacco and rice. (List the crops on the map as the students mention them.)

T: Yes, anything else?

S: I remember the book also talked about something used in blue jeans.

T: That's correct. The plantation owners also grew a plant used for blue dye. Who remembers what that plant is called?

S: Indigo.

T: Do manufactures still use indigo to dye your blue jeans?

S: No, today they use chemicals.

T: All right, so we have listed tobacco, rice, and indigo. Tell me about growing rice? What is required to grow rice?

S: The rice was grown in the swamps. So they had to drain the swamps and build dikes, before they could plant. Then the rice had to be irrigated and harvested.

T: Good explanation! So why did the plantation owners need slaves?

S: The plantation owners wanted slaves who knew how to grow rice because they had grown rice in Africa before they were brought to America.

T: What did rice have to do with the economy in the southern colonies?

S: They sold rice to other colonies.

T: That's right! They sold or exported the rice to the other colonies. Growing the crops was important to the economy because the southern colonies exported their crops to other colonies. Was it easy to grow rice in the southern colonies?

S: No, it was hard work. That's why they wanted the slaves to do it.

T: The hard work was one of the reasons the plantation owners wanted slaves to help them. As the plantations grew, more slaves were needed to complete all the work. What do you remember from the reading was another reason slaves were needed to grow rice?

T: Another important factor that relates to the economy and to the plantations is trade. (Add trade to the map.) How did they send the crops out and bring the slaves in?

S: By boat.

T: Exactly. Let's look at the map in your book on page 133. Notice all the rivers and waterways which ran through the southern colonies. Why were these rivers the key to the success of the southern economy?

S: They could export the crops and bring in the slaves on boats.

T: Right. Crops were exported and slaves were imported. Let's write a definition for these two terms: export and import. (Write the words and the definitions on the map.)

T: How do exports and imports influence an economy?

S: (Accept all reasonable answers)

T: What resources or products does the United States export now?

S: (Accept all reasonable answers)

T: What resources or products does the United States import now?

S: (Accept all reasonable answers)

T: What do you think would have happened in the southern colonies if they would not have had slaves?

S: (Accept all reasonable answers)

T: Today we have discussed the economy of the southern colonies. Looking at our map, we see there were two important aspects of the economy: farming and trade. The warm climate and the rich soil grew a variety of crops, which generally could not be grown in the other colonies. These farms were called plantations. The plantation owners made a living growing and selling the crops. However, as their plantations became larger, they needed help to work on the plantations. That is the main reason slaves were brought into the southern colonies. The vast waterways of the southern colonies made it relatively easy to transport resources and people. So crops were exported and slaves were imported, and the southern economy grew. Are there questions or comments?

S: Respond to all questions and comments.

T: Today we have discussed the economy of the southern colonies and talked about the importance of slaves to that economy. Tomorrow we will look at the culture of the southern colonies and discuss plantation owners' treatment of slaves.

---

behavior management. These strategies build on the strengths of students who are deaf or hard of hearing.

References

Bromley, K., Irwin-DeVitis, K., & Modlo, M. (1995). *Graphic organizers: Visual strategies for active learning.* New York: Scholastic Professional Books.

Carle, E. (1969). *The very hungry caterpillar.* New York: Philomel Books.

Downey, M. T., & Metcalf, F. D. (1999). *Colorado: Crossroads of the West* (3rd ed.). Boulder, CO: Pruett.

Dye, G. A. (2000). Graphic organizers to the rescue: Helping students link—and remember—information. *TEACHING Exceptional Children, 32*(3), 72–76.

Hodgdon, L. (1995). *Visual strategies for improving communication. Vol. 1. Practical support for school and home.* Troy, MI: Quirk Roberts.

Figure 7. An Explicit Graphic Organizer Created by Teacher and Students of Materials from *America's Past and Present*

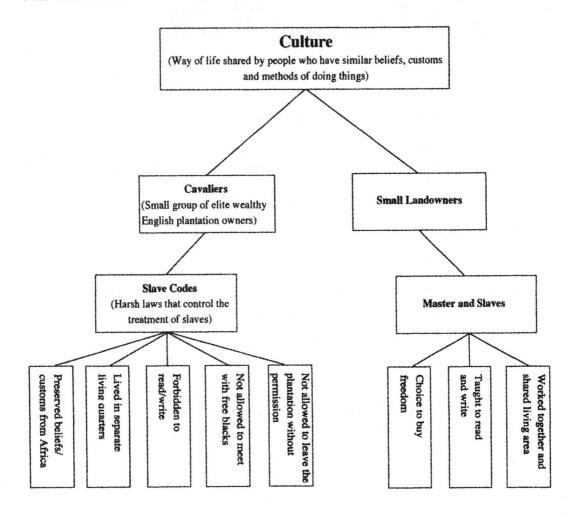

Kaskel, A., Hummer, P. J., & Daniel L. (1992). *Biology: An everyday experience.* Lake Forest, IL: Glencoe.

Lane, H., Hoffmeister, R., & Bahan, B. (1996). *A journey into the deaf-world.* San Diego, CA: Dawn Sign Press.

Mahshie, S. N. (1995). *Educating deaf children bilingually.* Washington, DC: Gallaudet University Pre-College Programs.

Mason, L. C., Garcia, J., Powell, F., & Risinger, C. F. (1998). *America's past and promise.* Evanston, IL: McDougal and Littell.

Nover, S. M., & Andrews, J. F. (1998). *Critical pedagogy in deaf education: Bilingual methodology and staff development.* Santa Fe: New Mexico School for the Deaf.

Paterson, K. (1977). *A Bridge to Terabithia.* New York: Harper Trophy.

Reeves, J. B., Wollenhaupt, P., & Caccamise, F. (1995). *Deaf students as visual learners: Power for improving literacy and communica-tion.* Paper presented at the International Congress on Education of the Deaf, Tel Aviv, Israel. (ERIC Document Reproduction Service No. ED 390 209)

Tarquin, P., & Walker, S. (1997). *Creating success in the classroom: Visual organizers and how to use them.* Englewood, CO: Teacher Ideas Press

John Luckner *(CEC Chapter #381), Professor;* **Sandra Bowen** *(CEC Chapter #382), Assistant Professor; and* **Kathy Carter**, *Doctoral Student, Division of Special Education, University of Northern Colorado, Greeley.*

UNIT 8
Multiple Disabilities

Unit Selections

Key Points to Consider

- Can paraeducators make a difference in the education of students with multiple disabilities? How can paraeducators be taught specialized skills quickly?

- How can teachers recognize loneliness in students with multiple disabilities? What solutions can they find?

- Can teachers access state-of-the-art technology to assist in their education of students with multiple disabilities? How?

 **Links: www.dushkin.com/online/**
These sites are annotated in the World Wide Web pages.

Activity Ideas for Students With Severe, Profound, or Multiple Disabilities
http://www.palaestra.com/featurestory.html

For most of the twentieth century, children with multiple disabilities (MD) were kept hidden in their parents' homes or put into institutions. Any father or mother presenting such a child at a public school for admission was ridiculed and turned away. The 1975 Individuals with Disabilities Education Act (IDEA) in the United States has turned this around. Such children may now be enrolled in general education classes if that is appropriate. They are entitled to a free education in the least restrictive environment that serves their needs. IDEA, in its years of existence, has allowed millions of students, who once would have been written off as "uneducable," to be given some form of schooling.

A child placed in the category of multiple disabilities may have cognitive developmental disabilities, speech and language impairments, autism, traumatic brain injuries, emotional and behavioral disorders, visual impairments, hearing impairments, orthopedic impairments, health impairments, or any combinations of these. While any child with multiple disabilities (MD) does not need to be disabled in every category set forth by IDEA in order to be so labeled, each child with MD is very special and very needy. Most of them have more than two co-occurring areas of exceptionality. The practice of deinstitutionalization (removing individuals from hospitals and large residential institutions and keeping them in their own homes) and the legal initiatives requiring free and appropriate public education in the least restrictive environment have closed some of the cracks through which these children once fell. The needs of many children with multiple disabilities, however, are not yet being adequately met.

The success of IDEA (bringing children with MD out of their hidden abodes and into the light of our consciousness) has been counterbalanced with the failure of schools to adequately educate children with MD. Their school dropout rate is unjustifiably high. Some of the reasons for the educational mismanagement of children with MD are shortages of qualified special educators, underfunding of programs, lack of knowledge about which methods and materials would work best for each individual child, frustration with accountability, reams of paperwork, less than perfect assessment tools, and a general resistance to implementing the provisions of IDEA.

One of the problems that looms largest in the collection of those factors that hinder appropriate education for children with MD is lack of acceptance and preparation by the school system for their inclusion. Advocates for the rights of disabled individuals have used the term "handicapism" to describe a similar prejudice and discrimination directed at disabled students. The greater the disability, the greater the evinced prejudice. A disability (not able) is not the same as a handicap (hindrance, not at an advantage). The words should not be used interchangeably. A person who is not able to do something (walk, see, hear) has a disability but does not have to be handicapped. Schools impose handicaps (hindrances) by preventing the student with the disability from functioning in an alternative way. Thus, if a student who cannot walk can instead locomote in a wheelchair, he or she is not handicapped. If a building or classroom has no ramps, however, and is inaccessible to a wheelchair user, then the school has imposed a handicap by preventing access to that particular property of the environment. There are millions of ways in which properties of our school environments and char-acteristics of our behavior prevent children with multiple disabilities from functioning up to their potentialities.

Public schools have resisted the regular education initiative (REI) that calls for general education classes rather than special education classes to be primarily responsible for the education of students with more severe and multiple disabilities. The inclusive school movement, which supports the REI, would have special education teachers become consultants, resource specialists, collaborative teachers, or itinerant teachers rather than full-time special education teachers. While arguments for and against the REI have not been resolved, most educators agree that an appropriate education for each child with a disability may require a continuum of services. Some children, especially those with multiple disabilities, may require an environment more restrictive than a general education classroom in order to get the type of assistance they need to function up to their potentialities. Teacher education typically does not offer comprehensive preparation for working with children with MD who require extensive special educational services. In addition, children with MD often require related services (for example, chemotherapy, physical therapy, psychotherapy, transportation) to enable them to learn in a classroom environment.

Many children and youth with MD suffer from a lack of understanding, a lack of empathy, and handicapist attitudes that are directed at them. They present very special problems that few teachers are equipped to solve. Often the message they hear is, "Just go away." The challenge of writing an appropriate individualized education plan (IEP) is enormous. Updating the IEP each year and preparing an individualized transition plan (ITP), which will allow the student with MD to function as independently as possible after age 21, is mandated by law. These students must be served. Excuses such as no time, no money, and no personnel to provide appropriate services are unacceptable. Teachers need to have the attitude of expecting progress and good results, even with the most multiply disabled.

The first article in this unit suggests that paraeducators can play a very important role in giving one-on-one services to students with MD in inclusive education settings, but it is necessary that inservice training be provided for paraeducators. This selection describes a one-day workshop that gives paraeducators an overview of effective methods of teaching adaptive skills to students with MD. Many highly successful teaching strategies can be learned quite quickly in this program.

The second article deals with the loneliness experienced by children with multiple disabilities. They frequently lack the knowledge of how to find someone trustworthy to talk to, how to make friends, how to assert themselves, and how to have confidence in who they are. Shireen Pavri discusses how teachers can recognize loneliness, find solutions, and help the students learn social skills, coping strategies, and self-respect.

The unit's final article discusses the uses of new technology to construct alternate portfolios for students with multiple disabilities. Four students with physical, cognitive, and behavioral characteristics of disability who were unable to learn on a standard computer were taught to use the assistive Intellikeys instead. They had a smorgasbord of other technological aids, and customized Intellikeys overlays. All four students showed increased achievement and independence.

Training Basic Teaching Skills to Paraeducators of Students with Severe Disabilities

A One-Day Program

Lakeisha beams at the teacher as she demonstrates her new skills at setting the table with plates, cups, forks, an napkins.

The new paraeducator can't wait to report that he successfully taught Jon to put on his coat independently.

Finally conquering the copy machine at her workplace, Susan proudly delivered 30 copies of the newsletter to her co-workers.

Marsha B. Parsons
Dennis H. Reid

Since the early 1970s, a technology for teaching students with severe disabilities has been evolving. Research behind the development of this teaching technology has indicated that the strategies for teaching students with severe disabilities are somewhat different from strategies used with students who have mild or moderate disabilities. Whereas the latter students may benefit substantially from teaching strategies based on verbal instruction, students with severe disabilities often require more individual instruction, using a high degree of physical guidance.

This article shows that when teachers and other staff members proficiently use physical guidance in conjunction with other teaching strategies, such as task analysis, prompting, reinforcement, and error correction, students with severe disabilities can learn useful skills (Parsons, Reid, & Green, 1993). And paraeducators can quickly learn to assist students with their learning.

The role of paraeducators is becoming even more important as greater numbers of students with severe disabilities receive their education in inclusive settings.

Paraeducators in Inclusive Settings

The valuable role paraeducators can play in teaching students with severe disabilities is currently well recognized and is becoming even more important as greater numbers of students with severe disabilities receive their education in inclusive settings. Whereas special education teachers often learn appropriate teaching strategies during their preservice training, paraeducators rarely have specific preservice training in how to use the teaching strategies that constitute "best practice" for these students. Hence, a major need in special education is to provide inservice training for paraeducators in effective methods of teaching adaptive skills to students with severe disabilities.

TSTP is efficient because the program can be conducted in one 8-hour workday.

Teaching-Skills Training Program

We developed the Teaching-Skills Training Program (TSTP) to ensure that human service personnel are adequately prepared to teach people with severe disabilities. We conducted research over a 5-year period to meet each of four criteria for successful staff training (see box, "Characteristics of Successful Staff Training Programs"; Jensen, Parsons, & Reid, 1997; Parsons et al., 1993; Parsons, Reid, & Green, 1996; Reid & Parsons, 1996).

In initial research conducted to validate the program's effectiveness, we taught 9 direct-support staff and 4 supervisors in a residential program for people with severe disabilities to apply basic teaching strategies, with at least 80% proficiency (Parsons et al., 1993). In subsequent research, we trained 24 staff members, including group home personnel, paraeducators, and undergraduate teaching interns, to teach with 80% proficiency using TSTP (Parsons et al., 1996). Acceptability research has indicated that staff respond favorably to the training procedures (Parsons et al., 1993; Reid & Parsons, 1996). Finally, TSTP is efficient because the program can be conducted in one 8-hour workday (Parsons et al., 1996).

Since the initial validation research, educators have used TSTP to successfully train more than 300 paraeducators and other support personnel. Equally important, students with severe disabilities have made progress toward acquiring adaptive skills when their paraeducators have used the skills they learned during the program (Parsons et al., 1993).

To illustrate, graduates of TSTP have taught children with severe disabilities in an inclusive preschool program the following skills:

- Wash hands.
- Recognize numbers and letters of the alphabet.
- Operate a cassette player.
- Eat with a spoon.
- Respond to one-step directions.

In a school classroom for students with severe multiple disabilities, other graduates have taught students the following skills:

- Drink from a cup.
- Press a switch to activate a radio or TV.
- Use augmentative communication devices.

Other graduates have used the teaching strategies developed through TSTP to teach job skills to adults with severe disabilities—at the workplace.

> ## Figure 1. Sample Activity Illustrating the Rationale for Using Task Analyses
>
> ### Why Is a Task Analysis Important When Teaching a New Skill?
>
> 1. If you were asked to teach someone to prepare a place setting incorporating a plate, cup, napkin, knife, fork, and spoon, draw the placement of the items on a placemat. Assume that the placemat is already on the table in the appropriate place.
>
> 2. Compare what you have drawn to the drawings of others in the group. How many place settings among the group were exactly like yours?
>
> 3. Draw a place setting following the task analysis provided by the instructor.
>
> 4. Compare what you have drawn by following the task analysis to the drawings of others in the group. How many place settings were exactly like yours?
>
> ### Task Analysis for Place Setting
>
> 1. Place the plate in the center of the placemat.
> 2. Place the napkin directly beside and to the left of the plate.
> 3. Place the fork on the napkin.
> 4. Place the knife directly beside and to the right of the plate.
> 5. Place the spoon directly beside and to the right of the knife.
> 6. Place the cup directly above the tip of the knife.

Teaching Skills

TSTP focuses on four basic teaching competencies: task analysis, least-to-most assistive prompting, reinforcement, and error correction.

Types of prompts range from mild forms of assistance, such as gesturing to the student, to more directive prompts, such as physically guiding the student through a skill.

Task Analysis

We teach staff that to use task analysis, they should list each specific behavior in performing a targeted skill sequentially, in the order the behavior should occur for the skill to be performed correctly. They teach the kinds of behavior, or steps, in the order specified in the task analysis to facilitate learning so that each step becomes a signal for the performance of each subsequent step in the task analysis. Figure 1 illustrates a task analysis for teaching students how to set a table for lunch or dinner.

Using the Least-to-Most Assistive Prompting Strategy

When teaching a student to put on her coat, the first step of the task analysis is to pick up the coat. If the student does not pick up the coat independently, the paraeducator might begin by saying to the student, "Pick up your coat."

If the verbal prompt does not result in the student's picking up the coat, the paraeducator might tell her to pick up the coat while simultaneously pointing to the coat.

Subsequently, if the combined verbal and gestural prompt as just described does not evoke the student's picking up the coat, the paraeducator might tell the student to pick up the coat while guiding her hand toward the coat (verbal and partial physical prompts).

Least-to-Most Assistive Prompting

Providing assistance on a continuum of least-to-most prompting involves giving a student only the assistance necessary to correctly complete each step of the task analysis. Types of prompts range from mild forms of assistance, such as gesturing to the student, to more directive prompts, such as physically guiding the student through a skill.

We teach staff that if the level of assistance they provide at first does not enable the student to correctly complete a step in the task analysis, they should gradually increase assistance—level of prompting—until the student successfully performs the step (see box, "Using the Least-to-Most Assistive Prompting Strategy").

Reinforcement and Error Correction

The third and fourth teaching competencies work together. *Reinforcement* is the means by which a paraeducator can increase the likelihood across successive teaching sessions that a student will perform the skill that the paraeducator is attempting to teach. We teach staff that a reinforcing consequence is more than a reward or provision of a preferred item. A consequence provided in the context of a teaching program can be regarded as a reinforcer only if student performance of the skill improves over time. Hence, one of the most important skills of paraeducators who teach people with severe disabilities is determining what constitutes reinforcement for a given student, and effectively providing that reinforcement to encourage student learning. Praise and attention are effective reinforcers for many students. Also, engaging in preferred activities following teaching sessions can function as a reinforcer.

TSTP focuses on four basic teaching competencies: task analysis, least-to-most assistive prompting, reinforcement, and error correction

---

When a student incorrectly performs a step within a skill, a staff member must deal with the *error* in a manner that promotes student learning. In essence, errors are opportunities for students to practice the wrong way of completing a skill and should be prevented whenever possible.

We teach paraeducators to prevent errors by increasing the assistance provided on a given step when they see that the student is about to make an error. When the staff member cannot prevent an error, he or she immediately stops the student and has the student repeat the step of the task while providing enough assistance to prevent the error from occurring a second time. For example, when a student who is learning to use a copier loads the paper incorrectly, the paraeducator should stop the student, remove the paper, and provide more assistance so that the student loads the paper a second time with no mistake.

Training Format

For paraeducators in our program, we use a training format consisting of classroom-based instruction, on-the-job monitoring and feedback, and follow-up supervision.

Classroom-Based Component

The primary purpose of the classroom-based training is to familiarize paraeducators with the *rationale* for each teaching competency (task analysis, prompting, and so forth) and the terminology used in describing the teaching process.

For example, using the activity shown in Figure 1, we show the rationale for using a *task analysis* to ensure that staff members teach students a skill in a consistent way. When several staff trainees draw a place setting without the task analysis, almost invariably the placement of cups, plates, and other items will differ across the staff trainees. Thus, if each trainee were teaching a student the task, the task would differ each time it was taught, so that a student with severe disabilities would find it difficult to learn to perform the task. If all trainees follow the task analysis when drawing the place setting, however, the completed drawings should look the same.

A second purpose of the classroom-based training is to begin training staff in the *performance skills* necessary to teach students with severe disabilities by having trainees practice the skills in a role-play situation. We limit the group size of classroom-based training to six trainees. Working with a small group allows the instructor sufficient time for the instruction, observation, and feedback necessary to ensure that each trainee acquires the teaching competencies.

During classroom-based training, we teach prospective paraeducators the skills of task analysis, prompting, reinforcement, and error correction, one at a time. We provide a rationale for using each skill to teach people with severe disabilities, and we demonstrate both correct and incorrect applications of each skill. Trainees practice and receive feedback about their performance from the instructor until each trainee can perform each respective teaching skill proficiently in a role-play situation (see box, "Modeling, Practice, and Feedback").

On-the-Job Monitoring and Feedback

The primary purpose of on-the-job monitoring and feedback is to ensure that trainees can apply the teaching skills learned during the classroom-based component in an actual teaching situation with their students. The instructor observes the trainee's teaching in the classroom and provides feedback regarding the trainee's application of the teaching skills. Through monitoring, the instructor determines the trainee's proficiency in applying each of the teaching competencies.

Modeling, Practice, and Feedback

Instructor demonstration of a teaching skill, followed by trainee practice of the skill with subsequent feedback from the instructor, is the most important aspect of classroom-based training.
Modeling. When training paraeducators how to use a least-to-most assistive prompting strategy, the instructor first demonstrates a prompting sequence in a teaching program with a staff trainee who plays the role of a student.
Practice. Each trainee practices implementing the prompting strategy, with another trainee playing the role of the student.
Feedback. After the trainee practices the prompting strategy, the instructor provides the paraeducator feedback regarding the accuracy of his or her prompting.

Using an Observation Form. To facilitate the instructor's job in this respect, we use the form shown in Figure 2, in conjunction with the criteria listed in Table 1. The form in Figure 2 guides the instructor in focusing on whether or not the trainee performs each of the teaching skills proficiently.

To use the observation form, the observing instructor lists steps of the task analysis (e.g., steps for setting a table) in the appropriate order along the left side of the form. As illustrated in Figure 2, the observer scores each teaching skill under the column labeled for the respective skill on the line corresponding to the designated step of the task analysis. The observer scores each performed skill as being either correct (+) or incorrect (-). Nonapplicable (NA) is scored if there is no opportunity to perform one of the teaching skills for a given step of the task analysis. Table 1 shows the specific criteria for scoring a teaching skill as correct.

In small groups, paraeducators role-play effective teaching strategies.

Providing Feedback. Following observation of the student-teaching session, the instructor provides the trainee with feedback by explaining the teaching skills that were correctly and incorrectly performed. For those teaching skills that the trainee performed incorrectly, the instructor describes or demonstrates how the skill should have been performed.

The trainee's teaching proficiency is calculated by dividing the total number of *correctly* implemented teaching skills across all program steps by the *total* number of all skills taught, and multiplying by 100%. This calculation results in a percentage of correct teaching skill application, as illustrated in Figure 2. We consider a staff trainee *proficient* when he or she scores at least 80% correct during two separate observations of student teaching.

Follow-up Supervision

We designed the final component of TSTP, follow-up supervision, to ensure that paraeducators maintain their teaching skills at the 80% proficiency level. Establishing maintenance procedures is essential for the long-term success of staff training programs (Reid et al., 1989, Chapter 4). This part of the program, of course, lasts longer than 1 day!

Follow-up supervision entails implementing a schedule for continued observation of staff teaching and provision of feedback. The frequency of follow-up sessions is determined by how proficiently a given paraeducator continues to teach—the more proficient the teaching skills, the

less frequently observations with feedback are needed, and vice versa.

Role of Special Education Teachers and Administrators

We have successfully implemented TSTP using two different staff training models: direct training and pyramid training.

Direct Training

A model that works well in settings where fewer than 10 staff require training involves having one instructor directly train all staff. The instructor is responsible for the classroom-based training, on-the-job observations, and follow-up supervision for all staff in a school or agency. The instructor may be a principal, supervising teacher, or educational consultant—essentially, anyone with experience using the teaching strategies, observing staff performance, and providing feedback. The *Teaching-Skills Training Program Instructor's Manual*, available from the authors, serves as a guide in implementing the program (Reid & Parsons, 1994).

Pyramid Training

In school systems where a large number of staff require training, other researchers have successfully used the *pyramid* staff training model (Demchak & Browder, 1990). Using the pyramidal model, one instructor initially trains all *supervising teachers*, who, in turn, directly train the paraeducators whom they supervise. The type of training teachers should receive is twofold:

- Teachers may need to complete TSTP to ensure that the teachers themselves are proficient in the skills they will be training to paraeducators.
- Teachers should be trained in the supervisory skills of systematically observing the teaching skills of others and providing feedback to improve the teaching process. This focused supervisory training for teachers is often essential to the successful training of paraeducators because, although teachers are expected to supervise paraeducators, few teachers have had training in effective strategies for supervision.

Figure 2. Sample of a Completed Form for Observing Teaching Proficiency

Teaching-Skills Observation Form

Trainee _Anna_   Instructor _Mary_   Student _Joe_

Skill _using a table napkin_ Date _5-22-98_

+ correct
- incorrect
NA nonapplicable

TRAINING STEPS	ORDER	PROMPTS	REINFORCES	ERROR CORRECTION
STEP 1 pick up napkin	+ ~ NA	+ ~ NA	+ ~ NA	+ ~ NA
STEP 2 wipe mouth	+ ~ NA	+ ~ NA	+ ~ NA	+ / NA
STEP 3 replace napkin in lap	+ ~ NA	+ ~ NA	+ ~ NA	+ ~ NA
STEP 4	+ ~ NA	+ ~ NA	+ ~ NA	+ ~ NA
STEP 5	+ ~ NA	+ ~ NA	+ ~ NA	+ ~ NA
STEP 6	+ ~ NA	+ ~ NA	+ ~ NA	+ ~ NA
STEP 7	+ ~ NA	+ ~ NA	+ ~ NA	+ ~ NA
STEP 8	+ ~ NA	+ ~ NA	+ ~ NA	+ ~ NA
STEP 9	+ ~ NA	+ ~ NA	+ ~ NA	+ ~ NA
STEP 10	+ ~ NA	+ ~ NA	+ ~ NA	+ ~ NA

OBSERVATION SUMMARY

$$\frac{\text{\# CORRECT TEACHING SKILLS}}{\text{\# CORRECT AND INCORRECT TEACHING SKILLS}} = \frac{6}{7} \times 100\% = \underline{86}\%$$

Feedback _Nice job! Appropriate prompting on step 1; use more assistance during error correction to avoid another error_

Table 1. Definitions for Correct Application of the Basic Teaching Skills

Teaching Skill	Definition for Correct Application
Order	The steps of the task analysis are taught in sequence so that each step taught is preceded by the specific step listed in the task analysis.
Prompt	Each successive prompt (if more than 1 prompt is used) provided for a given step in the task analysis involves more assistance than the previous prompt.
Reinforcement	A positive consequence is provided following the last correct step of the task analysis and is not provided following any incorrectly performed step. Reinforcement could be provided following any correctly performed step but must be provided following the last correctly performed step.
Error Correction	When the student incorrectly performs a step of the task analysis (i.e., a behavior incompatible with the step), the student is required to repeat the step; and a more assistive prompt is provided on the second trial. The prompt on the second trial should provide sufficient assistance so the student completes the step without another error.

Focused supervisory training (in observation and feedback methods) for teachers contributes to the successful training of paraeducators

Supervisory training for teachers should include practice in observing another staff member teach, completing the observation form, and giving feedback in a role-play situation. A protocol for teachers to use as a guide for giving diagnostic feedback is presented in Figure 3. Once a teacher is competent in observing and providing feedback in a role-play situation, the instructor observes the teacher on the job as the teacher observes the paraeducator conduct a teaching session. When the teacher can provide accurate feedback to the paraeducator regarding the latter's teaching skills, then the teacher independently observes and provides feedback to the paraeducator several times each week until the paraeducator can perform the basic teaching skills.

Research has indicated that when teachers complete TSTP, as well as the additional supervisory training, they can train paraeducators to implement the basic teaching skills through observation and feedback in the classroom and *without the paraeducators participating in the classroom-based component* (Jensen et al., 1997). Moreover, these researchers found that the supervisory training improved the teacher's *own teaching skills* when those skills were below the 80% proficiency criterion prior to training. The supervising teacher provides follow-up supervision for paraeducators through intermittent observations and feedback.

Figure 3 shows a checklist that supervising teachers can use to guide their feedback sessions. This form actually constitutes a "task analysis" for providing feedback, beginning with setting a positive tone and ending with making a positive statement.

Figure 3. Protocol for Giving Diagnostic Feedback to a Staff Member Following the Observation of a Teaching Session

Supervisor's Feedback Checklist

Staff Trainee _____ Student _____ Skill _____
Supervisor _____ Location _____ Time ____ Date ____

Feedback Components

Check each component included in your feedback to the trainee. Check NA (nonapplicable) for components 4 and 5 if no teaching errors were made.

	Yes	No	NA
1. Set a positive tone for feedback session			
2. Began diagnostic feedback with positive feedback			
3. Gave appropriate positive feedback.			
4. Identified each skill category with teaching errors			
5. For each category with teaching errors, described how the teaching skill should have been performed correctly			
6. Solicited questions for feedback from trainee			
7. Referenced current training status			
8. Ended feedback session with a positive statement			

Student and Parent Input

The highly effective teaching strategies espoused by the Teaching-Skills Training Program require brief teaching sessions involving one student at a time. Individual instruction, however, is only one component of a quality educational experience for students with severe disabilities. Students and family members should have significant input into which skills warrant teaching in this manner and how much time should be directed to individual teaching services versus other valuable educational supports.

When individualized teaching, embedded within the daily routine, is deemed necessary, the TSTP provides paraeducators with the requisite teaching skills to improve student achievement.

References

Demchak, M., & Browder, D. M. (1990). An evaluation of the pyramid model of staff training in group homes for adults with severe handicaps. *Education and Training in Mental Retardation, 25,* 150–163.

Jensen, J. E., Parsons, M. B., & Reid, D. H. (1997). *Multiple effects of training teachers to improve the data recording of teacher aides.* Manuscript submitted for publication.

Parsons, M. B., Reid, D. H., & Green, C. W. (1993). Preparing direct service staff to teach people with severe disabilities: A comprehensive evaluation of an effective and acceptable training program. *Behavioral Residential Treatment, 8,* 163–185.

Parsons, M. B., Reid, D. H., & Green, C. W. (1996). Training basic teaching skills to community and institutional support staff for people with severe disabilities: A one-day program. *Research In Developmental Disabilities, 17,* 467–485.

Reid, D. H., & Parsons, M. B. (1994). *Training to teach in a day: The teaching skills training program instructor's manual.* Morganton, NC: Carolina Behavior Analysis and Support Center, Ltd.

Reid, D. H., & Parsons, M. B. (1996). A comparison of staff acceptability of immediate versus delayed verbal feedback in staff training. *Journal of Organizational Behavior Management, 16*(2), 35–48.

Reid, D. H., Parsons, M. B., & Green, C. W. (1989). *Staff management in human services: Behavioral research and application.* Springfield, IL: Charles C Thomas.

Marsha B. Parsons, *Associate Director, Carolina Behavior Analysis and Support Center, Ltd., Morganton, North Carolina.* **Dennis H. Reid,** *Associate Professor, Louisiana State University Medical Center, New Orleans.*

Address correspondence to Marsha B. Parsons, Carolina Behavior Analysis and Support Center, Ltd., P.O. Box 425, Morganton, NC 28680.

Fostering Friendships

Loneliness in Children with Disabilities:
How Teachers Can Help

Shireen Pavri

Maria is a 10-year-old repeating fourth grade due to extremely limited reading skills. She is diagnosed as having a learning disability. Maria feels alone in the world, even when there are other people around her. She believes that she has nothing in common with the other kids at school, and that she has nobody to turn to when she needs help. Maria does not know how to begin a conversation with other students. She feels a desperate ache deep within her and wants to have friends.

Jake, a 14-year-old adolescent with hearing impairments, has always been a shy and quiet introvert. Of late he seems withdrawn and listless, mechanically going through life activities. He shuns social interaction and has stopped hanging out with the only other student he was friendly with. He recently wrote a poem about suicide as a way out of his silent and desolate world.

Jeremy is an 8-year-old second grader, recently diagnosed as having mental retardation. He had to change schools so he could attend a special program for students with mental retardation. Jeremy has found it difficult to adjust to the new school. He complains about missing his friends and activities at his old school. He says he doesn't have anyone to play with, and that nobody likes him. His parents report that he has become irritable and anxious and has frequent physical and verbal outbursts.

The students in the preceding scenarios are experiencing severe loneliness, an unpleasant emotional state that often goes unidentified in school-aged children (Asher & Gazelle, 1999; Peplau & Perlman, 1982). In most instances, lonely children are shy and quiet and do not disrupt classroom activities or call attention to themselves. Many students do not acknowledge feeling lonely and are resistant to sharing their feelings of loneliness with others; thus, their needs go unmet.

Loneliness in Children

Most children experience short-term, situational loneliness as a natural consequence of interacting in social situations (e.g., not getting invited to a birthday party, a best friend's leaving town, not being allowed to go outside to play at recess due to incomplete classwork). Only when loneliness becomes chronic and has serious emotional

consequences do teachers and other professionals view it as problematic, requiring intervention (Asher & Gazelle, 1999).

Consequences of Loneliness

Researchers have found several devastating consequences of loneliness on children's immediate and long-term adjustment. Many lonely students, like Maria, Jake, and Jeremy, have difficulty developing satisfactory peer relationships and friendships (Asher, Hymel, & Renshaw, 1984; Renshaw & Brown, 1993). Lonely children often experience poor self-esteem and increased anxiety and depression that may be accompanied by suicidal ideation (McWhirter, 1990).

Students who are lonely are at risk of poor later life adjustment, as well. For instance, lonely people are at an increased risk of engaging in criminal and delinquent

Social Problem-Solving

 Stop and Think
What is the problem?

 Brainstorm solutions to the problem

 Select and apply the best solution

behaviors in adulthood (Parker & Asher, 1987). Given these detrimental consequences of chronic loneliness, educators must identify students who are lonely and develop interventions to prevent and reduce loneliness.

This article describes the phenomenon of loneliness and its incidence in children with disabilities, and suggests techniques for detecting and dealing with loneliness at school (see box, "How Does Loneliness Affect Children with Disabilities?"). The strategies suggested for developing school-based interventions for students who are lonely are based on my personal experiences in working with students with disabilities, and from the extant literature. Additional research is needed to determine the effectiveness of the suggested intervention techniques in reducing feelings of loneliness in children.

Assessing Loneliness in Children

Because loneliness is a subjective experience that is not synonymous with social isolation or rejection, it is difficult to diagnose accurately. Some children enjoy their solitude and do not feel lonely when they are alone. Others experience intense loneliness even when they are in a room full of people. The lonely child has an ideal conception of the social relationships he or she desires, and believes that his or her present relationships fall short of

How Does Loneliness Affect Children with Disabilities?

Researchers have defined loneliness as a subjective experience that is unpleasant and distressing to the individual. It usually stems from dissatisfaction with social relationships and may vary from being brief and transient to becoming a persistent and life-disrupting experience (McWhirter, 1990; Peplau & Perlman, 1982).

Children with disabilities, particularly children with learning disabilities and mental retardation, are more vulnerable to feelings of loneliness than their peers without disabilities (Luftig, 1988; Margalit & Levin-Alyagon, 1994; Pavri & Luftig, 2000; Williams & Asher, 1992). Research evidence suggests that 10%–16% of students without disabilities report feeling lonely (Asher et al., 1984). Reports of loneliness experienced by students with mental retardation are as high as 25% (Luftig, 1988). Though most of the research has focused on students with learning disabilities and mental retardation, students with other disabilities are likely to experience similar levels of loneliness.

Students with disabilities experience a higher incidence of loneliness for two principal reasons:

- Many students with disabilities have *difficulty reading and processing social cues and developing social relationships*, and consequently they are less accepted in their peer group (Haager & Vaughn, 1995). Many students have difficulty expressing themselves appropriately in social situations and may display behaviors that result in their being rejected by their peers.

- Educators have traditionally not given students with disabilities equal opportunities for full participation in educational and extracurricular activities at school. Such a *separate education system* likely affects the extent to which students with disabilities feel a sense of belonging and acceptance in the school and classroom community. For instance, Jeremy, in the introductory scenario, may be reacting to his new placement in a more restrictive educational setting for students with mental retardation. He must adjust to a new school, teacher, and peer group, and has less opportunity for after-school activities where he could develop supportive friendships with a heterogeneous group of peers.

these desired relationships (Sermat, 1978). For instance, Maria, in the introductory scenario, feels socially alienated and dissatisfied with her existing social relationships and has a desperate need to make friends.

Family members, teachers, child care providers, and other school personnel might be the first to notice that the child is lonely. Some children are willing to talk to teachers about their loneliness and seek assistance with social participation. Other children, particularly those who are chronically lonely, do not initiate interventions, thereby making it more difficult to detect their loneliness.

Detecting Loneliness Symptoms

Researchers have found that students who display particular behavioral patterns experience greater levels of loneliness. For instance, students adopting a passive-withdrawn behavioral style or an aggressive behavioral style are more likely to be rejected by the peer group, and consequently experience higher levels of loneliness (Cassidy & Asher, 1992; Margalit & Levin-Alyagon, 1994; Renshaw & Brown, 1993). Students who are passive and withdrawn rarely initiate social interactions, often provide minimal encouragement to overtures of friendship, and in extreme cases perceive themselves as being persecuted by others. Jake, in the introductory example, would be considered to be passive and withdrawn. On the other hand, students like Jeremy who act out verbally or physically when their social goals are not met also tend to be rejected by their peers. Educators should look for signs of loneliness in students who tend to be shy and withdrawn or who are prone to aggressive behavior.

Look for signs of loneliness in students who tend to be shy and withdrawn or who are aggressive.

Assessment Techniques

Figure 1 illustrates four techniques that educators often use to assess loneliness in students with or without disabilities. As discussed in Figure 1, informal observations of students interacting with peers in naturally occurring social situations is an effective way for teachers and paraprofessionals to identify students who appear lonely. Bullock (1993) provided guidelines for school professionals to use while observing students to determine whether they are lonely. She recommended that teachers look for whether the student appears anxious or timid, lacks interest in his or her surroundings, is rejected by playmates, chooses to avoid other students, and lacks the social skills needed to initiate or maintain interactions or is reluctant to use these skills. The observer might also make a determination of whether these signs of loneliness are of recent onset or have been recurrent over a period of time. Observations should be conducted during academic class periods, as well as social or unstructured times at school. Interestingly, students with and without disabilities have reported feeling particularly lonely during structured classroom activities, such as reviewing math facts or working on an independent writing assignment (Asher,

Hopmeyer, Gabriel, & Guerra, 2001; Pavri & Monda-Amaya, 2001).

The second assessment strategy highlighted in Figure 1 is interviewing peers to determine a target student's social standing in a group. Same-age peers share several experiences and spend a large part of the school day with the target student. Informal conversations with peers give school professionals a sense for students' social relationships and events occurring in their social lives. Educators might also use more structured peer ratings and peer nominations in the classroom. Teachers can conduct peer ratings by providing all students in the classroom with a class roster and asking them to rate each class peer, according to how much they like them on a 5-point scale. Peer nominations are a little different, requiring students to generate names of class peers that meet predetermined descriptors (e.g., name three students whom you would like to sit next to in class).

Figure 1. Commonly Used Assessment Techniques to Identify Loneliness

1. Direct observation of the target student at different times at school, for example, recess, playground, academic class periods.
2. Interviews with peers to learn about the student's social behavior using informal interviews, peer ratings, peer nominations, and sociometric ratings.
3. Interviews with parents and other adults to learn about the student's social behavior and adjustment in different situations and settings, for example, home, school, extracurricular settings.
4. Interviews with the target student to learn about his or her self-perceptions of loneliness and social satisfaction using informal interviews, and self-report inventories, such as the following:
   a. *Children's Loneliness Scale* (Asher et al., 1984).
   b. *UCLA Loneliness Scale* (Russell, 1996).

Sociometric techniques are used to measure the extent to which class peers like a target student. This technique allows teachers to classify students into one of the following five groups based on sociometric status: popular, average, neglected, rejected, and controversial. The extent to which students are accepted by their peers influences their vulnerability to loneliness (Renshaw & Brown, 1993). Typically, students who are popular feel less lonely than do students who are rejected; and, contrary to common belief, not all students from a lower sociometric status group experience high levels of loneliness.

An effective assessment strategy is interviewing peers to determine a target student's social standing in a group.

The third assessment technique discussed in Figure 1 is interviewing family members and other adults, including teachers and paraprofessionals who work closely with the student. The family is aware of transient and long-term changes in the student's life and the effect these changes have on the student's social and emotional adjustment. For this reason, building a partnership with family members is extremely important in making an appropriate diagnosis. Educators should also solicit feedback from any other people who interact with the student in different settings (e.g., childcare providers, extended family members, neighbors, siblings, and after-school activity coordinators) and should take this feedback into account in determining whether a student is lonely.

The final assessment technique described in Figure 1 is interviewing the target student. This technique might be the most effective way to determine whether a student feels lonely. On a cautionary note, one should take into account that such self-report could be subject to temporal changes in a student's social interactions. For instance, Jessie, who has a fight with her best friend an hour earlier, may report feeling "extremely sad and lonely," but on making up with her friend in the next couple of hours might feel "happy and loved." Students might also be hesitant to be completely truthful about their feelings, particularly with adults they do not feel they can trust.

Self-report inventories could be used to assist teachers in diagnosing loneliness in students. These inventories provide a reliable and valid index of a student's loneliness and are less subject to the situational fluctuations described above. Two such inventories are described:

1. Educators have frequently used *The Children's Loneliness and Social Dissatisfaction Scale* (Asher, Hymel, & Renshaw, 1984) in assessing school-based loneliness in students without disabilities and in students with learning disabilities and mental retardation (Pavri & Luftig, 2000; Pavri & Monda-Amaya, 2001; Williams & Asher, 1992). This questionnaire includes 24 items on a 5-point Likert scale, 16 tapping into loneliness (e.g., "It's easy for me to make new friends at school"), and 8 filler or "neutral" items used to help the student feel comfortable in responding to the questionnaire (e.g., "I like to read"). Students respond to the items by checking one of five choices, ranging from "That's always true about me" to "That's not true about me at all." A total loneliness score ranging from 16 (low loneliness) to 80 (high loneliness) is obtained for students responding to the measure.

Pavri and Monda-Amaya (2000, 2001) modified the *Children's Loneliness Scale* for use with students with learning disabilities. To facilitate student's reading difficulties, the researchers individually administered the scale, read test items and response choices aloud to the student, and enlarged the response format to allow the student to more clearly distinguish between the five response options. The measure yielded high internal reliabilities for the group of elementary-age students with learning disabilities. To accommodate students with mental retardation, the scale might be further modified (e.g., having a 3-point scale comprised of a happy, neutral, and sad face instead of the standard 5-point scale). Although such a test modification would still provide rich qualitative information, it might affect the reliability and validity of the scale.

2. Educators have used The UCLA Loneliness Scale-Version 3 (Russell, 1996) and earlier versions to measure loneliness in adolescents, adults, and elderly people. This 20-item measure requires the respondent to indicate in writing (by selecting "never," "rarely," "sometimes," and "always") how often they feel a certain way (e.g., "How often do you feel alone?" or "How often do you feel close to people?"). Russell reported sound psychometric properties for this instrument, with high reliability and validity, and significant correlations with other loneliness measures. There are no reports of whether the UCLA Loneliness Scale has been modified for use with people with disabilities. It might be challenging for students with mental retardation to comprehend several items on this measure. Test presentation might also need to be modified for use with students with disabilities (e.g., reading items aloud, modifying response format), which might affect the psychometric qualities of the measure.

Teachers have also used other measures to assess loneliness in students. *The Loneliness in Contexts Questionnaire*, developed by Asher, Hopmeyer, Gabriel and Guerra (2001), provides an index of how students feel in different school contexts such as the classroom, lunchroom, playground, and physical education class. Marcoen and Brumagne (1985) developed a measure to assess loneliness across parent and peer contexts.

Interventions to Alleviate Loneliness

We must develop ways to reduce the debilitating effects of loneliness on the social functioning of students with disabilities. Unfortunately, few researchers have investigated how educators and other professionals can help reduce loneliness in students with and without disabilities (Bullock, 1993; Margalit & Levin-Alyagon, 1994; Page, Scanlan, & Deringer, 1994; Pavri & Monda-Amaya, 2001; Williams & Asher, 1992).

The following suggestions are based on a review of the literature on student- and teacher-generated interventions to provide social support and reduce loneliness in students, and on my personal experiences working with students with disabilities. Figure 2 summarizes these strategies.

Figure 2. Key Intervention Approaches to Working with Students Who Are Lonely

1. Social Skills Training
   - Initiating, maintaining, and terminating interactions.
   - Assertiveness training.
   - Conflict-resolution skills.
   - Social problem-solving skills.
   - Dealing with aggressive behavior.
2. Creating Opportunities for Social Interaction
   - Participation in extracurricular and after-school activities.
   - Structuring recess and play times.
   - Social interaction during academic subjects, for example, cooperative learning, peer tutoring.
3. Creating an Accepting Classroom Climate
   - Developing rapport with students.
   - Developing clear classroom rules and expectations.
   - Promoting classroom membership and belonging.
   - Promoting disabilities awareness and acceptance.
4. Teaching Adaptive Coping Strategies
   - Awareness of a range of coping skills.
   - Suggestions for adopting alternative strategies.
   - Changing self-perceptions and attributions through counseling.
5. Enhancing Student's Self-Esteem
   - Using positive reinforcement.
   - Encouraging social interaction and taking risks.
   - Assigning classroom jobs and responsibilities.

1. **Teach social interaction skills.** Students with good social skills are better accepted by their peers and find it easier to make and keep friends. Having even a single friend helps decrease a student's feelings of loneliness (Renshaw & Brown, 1993). Many educators have used social skills training to equip students with the skills they need to effectively interact with their peers. Schools have used social skills training groups run by school counselors or psychologists to help students overcome shyness and social inhibition (McWhirter, 1990; Page et al., 1994). The classroom teacher can also teach these skills to the students. Social-skill instruction can take various forms:

- Selecting a skill to be focused on each week, based on individual student needs.

- Making use of teaching opportunities as they naturally arise in the classroom.

- Using an established social skills curriculum (e.g., Skillstreaming), or schoolwide programs such as "Character Counts" or "Peaceable Schools."

When teaching social skills, you should determine why the student is not manifesting appropriate behaviors. The instructional strategies used to teach a student to acquire a desired social skill that is not already in his or her behavioral repertoire are different from strategies used when a student has acquired the skill but fails to perform the skill in an appropriate situation.

For instance, to go back to our scenarios, coaching and modeling techniques would be effective in teaching Maria to learn the new skill of initiating a conversation with her peers, whereas motivation or reinforcement strategies might be more effective when working with Jake, who appears disinterested in social interactions.

2. **Create opportunities for social interaction.** Work with family members and other school personnel to create socialization opportunities and build social networks and supports for students with disabilities. For instance teachers and school counselors could provide students with opportunities for meeting new people and making friends. You could encourage students to participate in activities like Boys and Girls Clubs, nature camps, after-school activities, Special Olympics, and other hobby groups. Such activities would provide opportunities for students like Maria, Jake, and Jeremy to meet other students and share a common interest with them.

Family members, teachers, childcare providers, and other school personnel might be the first to notice that the child is lonely.

Pavri & Monda-Amaya (2001), in interviewing 60 general and special educators, found these teachers using several techniques to engage students in social interaction at school. During academic class periods at school, teachers used cooperative learning groups, buddy systems, and heterogeneous seating arrangements to facilitate working with others, thereby reducing loneliness. During unstructured and free times at school, teachers facilitated group games and activities, assigned roles or jobs to students, and even spent time outside on the playground with vulnerable students teaching them important skills and encouraging other students to play with them.

Developing a relationship with parents is extremely beneficial for the teacher who wants to truly understand and help her students. In Jeremy's situation, teachers could work with his family to find ways to help him adjust to the new school, while arranging for him to coninue to participate in activities with friends from his former school.

3. *Develop an accepting classroom climate*. An accepting classroom environment nurtures a sense of belonging and membership where students feel respected and trusted by each other and their teacher. Establishing good rapport with students goes far in meeting academic, social, and emotional needs. Margalit (1994) identified three important variables of classroom climate that teachers can control:

- Foster relationships between classroom members so as to create a supportive environment with reduced conflict.
- Emphasize individual growth of each student and reduce competition in the classroom.
- Establish order, consistency, and clear expectations among the students regarding classroom rules and work habits.

In interviews with general and special educators, Pavri and Monda-Amaya (2001) found that teachers adopt several strategies to promote an accepting classroom climate. Some teachers reported eating lunch with small groups of students, or playing with them at recess, so they get to know and develop a relationship with each of their students. Others reported having open classroom discussions on issues concerning students, so as to reduce conflict and facilitate group problem-solving. Other teachers used videos and books featuring people with disabilities to foster disability awareness. Teachers invited guest speakers to talk to the class about individual differences and similarities among students.

4. *Teach adaptive styles for coping with loneliness*. Students tend to respond in different ways when they feel lonely. Some students take active steps to alleviate loneliness, and others adopt a more passive approach. Researchers have found that some students with learning disabilities use strategies similar to those used by lonely adults in coping with loneliness (Margalit & Levin-Alyagon, 1994; Pavri & Monda-Amaya, 2001). These coping strategies include the following:

- Active solitude or engaging in a creative activity while alone.
- Distracting oneself by engaging in a task such as shopping that takes one's mind off the distressing situation.
- Initiating social contact with others to overcome loneliness.
- Sad passivity or doing nothing, which serves to prolong the lonely experience (Rubenstein & Shaver, 1979).

As in Jake's scenario, students who adopt passive coping strategies tend to perpetuate their experience of loneliness, allowing it to become chronic. Other students like Maria and Jeremy also do not use effective ways to deal with their loneliness. Counselors and teachers can help

students become aware of the maladaptive nature of the strategies used and teach students to substitute ineffective and passive coping techniques with more adaptive and effective strategies. This change could be brought about by nonintrusive interventions, such as suggesting alternative ways to react in particular situations (e.g., "Maria, why don't you ask Dulce to join you at the computer?") or more intrusive interventions that might involve mental health professionals working with the student on changing their attributions and perceptions.

Students who are lonely are at risk of poor later life adjustment.

5. *Enhance self-esteem*. Students with a healthy self-concept are empowered to believe that they can take action to control important life outcomes. Such students engage in positive and constructive thinking and problem-solving and have an "I can do" approach. Teachers can enhance the self-esteem of students across all domains by providing them with appropriate classroom jobs and responsibilities, giving positive reinforcement when they accomplish a task, and encouraging them to be successful in new situations.

Teachers might need to consult with psychologists or mental health therapists in helping some students develop a positive attitude about themselves. Maria, Jake, and Jeremy would benefit from interventions that make them feel good about themselves and in control of their social functioning at school. This would encourage them to take risks in initiating interactions with their peers.

Interviewing the student might be the most effective way to determine whether a student feels lonely.

Final Thoughts

Teachers can use several strategies to promote a sense of belonging and acceptance for students with disabilities, thereby reducing feelings of loneliness and social isolation. Training in social skills helps those students who have not acquired the skills required to interact appropriately with their peers. Activities like art, drama, and free play allow increased peer contact and an avenue for expressing feelings in young students, while cooperative learning and peer tutoring are effective ways to facilitate social relationships in older students. Developing a positive classroom climate aids the acceptance of diversity and respect for all students. Teachers should monitor and guide group activities to optimize the learning and social development these activities offer.

Some students might need to build a network of support in both school and home settings to feel more a part of these communities. The teacher and school counselor can collaborate with parents in identifying out-of-school activities that the student could participate in. School professionals play a prominent role in developing much-needed interventions for lonely students to feel a connection with people in their lives and to develop fulfilling and meaningful relationships.

Additional Readings on Loneliness

Asher, S. R., Parkhurst, J. T., Hymel, S., & Williams, G. A. (1990). Peer rejection and loneliness in childhood. In S. R. Asher & J. D. Coie (Eds.), *Peer rejection in childhood* (pp. 253–273). New York: Cambridge University Press.

Weiss, R. S. (1973). *Loneliness: The experience of emotional and social isolation.* Cambridge, MA: MIT Press.

References

Asher, S. R., & Gazelle, H. (1999). Loneliness, peer relations, and language disorder in childhood. *Topics in Language Disorders, 19,* 16–33.

Asher, S. R., Hopmeyer, A., Gabriel, S., & Guerra, V. (2001). *Children's loneliness in different school contexts.* Unpublished manuscript submitted for publication.

Asher, S. R., Hymel, S., & Renshaw, P. D. (1984). Loneliness in children, *Child Development, 55,* 1456–1464.

Bullock, J. R. (1993). Lonely children. *Young Children, 48,* 53–57.

Cassidy, J., & Asher, S. (1992). Loneliness and peer relations in young children. *Child Development, 63,* 350–365.

Haager, D., & Vaughn, S. (1995). Parent, teacher, and self-reports of the social competence of students with learning disabilities. *Journal of Learning Disabilities, 28,* 205–215.

Luftig, R. L. (1998). Assessment of the perceived school loneliness and isolation of mentally retarded and nonretarded students. *American Journal on Mental Retardation, 92,* 472–475.

Marcoen, A., & Brumagne, M. (1985). Loneliness among children and young adolescents. *Developmental Psychology, 21,* 1025–1031.

Margalit, M. (1994). *Loneliness among children with special needs: Theory, research, coping and intervention.* New York: Springer-Verlag.

Margalit, M., & Levin-Alyagon, M. (1994). Learning disability subtyping, loneliness, and classroom adjustment. *Learning Disability Quarterly, 17,* 297–310.

McWhirter, B. T. (199). Loneliness: A review of current literature with implications for counseling and research. *Journal of Counseling and Development, 68,* 417–422.

Page, R. M., Scanlan, A., & Deringer, N. (1994). Childhood loneliness and isolation: Implications and strategies for childhood educators. *Child Study Journal, 24,* 107–118.

Parker, J., & Asher, S. R. (1987). Peer relations and later personal adjustment: Are low accepted children at risk? *Psychological Bulletin, 102,* 357–389.

Pavri, S., & Luftig, R. L. (2000). The social face of inclusive education: Are students with learning disabilities really included in the classroom? *Preventing School Failure, 45,* 8–14.

Pavri, S., & Monda-Amaya, L. (2001). Social support in inclusive schools: Student and teacher perspectives. *Exceptional Children, 67,* 391–411.

Peplau, L. A., & Perlman, D. (Eds.). (1982). *Loneliness: A sourcebook of current theory, research and therapy.* New York: Wiley

Renshaw, P. D., & Brown, P. J. (1993). Loneliness in middle childhood: Concurrent and longitudinal predictors. *Child Development, 64,* 1271–1284.

Rubenstein, C. M., & Shaver, P. (1979). Loneliness in two northeastern cities. In J. Hartog & R. Audy (Eds.), *The anatomy of loneliness.* New York: International Universities Press.

Using Technology to Construct Alternate Portfolios of Students with Moderate and Severe Disabilities

Anne Denham

Elizabeth A. Lahm

The 1997 Amendments to the Individuals with Disabilities Education Act (IDEA '97) require that all states include students with disabilities in their measures of account-ability. Such measures may be part of the statewide and districtwide general education assessment programs through appropriate accommodations or through alternate assessments for those who cannot complete the general education assessment (Kleinert & Kearns, 1999).

Inclusion in Statewide Assessments

Since 1992, Kentucky has been including all students in the statewide assessment and going beyond federal regulations by including all students in the accountability system. Students receiving special education services are assessed in one of three ways:
- Through participation in the general education assessment program.
- Through participation in the general assessment program with accommodations.
- Through participation in the alternate portfolio system.

This article shares how the students in one classroom achieved "Distinguished" ratings, the highest of ratings, on their alternate portfolios, using assistive technology (see box, "What Is an Alternate Portfolio?").

Student Profiles

We conducted multiple case studies in one Kentucky classroom for students with moderate to severe cognitive disabilities to explore the process of using the IntelliKeys keyboard as an alternative computer input device for the production of the alternate portfolio. The classroom is located in a small elementary school (430 fourth- and fifth-grade students) in rural Kentucky. The students receive instruction in the general education classroom, the community, and a special class. The teacher has 12 years' experience servicing students in both the general and special education environment, is a recent graduate of an assistive technology educational specialist degree program, and holds an Assistive Technology Practitioner certificate. The students use a selection of assistive technology devices commensurate with their needs, to include single communication aids; a variety of switches to access tape recorders, electric kitchen mixer, and television through an environmental control; and an adaptive keyboard with custom overlays to access the computer.

How do we provide alternate assessments for those who cannot complete the general education assessment?

Four of the seven students in the class were in the age groups of students in the fourth and eighth grades and were thus required to participate in the Kentucky assessment program. Three were 9-year-old females, and one was a 13-year-old male. Two students were classified as having severe cognitive disabilities and two as having multiple disabilities. Table 1 describes these students further, according to physical, cognitive, and behavioral domains. The teacher determined that they qualified to participate in the assessment by completing an alternate portfolio.

What Is an Alternate Portfolio?

The alternate portfolio showcases student work where educators can assess learning across life domain activities in a comprehensive way. It represents performance-based evaluation, using a multidisciplinary approach, and models the use of holistic scoring. As with the general education portfolio scoring system, educators score alternate portfolios on four different levels: novice, apprentice, proficient, and distinguished. To qualify for a distinguished score, the highest level, the student must show the following:

• Progress on specifically targeted skills that are meaningful in current and future environments.
• Planning, monitoring, and evaluating self progress.
• Evaluation used to extend performance.
• Extensive evidence of Kentucky Academic Expectations in all entries.
• Natural supports.
• Use of adaptations, modifications, and/or assistive technology to evidence independence.
• Performance occurring in a variety of integrated settings, within and across all entries.
• Clearly established mutual friendship(s) with peers without disabilities.
• Choice and control in age-appropriate portfolio products within and across all entries.

The alternate portfolio assessment was designed by Kentucky educators specifically for those students whose limitations in cognitive function prevented completion of the standard assessment program (see below "Alternate Portfolios in Kentucky"). Eligibility is determined by the IEP committee, by considering cognitive function, adaptive behavior, cause of limited function, application skill level, use of community-based instruction, and level of performance with supports. Kleinert, Kearns, and Kennedy (1997) stated that between 0.5% and 1.0% of the public school students meet such requirements.

In addition to becoming part of the school's accountability indexes, alternate portfolios serve as "an 'instructional organizer' to give clarity and focus to the student's daily educational program, and as a teaching tool for students to learn higher order self-management, planning, and self-evaluation skills" (Kleinert, Haigh, Kearns, & Kennedy, 2000, p. 24). Such organizers provide teachers with a solid framework from which to work.

Alternate Portfolios in Kentucky

For more information about alternate portfolios, as implemented in Kentucky, visit the following Web sites:
Kentucky Alternate Portfolio Online
   http://www.ihdi.uky.edu/projects/KAP/
Kentucky Alternate Portfolio Assessment Teacher's Guide (PDF format)
   http://www.ihdi.uky.edu/projects/KAP/downloads/ap%20book99.pdf

Each of the four students was required to produce five entries for their alternate portfolio, in addition to demonstrating their use of a daily schedule and writing a letter to the reviewers. Table 2 shows the activities selected for these students to illustrate Kentucky's academic expectations within four content areas. Statements in black are target skills, and statements in italic are questions they had to respond to in order to demonstrate that skill. For example, Amanda demonstrated her computation skills by responding to the question "Did I count the cans?" on her activity sheet for loading the soda machine. One curricular area entry for each student was the focus of the study and is used to demonstrate the assessment process.

Students used a smorgasbord of assistive technology: single communication aids; a variety of switches to access tape recorders, electric kitchen mixer, and television through an environmental control; and an adaptive keyboard with custom overlays to access the computer.

All four students were unable to use the standard computer keyboard effectively. The teacher determined that the IntelliKeys keyboard was an appropriate adaptation for each. Three of the students used switches plugged into the IntelliKeys, in addition to the IntelliKeys keyboard itself. The switches were used to highlight and read text on the activity sheet with the use of text reading software.

The teacher constructed a custom overlay for each student, using Overlay Maker (IntelliTools, 1996) to support each student's individual needs. The overlay provided response choices to be used in the completion of a data sheet that was displayed on the computer (see Figure 1). By pressing a response choice on the overlay, the student caused the text programmed into that cell to be entered into the data sheet. The amount of text in the response depended on the student's level of functioning. For example, one student was able to record a complete sentence by sequencing three response choices, whereas another had only "yes" or "no" programmed as response choices. Color and location were used on the overlays to provide visual cues as to which response choices should be used for each of the assessment questions. Figure 2 is an example of one student's overlay.

The teacher provided a short training session for each student and one peer buddy on all components of the assessment process. For each student, the IntelliKeys with a custom overlay was used to respond to the assessment

Table 1. Profile of the Students in the Study

Subject	Physical Characteristics	Cognitive Characteristics	Behavioral Characteristics	Disability
Sandra: Age 9	Hearing impaired; hyperactive; impaired speech	Exceedingly low academic ability compared with typical peers	Noncompliant; resists authority	Multiple: hearing impaired and severe cognitive disability
Christine: Age 9	Low to fluctuating tone; nonambulatory; verbal though not clearly understood by anyone other than parent	Exceedingly low academic ability compared with typical peers	Friendly but demanding; persistent presence	Multiple: physical and severe cognitive disability
Amanda: Age 9	Small, ample stamina to function well with peers	Very low academic ability; beginning academics; delayed language skills	Friendly, predominantly smiling; enjoys being the center of attention; loud; silly behaviors	Severe cognitive disability
Brent: Age 13	Very small and thin; exhibits self-stimulatory behaviors; nonverbal; ambulatory but resistant	Nonparticipatory	Self-stimulatory behaviors; little response to peers or adults; very little interaction with others	Severe cognitive disability

questions. The teacher created an activity data sheet using a word processor with table capabilities (Microsoft, 1997). Figure 1 shows one of these activity data sheets. The text-to-speech feature of the software (textHELP! 1999) was used to read each assessment question to the student. The student responded using the custom overlay, and their answer was read back to them so they could confirm the correctness of the answer.

The teacher provided a short training session for each student and one peer buddy on all components of the assessment process.

Each student had content area tasks for which they were responsible. One student was in charge of filling the soda machine; another, shopping for ingredients for a cooking activity. After the activities were completed, they rated and commented on their performance using the activity data sheet. With a peer, they sat at the computer workstation. They responded to the assessment questions that were read aloud by the computer, using the activity-specific IntelliKeys overlay to "type" their response to each question. The peer provided prompts and assistance when needed. On the activity sheet, independent responses were recorded in blue and assisted responses

were recorded in red. Based on that record, each student's level of independence was determined across four trials. Table 3 (page 14) shows the increase in independence across the trials for each student.

Examples of Student Use of Portfolio Entries

Amanda

We used Amanda's math entry for this study with the following activities: (a) filling the soda machine with a peer, (b) taking cans to the recycling center, and (c) purchasing items at the store. Targeting improvement in computation and money skills, Amanda planned, monitored, and evaluated her activities by using the IntelliKeys and the custom overlay to respond to the questions on the activity sheet. The activity sheets and overlays were designed to allow Amanda to read the text with the text-reading software and construct a variety of sentences in response to the questions posed on the activity sheet. The response keys on the custom overlay were grouped according to color and use to facilitate correct choice (Figure 3).

On the first trial activity sheet, 48% of Amanda's responses were made independently. By the fourth trial, Amanda had increased her independence to 88%. Figure 4 illustrates how on one response item, the quality of her responses also improved. Before using the IntelliKeys, Amanda was limited to handwriting her response, which was painstakingly slow. The IntelliKeys system allowed her to write 56 words in 20 minutes, a feat she could not have accomplished without it. Amanda's reaction to the IntelliKeys system was, "This is neat."

Table 2. Student Evidence of Performing Each of the Nine Criteria for a "Distinguished" Rating

Assessment Dimension and Requirements of the Alternate Portfolio	Amanda-Math • Loading soda machine • Recycling cans • Shopping at the store	Christine-Lang.Arts • Cooking • Purchasing items for cooking	Sandra-Soc.Studies • Art activity • Shoping for art supplies	Brent-Science • Pet care • Purchase items at the store
Performance:				
Progress on specifically targeted skills which are meaningful in current and future environments	Increased accuracy by 20% or more in computation and coin values Did I count the cans?	Increased accuracy by 20% or more in visual scanning ability Did I scan my pictures?	Increased frequency of requesting assistance in an appropriate manner by 20% or more Did I follow directions?	Increased accuracy by 20% or more in selecting the correct object Did I touch the correct object?
Planning, monitoring, and evaluating self progress	Evaluating performance Did I say I am ready?	Reporting and following a sequence of tasks What will I do first?	Following a sequence of tasks Do I know what to do?	Following a sequence of tasks Did I wash my hands when I finished?
Evaluation used to extend performance	Developing a goal for the next session Next time I will try harder with...	Making a quality choice using visual scanning Did I try harder with...	Making a quality choice related to a targeted skill Next time I will try harder with...	Making a quality choice related to a targeted skill Did I try harder with...
Extensive evidence of Kentucky Academic Expectations in all entries	E.G. Quantifying, How many cans did we need? Classifying, Did I put the soad in the right space?	E.g. Reading, Did I use pictures to read the recipe? Production, What am I making	E.g. Accessing information, Did I ask for help if I needed it? Democratic principles, Did I have good manners in class?	E.g. Constancy, Did I follow my schedule? What do I plan to do first? Speaking, Did I use my switch to ask for food?
Supports:				
Natural support	Peers working on estimation and mental math skills Who worked with me today?	Peers working on math skills wihtin the cooking activity What friend cooked with me today?	Peers exploring a variety of media within the art activity Who did I sit with today?	Peers learning about domestic animals within the pet care activity Which friend helped me today?
Use of adaptations, modifications, and/or assistive technology to evidence independence	Big key calculator; IntelliKeys to record performance on the computer	Switch controlled electric mixer; IntelliKeys to record performance on the computer	Modified goals; IntelliKeys to record performance on the computer	Auditory switch device; IntelliKeys to record performance on the computer
Settings:				
Performance occurring in a variety of integrated settings, within and across all entries	Teacher's lounge, office, stockroom, recycle center, store Where did I go?	Classroom, kitchen, store, office, other classrooms Where did I go?	Art room, classroom, cafeteria, store Where did I go?	Classroom, kitchen, restroom, store, recycle center Where did I go?
Social Relationships:				
Clearly established mutual friendship(s) with non-disabled peers	Time spent in activities with peers to facilitate friendships Who helped me today?	Time spent in activities with peers to facilitate friendships What friend cooked with me today?	Time spent in activites with peers to facilitate friendships Who did I sit with today?	Time spent in activities with peers to facilitate friendships Which friend helped me today?
Context:				
Choice and control in age-appropriate portfolio products within and across all entries	Multiple opportunities for choice and decision making Did I make a choice?	Multiple opportunities for choice and decision making Did I say I was ready?	Assuming personal responsibility Did I ask for help correctly?	Multiple opportunities for choice and decision making What do I plan to do first?

Table 3. Level of Independent Performance During Completion of Activity Sheets

		Percentage of Responses Made Independently				
Student	Activity	Trial 1	Trial 2	Trial 3	Trial 4	Overall Gain
Amanda	Soda	48	56	72	88	25%
	Recycle	55	66	82	71	
	Store	62	72	85	82	
Christine	Cooking	25	54	60	75	43%
	Store	35	53	71	--	
Sandra	Art class	4	24	16	35	22%
	Store	18	22	31	30	
Brent	Pet care	7	25	44	56	32%
	Store	40	40	50	56	

Figure 1. Soda Machine Activity Sheet

Prompt	Response			
Date				
Did I use my schedule?				
Did I say I am ready?				
What will I do first?				
Did I use my sheet so I know what to do next?				
Where did I go?	Office Lounge	Office Lounge	Office Lounge	Office Lounge
Did I write what sodas were needed?				
Did I use my list to say what sodas were needed?				
Did I count the cans?				
Did I make a choice?				
How many cans did we need?				
Did I put the can in the right place?				
Did I do a good job?				
Did I try harder?				
Next time I will do better at …				
Who helped me today?				
What did my friend do?				

Christine

Christine's alternate portfolio activities targeted her language arts objectives. She engaged in two activities to demonstrate her achievements: cooking and buying items from the store. Before using the IntelliKeys for recording responses. Christine was limited to using a rubber stamp to indicate a yes/no response to questions on the activity

sheets. That was accomplished with physical assistance from a peer or adult to assist in stamping and reading the questions. The overlay was designed to be simple, with large keys outlined in black. The keys were arranged by color and location to facilitate correct responses. The overlay keys also directly addressed her individualized education program (IEP) objectives—to visually scan pictures or objects from left to right or from top to bottom. Christine also used two color-coded single switches plugged into the IntelliKeys, to highlight activity sheet cells on the computer and to have it read each question.

Sandra's initial trial with the art class activity showed that 4% of her responses were made independently. By the fourth trial she increased her independence to 35%.

As with Amanda, by the fourth trial Christine had increased her performance level substantially, achieving 75% of her responses independently with the cooking activity sheet. Christine attended well to the reporting activity and appeared to enjoy the print output. She asked to take it home with her.

Sandra

Sandra's portfolio demonstrated her achievements in social studies. She participated in two activities: shopping for art supplies, and participating in a general education art class. Sandra's overlays were simple, using color coding and

Figure 2. Amanda's IntelliKeys Overlay

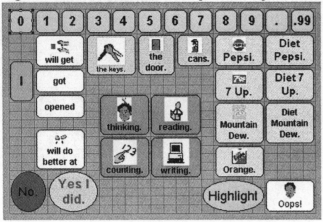

**Figure 3.
Amanda's Additional IntelliKeys Overlay**

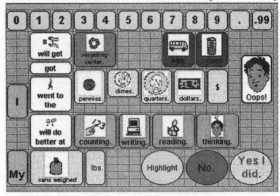

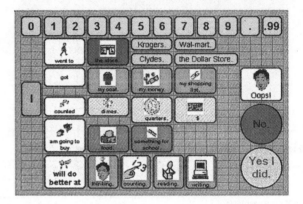

location, to facilitate correct responses. When using the IntelliKeys, Sandra listened to the peer who cued her verbally and with gestures, as necessary. She also used switches to highlight and read the text. Sandra responded well to peer cues, tolerating their guidance, following their directions, and remaining seated during the activity. Sandra's initial trial with the art class activity showed that 4% of her responses were made independently. By the fourth trial she increased her independence to 35%. A similar gain was found in the shopping activity. She apparently enjoyed working on the computer with the IntelliKeys. She grinned and clapped as each entry was keyed into the cell, and read with the text reader as it was typed. She anxiously waited for the printed output so she could take it from the printer's paper tray.

The design of the custom overlay is an important consideration in the success of student use of the IntelliKeys.

Brent

Brent's example is for his science entry. Two custom overlays were used—one overlay was restricted to two cells demonstrating a yes/no response to the activity sheet questions, and the other with five keys giving Brent the opportunity to document a high-quality independent choice over his area of improvement (Figure 5). Two

switches were used to highlight and read the text as with the other students.

Brent averaged a 32% gain in independent performance. Brent's responses were more erratic than the others, but this is typical for Brent. He requires consistent cueing and often hand-over-hand instruction with physical cues. Brent is nonverbal and at present has an inconsistent system of communication. He required physical guidance to be seated and consistent cueing to remain seated. Brent's response to the question regarding improved performance was generated through activation of two out of five keys linked to his IEP goals and targeted skills. He consistently chose either the "choose the right one" or "look" key, both located at the bottom of the overlay toward the left (Figure 6 on page 16). It is not clear if the location of the activated keys on the overlay was a factor.

Figure 4. Example of Amanda's Responses to One Activity Question

Prompt	Student Response			
	Day 1	Day 2	Day 3	Day 4
Did I use my money?	Yes I did.	Yes I did. I $	Yes I did.	Yes I did. I counted $ 1.

External Review

Each alternate portfolio in this study was scored at the regional level by trained teams of scorers using a double-blind method. Table 4 presents the two scores awarded each portfolio. Out of a total of 40 possible scores when including each dimension, the portfolios carried 36 distinguished ratings and 4 proficient ratings. This results in a 90% distinguished rating when considering each dimension separately. The alternate portfolio is scored holistically, however, assigning one score to each complete portfolio. These four students received a rating of "distinguished."

The design of the custom overlay is an important consideration in the success of student use of the IntelliKeys.

Overlay Design

The design of the custom overlay is an important consideration in the success of student use of the IntelliKeys. Thorough knowledge of student need and capabilities of the device is essential to use the customizing features and maximize student potential. As a result of this study, we can share several design tips (see box "Design Tips for Customizing IntelliKeys Overlays"). Experimentation based on observation, however, is the most important element.

First, overlay design must be student centered. Motor and cognitive abilities guide the spatial arrangement of the overlay. Range of motion and reach are considerations for the placement of buttons. Items that will be needed more frequently should be easily within reach to avoid fatigue and frustration. Fine motor abilities are factored into button size. For students with cognitive impairments, color and clustering can facilitate use. Buttons in close proximity should be related to a single task and may be highlighted in a specific color to provide cues to the student for their use.

Figure 5. Brent's IntelliKeys Overlay

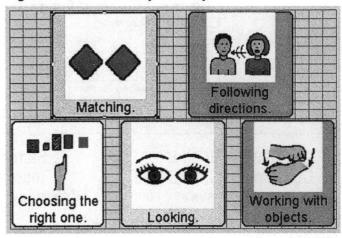

These design considerations are especially useful with more complex overlays.

Cognitive abilities play a role in the number of buttons or response options, and the design of the button depends on the student's cognitive level (for example, contrast Amanda's overlay in Figure 2 with Brent's in Figure 5). Type of graphic representation of a response option is critical. Pairing the written word with the picture will be beneficial for some students, but detrimental to others.

If using different layouts for different tasks, it is important to maintain as much consistency across the layouts as possible. For example, you may always put program commands (e.g., enter, space, delete) in the upper left quadrant and task-specific content keys in the lower right. In doing so, you reduce the cognitive load on the students as they complete each response. Taking both cognitive and motor abilities into account, you facilitate increased accuracy and reduction of time, which both contribute to fatigue.

Table 4. Scores Received from Two Reviewers on the Alternate Portfolio Dimensions

Student	Amanda	Christine	Sandra	Brent
Performance	Distinguished Distinguished	Distinguished Distinguished	Distinguished Distinguished	Distinguished Distinguished
Support	Distinguished Distinguished	Distinguished Distinguished	Proficient Distinguished	Distinguished Distinguished
Settings	Distinguished Distinguished	Distinguished Distinguished	Distinguished Distinguished	Distinguished Distinguished
Social relationships	Proficient Distinguished	Distinguished Distinguished	Distinguished Proficient	Proficient Distinguished
Contexts	Distinguished Distinguished	Distinguished Distinguished	Distinguished Distinguished	Distinguished Distinguished

Figure 6. Example of Brent's Responses to One Science Activity Question

Prompt	Student Response			
	Day 1	Day 2	Day 3	Day 4
Next time I will try harder with …	Choose the right one.	Choose the right one.	Look.	Look.

Design Tips for Customizing IntelliKeys Overlays

- Student needs and functioning level must drive the content and format.
- Use voice output to read the prompt and read the response back to the user.
- Group keys according to color to facilitate correct responses.
- Enable the "nonrepeat" function to ensure only one entry per response.
- Use left-to-right formats to naturally facilitate sentence construction.
- Size the text and the keys to match the visual abilities of the user.
- Program whole words and phrases into the keys to speed responses.
- Match the programmed responses to the student's cognitive ability (e.g., single-word responses limit the construction of complete sentences).
- Outline keys in black to improve contrast.
- Place frequently used keys on the user's dominant side of the keyboard.
- Include graphics on the keys with the text for the nonreader.
- Consider the complexity of training issues when choosing keys (e.g., arrow keys for directional movement are very difficult to teach).
- Place keys that are common across overlays in a consistent location on each.

Sample Peer Responses to Interview Questions

Six general education peers helped the students use the IntelliKeys during recording sessions. The overwhelming consensus was that the peers liked using the IntelliKeys with the students, primarily because it enhanced the student level of performance and increased their independence. The following are some of their responses:

- One peer appeared quite shocked at Amanda's performance within her math entry, and remarked that he did not know "she could do all that."
- Most peers were surprised with work that the students were able to produce with the IntelliKeys, and admitted that it elevated their opinion of the students' ability.
- Observations indicated that the peers enjoyed the process of working with the students, though this was in the form of a peer-tutor relationship.
- Each peer reported that working with a student helped him or her to get to know the student better, since they spent more time together. Spending time with one another provided the opportunity for relationships to develop, an important element within the social relationships dimension of the alternative portfolio.

Sample Student Responses Recorded in Observation Notes

- "Amanda appears to enjoy the technical aspects of the program; perhaps it gives her a sense of independence that she cannot get from other methods of reading and writing."
- "Amanda appears pleased with her work. At no time does she appear hurried or anxious to get finished. The teacher does not have to remind her to remain on task."
- "Christine was compliant in coming to the computer. She appears to enjoy computer tasks since it does give her an avenue for written expression and she likes to take things home."
- "Christine's mother came into the classroom when she was completing the activity sheets and Christine became animated and demanded that her mother watch what she was doing."
- On her first trial with the IntelliKeys, Sandra "grinned and clapped as each entry was keyed into the cell and read with the text-to-speech software as she typed."
- During Brent's first trial completing the science activity sheet, "Brent voiced and resisted being seated in the chair by the computer. He looked upwards at all times and avoided contact with the IntelliKeys and the monitor."
- Brent "does better on the computer than he does with the stamps since he is selecting the key and is the cause of the entered text."

Final Thoughts

In addition to the data showing the achievements of the students with disabilities, observations of the students working with their peers on these tasks confirmed other benefits of the program. Overall, the peers gained a better perspective on the students' abilities, and the students responded positively to their accomplishments and interactions with their peers (see boxes, "Sample Student Responses," for student observations and peer interviews).

This series of case studies denotes a beginning level of research, and is an indication for further definitive research at a critical time when states are looking to include students with moderate and severe disabilities in their accountability indexes. Studies of a more rigorous method of inquiry and more reliable data collection in the area of student support and assistive technology and assessment are essential. Kentucky is the only state fully including the assessment of this population in their school accountability indexes, and thus provides an excellent base for research.

Another area of focus for future research is on overlay design issues, because it is apparent that they influence output. Researchers and practitioners might look at overlay design and attempt guidelines to facilitate increased independence, increase output, and minimize the potential for student error.

References

IntelliTools. (1996). Overlay maker. [Computer software]. Novato, CA: Author.

Kleinert, H., Haigh, J., Kearns, J., & Kennedy, S. (2000). Alternate assessment. Lessons learned and roads not taken. *Exceptional Children, 67*, 51–66.

Kleinert, H., & Kearns, J. (1999). A validation study of the performance indicators and learner outcomes for Kentucky's alternate assessment for students with significant disabilities. *Journal of the Association for Persons with Severe Handicaps, 24*(2), 100–110.

Kleinert, H., Kearns, J., & Kennedy, S. (1997). Accountability for all students: Kentucky's alternate portfolio assessment for students with moderate and severe cognitive disabilities. *Journal of the Association for Persons with Severe Handicaps, 22*(2), 88–101.

Microsoft Corporation. (1997). WORD 97. [Computer software]. Redmond, WA: Author.

textHELP! (1999). Read & write. [Computer software]. Antrim, N. Ireland: Author.

Anne Denham *(CEC Chapter #5), Teacher, Mason County Public Schools, Maysville, Kentucky.* **Elizabeth A. Lahm** *(CEC Chapter #180), Assistant Professor, Department of Special Education and Rehabilitation Counseling, University of Kentucky, Lexington.*

Address correspondence to Elizabeth A. Lahm, Department of Special Education and Rehabilitation Counseling, University of Kentucky, 229 Taylor Education Building, Lexington, KY 40506-0001 (e-mail: ealahm1@pop.uky.edu).

From *Teaching Exceptional Children,* May/June 2001, pp. 10-17. © 2001 by The Council for Exceptional Children. Reprinted with permission.

UNIT 9

Orthopedic and Health Impairments

Unit Selections

Key Points to Consider

- What is the importance of giving young children with orthopedic disabilities mobility instruction within the context of typical daily activities? Describe the MOVE program.

- What kinds of accommodations are appropriate for students with health impairments (e.g., cancer, asthma, epilepsy)?

- What are some techniques that teachers can use to help students with ADHD adjust to their regular education classrooms?

 **Links: www.dushkin.com/online/**
These sites are annotated in the World Wide Web pages.

Association to Benefit Children (ABC)
http://www.a-b-c.org

An Idea Whose Time Has Come
http://www.boggscenter.org/mich3899.htm

Resources for VE Teachers
http://cpt.fsu.edu/tree/ve/tofc.html

Try using the word "handicapped" on a computer with a spell check. Today's computers are programmed to advise you that this is a derogatory term when applied to any individual. Older dictionaries defined "handicapped" as inferior and in need of an artificial advantage. People were described as handicapped if they were encumbered by physical limitations. Today, handicapped means limited by something in the environment. Handicap is synonymous with hindrance. If a property of the environment prevents a person with an orthopedic or health impairment from functioning to the best of his or her abilities, then the environment has imposed a handicap.

Children and youth with orthopedic and health impairments can be divided into classifications of mild, moderate, and profound. Within most impairments, the same diagnosis may not produce the same degree of disability. For example, children with cerebral palsy may be mildly, moderately, or profoundly impaired.

Orthopedic impairments are usually defined as those that hinder physical mobility or the ability to use one or more parts of the skeletomuscular system of the body. Orthopedic problems may be neurological (brain or spinal cord) or skeletomuscular (muscles or skeletal bones). Regardless of etiology, the child with an orthopedic impairment usually has a problem with mobility. He or she may need crutches or other aids in order to walk or may be in a wheelchair.

Health impairments are usually defined as those that affect stamina and predominantly one or more systems of the body: the cardiovascular, respiratory, gastrointestinal, endocrine, lymphatic, urinary, reproductive, sensory, or nervous systems. Children with health impairments usually have to take medicine or follow a medical regimen in order to attend school. The degree of impairment (mild, moderate, profound) is usually based on limitations to activity, duration of problem, and extent of other problems.

Attention-deficit hyperactive disorder (ADHD) is formally recognized as a health impairment, as well as a learning disability. Often children with ADHD are also assessed as gifted or as emotionally-behaviorally disordered. It is possible for a child with ADHD to have characteristics of all of these categories. ADHD will be covered in this unit.

Orthopedic and health impairments are not always mutually exclusive. Many times a child with an orthopedic impairment also has a concurrent or contributing health impairment, and vice versa. In addition, children with orthopedic and health impairments may also have concurrent conditions of educational exceptionality.

Some children with orthopedic and health impairments have only transitory impairments; some have permanent but nonworsening impairments; and some have progressive impairments that make their education more complicated as the years pass and may even result in death before the end of the developmental/educational period.

Each of the dimensions defined in the preceding paragraphs makes educational planning for children with orthopedic and health impairments very complicated.

The reauthorization of IDEA mandated that schools must pay for all medical services required to allow orthopedically or health impaired students to attend regular education classes. The only exceptions are the actual fees for physician-provided health services. Thus, if children need ambulances to transport them to and from school, the schools must pay the tab. Federal appropriations for special educational services only pay about 10 percent of the bills. Thus high-cost special needs students can quickly drain the funds of state and local education departments.

Teachers may resent the need to spend teacher time giving medications or providing quasi-medical services (suctioning, changing diapers) for students with health impairments in the many U.S. schools that no longer have school nurses.

Resentment is common in parents of nondisabled students who feel that the education of high-cost disabled students robs their children of teacher time, curriculum, and supplies to which they should be entitled. More than 95 percent of special needs students attend regular schools today. About 3 percent attend separate schools and about 2 percent are served at home, in hospitals, or in residential facilities.

When orthopedic or health impairments are diagnosed in infancy or early childhood, an interdisciplinary team usually helps plan an individualized family service plan (IFSP) that includes working with parents, medical and/or surgical personnel, and preschool special education providers.

When the orthopedic or health impairment is diagnosed in the school years, the school teachers collaborate with outside agencies, but more of the individualized educational planning (IEP) is in their hands. Children who have orthopedic or health impairments need psychological as well as academic support. Teachers need to help them in their peer interactions. Teachers should also work closely with parents to ensure a smooth transition toward a lifestyle that fosters independence and self-reliance. By middle school, individualized transition plans (ITPs) should be developed. They should be implemented throughout high school and until age 21 when the students move to adult living, and they must be updated every year. Schools are held accountable for their success in helping students with orthopedic and health impairments to make smooth transitions to maturity.

The first article emphasizes the importance of giving young children with orthopedic disabilities mobility instruction within the context of typical daily activities. Keith Whinnery and Stacie Barnes recommend the MOVE curriculum, an integrated therapy with high expectations that supports and motivates children. A case study of 4-year-old Breanna, who has cerebral palsy, illustrates how it works.

The second selection for this unit suggests some of the accommodations that school systems must make to ensure that students with orthopedic and health impairments receive an appropriate education. It explains the 504 plans required under the Americans with Disabilities Act. MaryAnn Byrnes points out that the teaching profession is about allowing students to learn. Removing barriers will do that.

The last selection in this unit addresses the need to help students with attention deficit hyperactive disorder (ADHD) adjust to their regular education classrooms. Despite the use of medication (usually Ritalin) to help them attend better and fidget less, students with ADHD may contribute to chaos during their lessons. The Schlozmans suggest a number of teaching techniques that can reduce confusion and help children with ADHD learn more effectively.

Mobility Training Using the MOVE® Curriculum

A Parent's View

Keith W. Whinnery, Stacie B. Barnes

Breanna is a 4-year-old girl who loves playing outside. Today she and her mom, Trellis, are taking a walk to feed the dogs, chase the chickens, and pick flowers. Though this might seem like a fairly common scenario for a parent and young child, it is quite extraordinary for Breanna and Trellis. Breanna contracted meningitis and encephalitis at 3 1/2 weeks of age, resulting in cerebral palsy with a mixture of high and low muscle tone, limited strength for standing or sitting upright, and difficulty holding her head upright. Since that time, life for Breanna and her family has consisted of numerous doctors' appointments, regular therapy sessions at a child development center, and constant strengthening and stretching exercises at home.

This article presents an interview with Trellis, Breanna's mother, who is using a new mobility curriculum with her daughter. The interview provides a glimpse into Trellis's concerns and expectations for Breanna's future independence, as well as her feelings about the use of the curriculum. The article also provides an overview of the curriculum and discusses Breanna's mobility progress.

A Parent's Search for Help

Despite continuous therapy sessions and Trellis's diligent home therapy program, Breanna still required significant physical assistance and was at risk for eventual hip dislocation. High muscle tone in her legs was causing "scissoring," which was increasing the degree of separation in her hip joints. Recently one of Breanna's doctors had recommended surgery to resolve the problem.

As with many parents of children with disabilities, Trellis was constantly searching for ideas and programs to help Breanna. After reading about the MOVE program (see section "How MOVE Works") in a Rifton Company catalog (1999), Trellis requested information on the program. She was sent literature and videotapes and was also given the names of two university professors in her area who were involved with training and research on the program.

Mobility instruction should occur within typical daily activities that are functional for the child.

A Find: How to Facilitate Mobility

After an introduction to MOVE, Trellis went through a 2-day training program to better understand the curriculum and how to implement it. As part of the MOVE program at home, Trellis was encouraged to think of activity-based instruction opportunities. It was explained that mobility instruction should occur within typical daily activities that were functional for Breanna. Initially, Trellis selected activities if Breanna enjoyed them, and if mobility skills could be embedded within them. This included daily dressing, eating, bathing, and playing activities. Although Breanna was able to participate only partially in these activities and needed extensive physical support, Trellis continued to be interested and participate because of the motivation of the activity.

The physical supports or prompts used in the MOVE curriculum are designed to *facilitate* the use of mobility skills, not to *replace* them. In this case, prompts to help support weight, provide balance, and guide the legs for reciprocal steps were provided. These prompts were fre-

Figure 1. Breanna's Mobility Progress

First Week--11/8/99 to 11/15/99	Last week*--4/16/00 to 4/23/00 *end of data collection and recording
Mean Number of Steps Taken (with adult assistance)	**Mean Number of Steps Taken** (with adult assistance)
15	509
Mean Number of Steps Taken (with gait trainer)	**Mean Number of Steps Taken** (with gait trainer)
0	125
Mean Time Standing	**Mean Time Standing**
45 seconds	4.02 minutes

quently provided by the mother and sometimes by the use of a gait trainer. The curriculum provides a guide for the use of prompts; however, as soon as prompts are implemented, a systematic plan for their removal is also developed.

In these activity-based learning opportunities, Trellis took every opportunity to let Breanna physically participate to the fullest degree possible.

Some of the activities Trellis selected to teach Breanna walking skills included feeding the dogs, feeding the chickens and checking for eggs, walking across the yard to Grandma's house, and picking flowers in the yard. Activities that required standing included washing hands at the sink, playing at the sink, and standing at the blackboard to play letter and number games. In these activity-based learning opportunities, Trellis took every opportunity to let Breanna physically participate to the fullest degree possible. For example, when learning games were to be played in the bedroom, the activity might start with Trellis helping Breanna to transfer from a sitting position to a standing position in the living room. Breanna would then walk with support to the bedroom and stand at the board while playing the game. Although it would have been easier for Trellis to have picked her up and carried her to the bedroom, the anticipation of playing the games motivated Breanna to participate in the mobility practice.

The MOVE Curriculum is typically used in school settings, where the team can measure and chart the students'

progress. During this home-based implementation of MOVE, we asked Trellis to keep records of the progress that Breanna made while using the MOVE Curriculum. She recorded the number of steps taken during activities that required walking inside and outside. She also recorded the number of seconds of weight-bearing during standing activities throughout the day (see Figure 1). In addition, we conducted an interview with Trellis to present her perspectives on MOVE. A portion of the interview follows.

A Concerned Parent's Words

We know you were doing a lot with Breanna before MOVE. What made you want to try MOVE?

After I watched the tape of *Kids on the MOVE* (Barnes, 1997) and saw how much they were able to do, I was willing to try just about anything. It seemed like those kids were able to do so much after MOVE; and I thought, if they can do it, then so could Breanna.

Was this approach, the MOVE Program, different from what you were doing?

They [the people on the video] were doing things I wasn't doing. After I saw it, I thought, this makes a lot of sense. Before, I was getting Breanna to stand up and sit down from a chair and walk, but it was just a lot of therapy exercises. The kids in the video were doing these things in regular activities. Now I can have Breanna stand up and sit down from the potty chair—she's being potty trained now! I was just moving her, but now we do these things all through the day in our regular routine. It's so much easier now that it is just part of what we do during the day, and we can practice standing and walking while playing.

We know that in the past you were discouraged because you were doing so much for Breanna and you were worried about the future.

I had gotten frustrated because it's like I told my husband: I said that I don't want to sit here and hold Breanna for the rest of her life. I want her to get up and walk; I want her to be independent. I want to have a little time to do something I want to do, and that's the reason I'm pushing her now and doing what I do. I don't want to do this for the next 20 years. I got discouraged and talked to the doctor about it one time, and she told me I needed to just take a little break and find a hobby or do something.

Did you follow the doctor's advice?

I have backed off, and I don't do as much as I did before; and the reason is last year I got really stressed out. I just wore down. We were doing so much on weight-bearing a day and so much of this and so much of that. By night if I didn't do everything I had planned, I would just almost freak out because I didn't do what I wanted to do; and I just thought the more I do, the better she's going to be. I guess that's true to a point, but I've also realized that after speaking with a therapist and a doctor, I've got to let her be a little girl too and let her have some free play time. So now I try to incorporate training when she's having a fun activity; I make her walk to it, I don't push her, and we take our time a little more. I just don't rush her from place to place like I did before, because I had these goals set that by a certain time I would have this done or that done, and I was just wearing myself out.

So maybe now you're accomplishing as much but enjoying it more?

I think so; I don't feel guilty now—I feel better. I used to have my list of exercises and practice to do, and if I didn't do my list, I felt frustrated. I just wanted a break, but now the practice is like playing. It's more enjoyable for the whole family. My husband, Jeff, has always wanted to be involved with this, but he wasn't sure what to do. Now we go outside and play hide and seek. We've found that one thing she likes is our pond. We can go catch fish in the pond, and we'll drive th golf cart down because it's a pretty good ways down the hill. Jeff will drop us off at one point, and he'll go somewhere else. We'll have to walk to where he is to help get the fish off [the hook], and she thinks that's fun. So she's getting in walking while we have fun and play together.

Now that you've been through the MOVE training and after you've been using the MOVE Curriculum, what are your thoughts about the program? Do you think it has helped you accomplish any of your goals?

Oh, I know it has. For instance, like the steps in front of the sink. You know, I never thought about putting steps in front of a sink and making her walk up the steps to wash her hands. Normally, what I would have done is pick her up and hold her over the sink and wash her as best I could. Now if she wants to go somewhere, you know, I'll stand her up, and instead of just picking her up, I'll make her push up with her legs and use her muscles to stand up; and then we'll walk to where she wants. If she wants to go to her room, I make her walk. I don't just pick her up and carry her like I did most of the time, and I think that's why she's developed the strength that she has in her legs because she's using them more.

Can you give us an example of one thing that she wasn't doing before starting the MOVE program that she is doing now?

When we first started her measurements in the hallway, like with me holding her arms, her most steps when we first started was about 20. Then I remember when it got up to 50 and 60, the length of the hallway; and we were running out of space to measure. So now we measure outside, and she has gone 500 steps without stopping for more than 20 seconds.

"I want her to know that I know she's going to do it, and I push her and challenge her to do it."

—Breanna's mother

In the year that we have known you and have worked with you, we have become aware of your expectations for your daughter. In general, do you think adult expectations of a child's success or failure has an effect on the child's overall performance?

I do. I say that I have high hopes for Breanna. She's already successful in moving from where she was to where she is now. She's done nothing but improve. I don't ever see her getting any worse, or I hope I don't. Because I see her improving, I push her. I want her to know that I know she's going to do it, and I push her and challenge her to do it. If I thought she wasn't able to do it, then we wouldn't even attempt it; and then, who would know? She might not ever do it.

Has this project made you change your expectations?

I still have high expectations for Breanna, and I always wanted her to walk independently without any supports. I guess I had too many expectations a year or a year and a half ago, because I thought she would walk by age 5 or 6; but I really don't think now that that is a realistic goal. She has progressed, but more slowly. Now I think it will be later. That's changed, but I don't think it's because of the MOVE program. It's just that I think I was expecting too much. I wanted too much too early.

Do you feel okay with this slower rate of progress?

Yes, I'm fine with that. I want her to be as independent as possible, and if she never walks without supports—I mean if she has to walk with a walker, or crutches, or a cane—that's fine because I don't want her to always have to rely on me to hold her. I want her to get around and be the most that she can. If she's 10, that's fine; I mean, she has many years after 10, I hope, to live and enjoy life.

You've mentioned in past conversations that a few people have tried to discourage you. Can you think of anything specific that anyone has said that has discouraged you or that has made you...

Mad?

Yes.

Yes, one of her orthopedists. He told me this child would never walk; and I said, "No, you're wrong, and one day I'm going to bring her to your door; and you're going to see her walk to the opposite end of the room." I don't take that lightly. No, every child is different, and she may not walk without supports; but if she's able to walk at all independently and in any shape or form, she's walking.

Did he say why he thought that?

He said that from his experience, and he said that he could tell by his experience that she would never walk, comparing her with all the other kids. That was basically what he told me. He said that she would not be able to sit up independently, and he sat her up on his table. Well, for one thing, she was crying and screaming her head off, and she was so upset that she just reared back and she wouldn't even try to do anything for him. And he just said, "Well, I tell you, she's never going to walk."

When we started this process you had switched doctors. The doctor that you were seeing at that time was thinking that surgery might be needed.

Yes, let me tell you, we went back to the doctor, and when she went, she had subluxation on her right hip at 28%. That's what it was calculated at. When we went to the doctor in March, it was down to 23%; and it's actually gone back in a little into her socket.

That's wonderful. Did the doctor comment about that?

He said it was because she was up and mobile and getting weight through her legs and hips. He said that she was improving.

That's great

So he told us that because her hip was doing well, we wouldn't need another visit for 6 to 8 months.

So now he's not considering surgery this time?

No.

Good. So all of that walking that you have been making her do seems to be helping. What was it like trying to get Breanna to walk more when she had been used to being carried?

I think it was hard for her, and she wouldn't try as much; but now because she is so much stronger and her muscles are not as tight, she's got more control. Weight shifting is easier for her, so she's going to do more. Now, she knows she can.

"If it's something that she wants to do, like play hide and seek, or go outside and pick something, or chase a ball, or chase a rooster, she'll do it"

—*Breanna's mother*

And does she seem to enjoy walking more now?

Oh, yes, she likes to do things she's not supposed to. If it's something that she wants to do, like play hide and seek, or go outside and pick something, or chase a ball, or chase a rooster, she'll do it. One day, when we were walking down the road, she started looking in the direction of my parents' house, so I asked her if she wanted to go; and she gave me a kiss for yes. I said okay, we'll go and walk down there (about 600 feet). So we did. She was very determined, and she got almost all the way—she got to their yard before she gave out. But she wanted to go.

You have found that there are more things that she wants to do now. Do you think motivation plays a role in her accomplishments?

If she doesn't want to do something, there's really no competition. That's why I've got to find things that are fun and motivating. Because if I tell her, let's walk to your room, we're going to get on the bolster and wedge to exercise, she's not going to go. And I know she's not. But if I tell her to go to her room because we're going to paint, she'll go.

You have mentioned that she seems to have better head and trunk control now. Has this made it easier to do other things around the house?

Yes, I can… just hold her. I mean, if we're standing and not walking, I have let her go and not helped her; and she has stood on her own for a couple of seconds. I can just barely have my arms on her, and she's fully supporting herself. I mean she's supporting herself even when I have my arms wrapped around her; but if I just let go and loosely touch her just so she knows I'm there, she'll stand. She's got so much more strength and control and balance.

Now that Breanna is more mobile, do you see changes in her relationships with other people?

I know I've told you before that Breanna is hard to handle physically. I mean, she has her special needs; and other people didn't know how to do her therapy. They would just carry her, but now they can walk with her because she can stand upright more. They can stand her on the ground and hold her arms rather than just carry her.

What would you recommend to other parents who have children with similar disabilities?

I think all parents ought to know that the more they do for their children when they are young, the more independent they're going to be and be able to do. Breanna's improved a lot since you first met her. I want parents to know that if they worked with their children, they can do better, and they will improve.

Trellis, this is wonderful information. Is there anything else that comes to your mind?

Well, you gave me some ideas when we started the [MOVE] program, and I thank you both for helping her and helping us. You gave me a lot to think about. Before, I was more interested in saving time, and that's maybe why I would pick her up and carry her instead of waiting for her to walk. But I found that she got so much more out of it when I helped her to walk from here to there. Instead of trying to save 9 minutes of time, we were better off taking the 10 minutes. Before I started the program, I didn't make her walk as much because I would carry her a lot to quickly get to the place where we would do our exercises. Now I make her go that extra distance and I think that's why she's improving like she is.

The MOVE Curriculum helps to provide the support, the motivation, and the high expectations to facilitate the development of functional motor skills.

Another example of what she is doing now happened just the other day at my sister's house. I had to run to the bathroom before lunch to wash up. My mom and my sister were in the kitchen fixing us some sandwiches. I put Breanna on the couch with Jordan, her cousin, I told Jordan to sit beside Breanna and not to let her fall off. She wouldn't fall off anyway because she can sit on a couch by herself now. So I went to the bathroom, and the next thing I knew my mom and sister were hollering, "Come here, come here, look at Breanna!" She had gotten off the couch and was standing holding the couch and just laughing. And they swore up and down that they did not help her, and Jordan had gotten down and come to the kitchen. When she did, they looked to make sure Breanna was still okay, and she was sitting on the couch. And the next time they looked, she had gotten off by herself. I think she must have seen Jordan getting off, and she did it, too. I put her on the couch and told her to do it again, and she wouldn't do it. But, she's done it once, she's going to do it again.

That's like when she walked from here to my parents'—she can do it again. It may not be today, and it may not be tomorrow. It may take her a few days, but she will do it again.

How MOVE Works

The MOVE Curriculum helps to provide the support, the motivation, and the high expectations to facilitate the development of functional motor skills. Although this can be accomplished in a variety of settings, such as the home, the curriculum is ideally suited for the school environment (see box, "MOVE Foundations").

Team Approach

Adopting the MOVE Curriculum allows the school team to develop a common focus based on the family's goals and dreams. Related services, such as occupational therapy and physical therapy are then embedded into meaningful activities that incorporate the skills needed to achieve the goals. MOVE uses data-based instruction in which repeated measures are taken on both student progress and the level of support required. Physical support from adults or equipment is provided to allow partial participation in the activity; and the support is reduced as skills increase. In this approach, eating lunch may change from a daily routine to a daily instructional opportunity, as follows:

- Transitioning from sitting to standing.
- Bearing weight (to wash hands at sink).
- Taking reciprocal steps (walking to and from table).
- Maintaining balance in a traditional classroom chair (while eating).

Within the structure of meaningful activities, the team can also incorporate functional academic, communication, and socialization goals. This allows educational teams to write integrated goals that focus on the needs of the individual, rather than on the isolated skills of specific disciplines.

Integrated Curriculum

MOVE is a top-down, activity-based curriculum designed to teach people with physical disabilities the basic, functional motor skills needed for greater participation within home, school, and community environments (Kern County Superintendent of Schools, 1999). The curriculum was developed by Linda Bidabe, a teacher in Bakersfield, California, who was frustrated with the lack of progress of many of her students who had severe disabilities. She recognized that small developmental gains in motor skills frequently gave way to growing bodies and that many of these students remained in wheelchairs, or returned to them, before they ever achieved independent mobility.

Bidabe's solution to this situation was to focus on the functional skills of standing, walking, and sitting, as opposed to prerequisite or developmental skills, such as raising head from a prone position, rolling over, and crawling. In this "top-down" approach to program planning, the team selects instructional activities and basic skills, based on functional outcomes, and incorporates events dispersed throughout the day. Assessment, planning, and instruction are accomplished through transdisciplinary teams that include parents, educators, and therapists who work together to achieve the family's goals for the student.

MOVE was developed on the following foundations:

- *Functional Curriculum*—Learning occurs within meaningful activities.

- *Natural Environments*—Skills are practiced where they will be used.

- *Family Centered*—Family priorities are an essential part of MOVE.

- *Integrated Therapy*—Team collaboratively plans, sets goals, and intervenes in students' natural environments.

- *Partial Participation*—Students participate in meaningful activities to the greatest degree possible.

MOVE uses motivating activities to teach functional mobility skills that

- Are age-appropriate.

- Increase independence.

- Increase access to the community.

- Reduce custodial care.

- Promote communication, social, and daily-living skills.

Final Thoughts

When working with individuals with limited mobility, it is important that the adults who are facilitating learning have high expectations and provide multiple opportunities for practice. This task can be challenging.

As an integrated, engaging, and motivating approach to education for students with mobility and other needs, MOVE holds great promise for teams of educators, students, and families. As Breanna and her mother discovered, learning independent skills can be fun and can lead to great strides in learning and improvement.

References

Barnes, S. B. (Producer). (1997). *Kids on the MOVE: Holm elementary* [Video]. (Available from MOVE International, 1300 17th Street, City Centre, Bakersfield, CA 93301-4533.)

Barnes, S. B., & Whinnery, K. W. (1997). Mobility Opportunities Via Education (MOVE): Theoretical foundations. *Physical Disabilities: Education and Related Services, 16*, 33–46.

Barnes, S. B., & Whinnery, K. W. (in press). Effects of functional mobility training for young students with physical disabilities. *Exceptional Children.*

Bidabe, D. L., Barnes, S. B., & Whinnery, K. W. (2001). M.O.V.E.: Raising expectations for individuals with severe disabilities. *Physical Disabilities: Education and Related Services, 19*, 31–48.

Campbell, S. K., Vander Linden, D. W., & Palisano, R. J. (2000). *Physical therapy for children* (2nd ed.). Philadelphia: W. B. Saunders.

Dunn, W. (1991). Integrated related services. In L. H. Meyer, C. A. Peck, & L. Brown (Eds.), *Critical issues in the lives of people with severe disabilities* (pp. 353–377). Baltimore: Paul H. Brookes.

Heriza, C. (1991). Motor development: Traditional and contemporary theories. In M. J. Lister (Ed.), *Contemporary management of motor control problems: Proceedings of the II Step Conference* (pp. 99–126). Alexandria, VA: Foundation for Physical Therapy.

Horak, F. B. (1991). Assumptions underlying motor control for neurologic rehabilitation. In M. J. Lister (Ed.), *Contemporary management of motor control problems: Proceedings of the II Step Conference* (pp. 11–27). Alexandria, VA: Foundation for Physical Therapy.

Kern County Superintendent of Schools. (1999). M.O.V.E.: Mobility Opportunities Via Education. Bakersfield, CA: Author.

Orelove, F. P., & Sobsey D. (1996). *Educating children with multiple disabilities* (3rd ed.). Baltimore: Paul H. Brookes.

Rainforth, B., & York-Barr, J. (1997). *Collaborative teams for students with severe disabilities: Integrating therapy and educational services.* Baltimore: Paul H. Brookes.

Rifton: Community Playthings. (1999). *Rifton equipment* (catalog). Rifton, NY: Community Products LLC.

Snell, M. E., & Brown, F. (2000). *Instruction of students with severe disabilities* (5th ed.). Upper Saddle River, NJ: Prentice-Hall.

Vockell, E. L., & Asher, J. W. (1995). *Educational research* (2nd ed.). Englewood Cliffs, NJ: Merrill.

Keith W. Whinnery (CEC Chapter #770), Associate Professor; and **Stacie B. Barnes**, (CEC Chapter #770), Assistant Professor, Special Education Department, University of West Florida, Pensacola.

Address correspondence to Keith W. Whinnery, Special Education Department, University of West Florida, 11000 University Parkway, Pensacola, FL 32514 (e-mail: kwhinner@at@;uwf.edu).

From *Teaching Exceptional Children*, January/February 2002, pp. 44-50. © 2002 by The Council for Exceptional Children. Reprinted by permission.

Accommodations for Students with Disabilities: Removing Barriers to Learning

Secondary school principals frequently encounter questions about educating students with disabilities. Sometimes the questions revolve around seeking a deeper understanding of the disability and the best way to meet student needs. Other times, the questions focus on all the changes that must be made to ensure students receive an appropriate education. What questions do teachers ask about accommodations for students with a disability?

By MaryAnn Byrnes

Think about taking a driver's test without wearing glasses (if you do, that is). Not fair, you say; you need the glasses to see. You have just identified an accommodation that you need. Wearing glasses does not make a bad driver better or make driving easier; rather, wearing glasses makes driving possible. Glasses are so much a part of our lives that we do not even consider that they remove a barrier caused by a disability.

Secondary school teachers encounter students every day on an Individualized Education Plan (IEP) or 504 Plan, both of which address programs for students with disabilities. Most likely, the person charged with monitoring this plan has indicated that particular students need changes in teaching style, assignments, or testing strategies.

It is usually easy to understand the need for glasses or wheelchairs or hearing aids. These sound like changes the student must make. Other adjustments, modifications, or accommodations on these plans, such as extended time, may not be as clear.

What is an accommodation?

An accommodation is an adjustment, to an activity or setting, that removes a barrier presented by a disability so a person can have access equal to that of a person without a disability. An accommodation does not guarantee success or a specific level of performance. It should, however, provide the opportunity for a person with a disability to participate in a situation or activity.

Think of that pair of glasses, or the time you broke your leg and could not drive. Think of how your life was affected by these conditions. Your competence did not change. Your ability to think and work did not change. Your ability to interact with (have access to) the reading material may be very limited without your glasses. Your ability to get to (have access to) work or the grocery store may be very limited without someone to transport you. The support provided by the glasses—or the driver—made it possible for you to use your abilities without the barrier presented by less than perfect vision or limited mobility.

An accommodation is an adjustment, to an activity or setting, that removes a barrier presented by a disability so a person can have access equal to that of a person without a disability.

The accommodations in IEPs or 504 Plans serve the same purpose. They identify ways to remove the barrier presented by a person's disability.

Why do we need to provide accommodations?

Accommodations are required under Section 504 of the Federal Rehabilitation Act of 1974 as well as the Americans with Disabilities Act. Both these federal laws prohibit discrimination against individuals who have a disability. Situations that limit access have been determined to be discriminatory.

Accommodations must be provided not just by teachers to students, but by employees for workers and governments for citizens. Curbs have been cut to provide access. Doors have been widened and door handles altered to provide access to people for whom the old designs posed a barrier. Employers provide computer adaptations or other adjustments in work schedules and circumstances.

For employers and schools, individuals with disabilities may have a document called a 504 Plan, which details the types of accommodations that are required. Students who have a 504 Plan will not require special education services, just changes to the environment or instructional situation.

Students who have a disability and require special education services in addition to accommodations will have this information contained in an IEP, which also details the types of direct services that need to be provided and the goals of these services. Accommodations will be listed within this IEP.

With the recent changes in IDEA '97, the federal law governing special education, you will be addressing accommodations that must be made so a student with a disability can participate in large-scale districtwide or statewide assessment systems as well as classwork and school life.

Who needs accommodations?

According to Section 504, an individual with a disability is any person who has "a physical or mental impairment that limits one or more major life activities." IDEA '97, the federal special education law, lists the following disabilities: autism, deaf-blindness, deafness, hearing impairment, mental retardation, multiple disabilities, orthopedic impairment, other health impairment, serious emotional disturbance, specific learning disability, speech or language impairment, traumatic brain injury, and visual impairment.

Students who have a 504 Plan will not require special education services, just changes to the environment or instructional situation.

Some conditions are covered by Section 504, but not special education. These can include attention deficit disorder—ADD, (also attention deficit hyperactivity disorder—ADHD); chronic medical conditions (such as cancer, Tourette Syndrome, asthma, or epilepsy); communicable diseases; some temporary medical conditions; physical impairments; and disorders of emotion or behavior. To qualify, there must be a demonstrated and substantial limitation of a major life activity.

Students (or adults) who have disabilities may require accommodations to have equal access to education. Not every student with a disability will require accommodations, and not every student with a disability requires the same accommodation all the time.

Think of Jim, a student who has limited mobility in his hands, affecting his ability to write. This disability will present a barrier in a class that requires the student to take notes quickly or write long essays in class. In a class that does not require either of these activities, no barrier may be present. Equal access is possible without accommodation. The student can learn and demonstrate what he knows and can do unaffected by his disability.

What kind of accommodations are there?

Just as there is no limit to the range of disabilities, there is no limit to the range of accommodations. The point is to understand disability and determine if it presents a barrier to equal access. If so, decide whether an accommodation can be identified to remove the barrier—and make sure the accommodation is implemented.

Not every student with a disability will require accommodations, and not every student with a disability requires the same accommodation all the time.

Think of the student described above. The limited mobility in Jim's hands presents a barrier in a class that requires rapid note taking or the writing of long essays in class. There are several accommodations that can result in equal access. Jim might tape the lesson and take notes later. These notes could be written or dictated into a computer. Essays could be composed verbally at a computer workstation or dictated into a tape recorder or to a scribe. A computer might be adapted so typing becomes an effective way to record information on paper. In yet another type of accommodation, essays could be replaced by oral reports.

Are there some accommodations that should not be used?

Like many difficult questions, the answer depends on the context. An accommodation should not alter the essential purpose of the assignment. If the skill you want to measure is the ability to make multiple rapid hand movements, then there is probably no accommodation that is appropriate. Jim will not do well because of his disability. Alternately, if the purpose of a task is to see if someone has perfect vision without glasses, using those glasses is not an appropriate accommodation. If the purpose is to see if you can read, the glasses become a reasonable accommodation.

Who decides about accommodations?

The team that writes IEPs and 504 Plans reviews the disability and determines what accommodations, if any, are necessary. These are then written into the EIP or 504 Plan.

Once more, return to Jim. As you consider the requirements of your class, think of the most appropriate way to remove the barrier that is presented by the limited mobility Jim has in his hands.

If we use accommodations, how will the student ever be prepared for independent life in college or the world of work?

Some people are concerned that the supports provided in school will result in the student being unable to work productively when he or she leaves school. As a matter of fact, Section 504 applies to colleges and employers as well. Colleges offer support centers and provide accommodations upon documentation that a disability exists. Employers are required to provide reasonable accommodations to any person who is otherwise qualified to fulfill the elements of the job.

If companies remove barriers at the workplace, educators should be willing and able to take barriers out of the school activities that prepare a student for the workplace. Teachers can help a student identify the type of accommodation that will be the least cumbersome for everyone, and those that will permit the student to be most independent.

Don't accommodations just make school easier?

That depends on how you view the world. Does wearing glasses make driving easier? Not really—for a person with limited vision, wearing glasses makes driving *possible*. With or without glasses, you need to be able to drive to pass the test. The same is true of an academic accommodation; whether or not the accommodation is provided, the students still must demonstrate that they know required material.

An accommodation should not alter the essential purpose of the assignment.

Think about the important elements of your class: Is it more important that Jim take notes in class or understand the material? Is it more important that Jim demonstrate good handwriting or the ability to communicate thoughts in print? Often, when you identify the main purpose of your assignments and consider the skills and abilities of a student, you will see that an accommodation lets you determine more clearly what a student knows, understands, and can do.

Does a student need to follow the IEP accommodations in all classes?

The IEP or 504 Plan needs to address any area in which the student's disability affects life in school. Sometimes this means in all classes, but not always. For example, a student who was blind would need to use Braille in all classes dealing with written material. Jim, our student with limited mobility in his hands, might not require accommodations in world languages or physical education.

Can we make accommodations without having students on an IEP?

Many accommodations are just different ways of teaching or testing. You should be able to have this freedom in your classes. In some cases, the way in which a class is taught makes accommodations unnecessary. Accommodations change the situation, not the content of the instruction. However, accommodations on standardized tests must be connected to IEP's or 504 Plans.

May teachers give different assignments on the same content as a way to meet the needs of different learning styles without lowering standards?

Absolutely. The point is to remove the barrier of the disability; this is one way to accomplish that. Some teachers find they tap student knowledge best in active projects; others find that written work is best. Many secondary schools are using portfolios or performance activities to document student learning.

These assessment activities can be very compelling and they do tap different methods of expression. A student like Jim, for example, might communicate depth of understanding and analysis to a social studies debate with a disability in the area of speech or language might find barriers in the performance activities that do not exist on a paper-and-pencil task.

. . . educators should be willing and able to take barriers out of the school activities that prepare a student for the workplace.

What if accommodations are not implemented?

Since accommodations allow equal access, refusing to provide them can be viewed as discrimination. Individuals who knowingly refuse to implement accommodations make themselves personally liable for legal suit.

This sounds serious, and it is serious. Once the accommodations are found to be necessary, everyone must implement them in situations where the student's disability poses a barrier that prevents equal access.

If no barrier exists in your class, the accommodation is not necessary. No one has the option, however, of deciding not to implement a necessary accommodation. Telling students they could not wear glasses or use a hearing aid is unthinkable. Just as inappropriate is a decision not to allow Jim to use accommodations to remove the barrier posed by his disability, even though it means making some changes to your own work.

Questions About Specific Accommodations

Now that the issues underlying accommodations have been addressed, it is time to talk about frequently-encountered accommodations that raise questions and concern. All these questions have come from secondary school faculty members in a variety of school systems.

Why is it fair to read material aloud to some students?

Some students have a learning disability that makes it difficult for them to decode print. They can understand the concepts; they can comprehend the material when they hear it; they can reason through the material. They just can't turn print into meaning. If the task is to determine if the student can read, you already know they will have difficulty. If the task is to determine if the student has content knowledge, reading material aloud removes the barrier of the learning disability. Reading material aloud to a student who does not understand the material will not result in a higher grade.

Why is it fair to give some students extra time on tests?

Some students have motor difficulties that make writing an enormous challenge. They may not be able to form the letters correctly. They may not be able to monitor their thoughts while they work on the physical act of writing. They understand the material, and they know what they want to respond; it just takes longer to write the answer. If the task is to determine how quickly the student can respond, you already know they will have difficulty. If the task is to determine if the student has the knowledge, providing extra time removes the

barrier of the motor disability. Providing extra time to a student who does not understand the material will not result in a higher grade.

Why is it fair to permit some students to respond orally to tests?

Think about the example above. For some students, responding orally would be a comparable accommodation. In this case, allowing an oral response will not result in a higher grade if the student does not know the material.

A student with a disability in the area of speech or language might find barriers in the performance activities that do not exist on a paper-and-pencil task.

The Bottom Line

It all comes down to deciding what is important. Think about your assignment and expectations. Think about the disability. If the disability provides a barrier, the accommodation removes it. The accommodation does not release a student from participating or demonstrating knowledge—it allows the student to be able to participate and demonstrate knowledge. And isn't that what school is all about?

References

Americans with Disabilities Act of 1990, P.L. 101–336, 2, 104 Stat. 328.1991.

Individuals with Disabilities Education Act Amendments of 1997, P.L. 105–17, 20 U.S. Code Sections 1401–1486.

Livovich, Michael P. *Section 504 of the Rehabilitation Act of 1973 and the Americans with Disabilities Act. Providing access to a free appropriate public education: a public school manual.* Indianapolis, Ind.: 1996.

Vocational Rehabilitation Act of 1973, 29 U.S.C. 794.

*MaryAnn Byrnes (**byrnes@mediaone.net**) is assistant professor at the Graduate College of Education, University of Massachusetts-Boston.*

From *NASSP Bulletin,* February 2000, pp. 21-27. © 2000 by NASSP Bulletin. Reprinted by permission. For more information concerning NASSP services and/or programs, please call (703) 860-0200.

Chaos in the Classroom: Looking at ADHD

Diagnosing and helping students with ADHD requires the collaboration of parents, clinicians, teachers, and students.

Steven C. Schlozman and Vivien R. Schlozman

Students increasingly walk through the classroom door wearing invisible labels and prescriptions. A list of psychiatric and learning disorders that was intended to clarify the difficulties different students experience has instead bewildered teachers and administrators. Educators must make sense of their students' new diagnostic criteria and glean from this information the most effective ways to assist their pupils. Given the enormous increase in the diagnosis and treatment of attention deficit hyperactivity disorder (ADHD) among school-age children, neuropsychiatric problems characterized by inattention and hyperactivity are pressing classroom issues.

Students diagnosed with ADHD often arrive in the classroom with medication and teaching recommendations that are based on completed psychological testing. In spite of these recommendations, teachers frequently have little or no contact with their students' clinicians. Tight budgets, large classrooms, and often multiple students with the same diagnosis who require different teaching strategies substantially challenge the educator's primary objective: to teach and inspire every student dynamically and efficiently. Reaching that goal starts with an understanding of ADHD and how teachers can help students who have been diagnosed with the disorder.

Describing and Diagnosing ADHD

ADHD is a neuropsychiatric disorder that begins before 7 years of age (American Psychiatric Association, 1994). Problems in the three core domains of *inattention, hyperactivity*, and *impulsivity* characterize the disorder.

Clinicians define *inattention* as age-inappropriate poor attention span and *hyperactivity* as age-inappropriate increased activity in multiple settings. For example, an inattentive child may pay poor attention to details or appear as though his or her mind is elsewhere. Often, the child has difficulty sustaining a single activity. One mother describes her son's bedtime difficulties: He starts to brush his teeth, follows the cat into the playroom while his mouth is full of toothpaste, notices the blocks and sits down to play, and in two minutes turns on the computer at the other end of the room.

> **Most children will occasionally display many of the aspects ascribed to ADHD, and this recognition may account for much of the controversy surrounding the disorder.**

Hyperactive children may fidget excessively and have difficulties playing quietly. Children with ADHD display, sometimes paradoxically, a level of inflexibility that leads them to experience intense frustration when asked to break from one activity and move on to something new. The child will appear to have well-honed attentional skills, but his or her rigidity will increasingly lead to tantrums and agitation.

Impulsivity refers to the tendency to act rashly and without judgment or consideration. A child might frequently interrupt others, take other children's toys, or appear consistently impatient and frustrated.

As these descriptions suggest, the symptoms of ADHD exist along a spectrum. Most children will occasionally display many of the aspects ascribed to ADHD, and this recognition may account for much of the controversy surrounding the disorder. To standardize the diagnosis, the Diagnostic and Statistical Manual-IV (DSM-IV) lists formal criteria (American Psychiatric Association, 1994). ADHD can be characterized as three types: predominantly inattentive, predominantly hyperactive-impulsive, or a combination of the two types. To some extent, these differentiations account for the increasingly recognized population of children—often girls—who display what appear to be difficulties primarily with attention but who respond to conventional treatments.

The brief adolescent tantrum or the distraction of an 8-year-old before vacation does not constitute sufficient data for a diagnosis of ADHD.

Finally, one of the most difficult and important aspects of understanding ADHD is to consider the child's developmental expectations. Obviously, we don't expect the same judgment or attention span from a 6-year-old and a teenager. In addition, symptoms must persist over time and exist in more than one setting. The brief adolescent tantrum or the distraction of an 8-year-old before vacation does not constitute sufficient data for a diagnosis of ADHD.

In fact, the heterogeneity and developmental aspects of ADHD make the diagnosis of the disorder potentially quite complicated (Cantwell, 1996). Ideally, the clinician should take a very careful history from as many sources as possible and note such important factors as the persistence of the symptoms and the extent to which these symptoms cause problems. Because emotionally troubled children often appear inattentive or agitated, the clinician should ask about difficulties in the child's life that might account for a change in the child's behavior. We must also remember, however, that many children experience difficult life changes but do not display symptoms of agitation or inattention.

Although research addresses the efficacy of specific laboratory tests, the descriptive criteria of ADHD remain the most effective means of making an accurate diagnosis. Clinicians must take the time to speak with parents and teachers, noting that children with ADHD will often appear normal in a brief office visit or in a one-on-one situation. As evidence mounts of a strong genetic component to the disorder, clinicians should ascertain whether siblings, parents, or close relatives suffer similar symptoms. Because many parents were not diagnosed as children, simply asking whether they were diagnosed with something similar to ADHD is usually not sufficient (Biederman et al., 1992). The clinician must probe parents for their memories of their childhood behavior.

Do inattention and hyperactivity always equal ADHD? In addition to the heterogeneity of ADHD, we must note that other psychiatric processes may account for many of the disorder's symptoms. Children with intense anxiety or depression are particularly likely to have problems that appear similar to ADHD, and evidence also exists that suggests that symptoms of depression—as the child's self esteem suffers in the face of continuing social and developmental failures—can complicate ADHD (Zametkin & Monique, 1999). Clinicians should also screen for problems with substance abuse, Tourette's syndrome, and psychosocial stressors. Clinicians, parents, or teachers may mistakenly attribute symptoms of these conditions to ADHD, and the symptoms may complicate the course of a child who happens also to suffer from ADHD.

In general, younger children with ADHD are happy. The preteen diagnosed with ADHD who is not generally in good spirits should be carefully scrutinized for other or additional psychological problems. Conversely, as children with untreated ADHD age, they may develop significant self-image problems. These difficulties come about as the young people continually endure academic and social failures; simply treating their ADHD will often not meet all of their social, developmental, and learning needs.

Although we don't clearly understand the causes of ADHD, current research suggests evidence of potentially causative brain abnormalities. Many of these studies implicate problems with frontal lobe function (Rubia et al., 1999). In general, the frontal lobe region of the cerebral cortex allows for the planning and execution of complex and complicated tasks. We often refer to the activity of this portion of the brain as executive function, and we think that children with ADHD have deficits in executive functioning.

Evidence for these deficits has been generated both by neuropsychological testing and by neuroimaging studies, as well as by the observation that individuals with frontal lobe injuries display behavior similar to that of people with ADHD. As stated earlier, strong evidence for a genetic component of the disorder also exists (Biederman et al., 1992). Further, mounting evidence suggests that psychological and environmental stress can lead to the development of the syndrome (Weiss, 1996). Although we know of no clear cause for the disorder, most theorists would argue that both environmental and biological factors play substantial roles in the development of ADHD.

Treating ADHD

Treatments for ADHD include behavioral and medical therapies. Stimulants such as methylphenidate (Ritalin) and dextroamphetamine (Dexedrine) continue to be first-line medical treatments, with more than 40 years of experience confirming the relative safety and effectiveness of these medications. Although the number of stimulants on the market proliferates, response to a specific stimulant remains idiosyncratic; some children will do better on one stimulant than the other, and it is difficult to predict which medication will work best. In addition to the stimulants, tricyclic antidepressants such as desipramine can be very effective, though their use is somewhat limited in younger children. Medications such as clonidine (Catapress) and guanfacine (Tenex), both high blood pressure medications, appear to treat the impulsive symptoms of the syndrome, but are not effective for inattention.

In general, if medical therapies work and the child receives the appropriate dose and stimulant, the child's behavior should improve relatively quickly. If a child does not improve or improves only minimally, both the proposed treatment regimen (dose and/or medication) and often the diagnosis itself should be re-evaluated. Nevertheless, we need to understand the limitations of medical therapies. Although such symptoms as overactivity, attention span, impulsivity, aggression, social interaction, and academic performance will often improve, such specific skills as reading and such antisocial behavior as cheating or stealing may not show marked progress without additional interventions (Zametkin & Monique, 1999). Children still must master the fundamental developmental task of learning to focus on activities or subjects that are not of immediate interest. No medication can take the place of the mastery of skills and attainment of maturity necessary for academic and social success.

Behavioral treatments of ADHD include daily report cards, positive reinforcement, social skills groups, and individual therapy (Barkley, 1990). As the child matures, these treatments may also address the child's self-image. Although psychodynamic therapies (play or talk therapies) may not be directly effective, we have found that the relationship between a child and an effective therapist often ameliorates many of the problem behaviors associated with ADHD.

Finally, when deciding on treatment, the parents and the child must take part in the decision-making process. Some families prefer behavioral remedies; others may request medications. Attention to such details as the meaning of each treatment modality, as well as the hopes and concerns of both the parents and the child, will have enormous benefits. Adolescents may not wish to take medications, for instance, but may be willing to implement equally effective study and behavioral strategies. Conversely, both time and financial constraints may limit the efficacy of psychotherapy. Clinicians must educate families about ADHD and its treatment and help the families make informed decisions. Clinicians should leave time at the end of an appointment for questions—if families cannot ask questions, their understanding of and compliance with treatment is severely threatened.

The issue of alcohol and drug abuse and ADHD deserves special mention. Because stimulants are addictive substances, we often worry that prescribing these medications will predispose children to addictive problems. Although caution is always necessary when using stimulants, recent research suggests that, in fact, the number of children developing substance abuse problems is substantially higher in those with ADHD who do not receive adequate treatment (Biederman, Wilens, Mick, Spencer, &

Faraone, 1999). Nevertheless, in adolescents with pre-existing problems with substances, clinicians often prefer treatment with medications other than stimulants.

ADHD in the Classroom

Just as diagnosing and treating children with ADHD is complex, working with the inattentive and hyperactive child challenges all teachers. The problems that children with ADHD experience may lead to chaotic classrooms, missed and incomplete assignments, and miserable teachers and students alike. Educators have found, however, a number of useful classroom techniques.

To assist the student with ADHD, educators need to exercise caution, creativity, and vigilance.

First, teachers must view the child as a whole person. The child is not a person with ADHD, or an "ADHDer," but a complete and unique individual. Although seemingly obvious, teachers must resist the tendency to label a child with unfair expectations. Most important, teachers can remind students that they are capable of learning and of enjoying the learning process. Many students diagnosed with ADHD will arrive in the classroom severely demoralized, having gleaned from their parents and peers that they are unable to excel academically. On the other hand, telling students that they can learn as easily as students without attentional deficits might reintroduce a pattern of failure and disappointment.

Educators, therefore, should be proactive when they suspect a psychiatric reason for a student's difficulties. Studies have demonstrated that teachers are valuable sources of clinical information. At the same time, teachers should be aware of their own biases. Many of the studies, for instance, suggest that teachers frequently suspect ADHD in boys more often than in girls (Dulcan, 1997).

To assist the student with ADHD, educators need to exercise caution, creativity, and vigilance. Teachers must employ all of their professional skills to structure classrooms and make assignments clear. Educators should let students with ADHD know that they will work creatively with the students to explore learning and organization strategies. An honest relationship between teacher and student is essential.

To be most effective, teachers should discuss the strategies with the student outside of class so that the student understands the teacher's expectations and the kinds of support the teacher will offer. Specific strategies might include nonverbal reprimands for out-of-control behavior. A simple and silent hand on the student's shoulder inconspicuously tells the student that his or her behavior is inappropriate. Similarly, relying on such cues as lost eye contact between a student and teacher might help a teacher recognize wavering attention. If a child is persistently unable to focus, move his or her seat to a less distracting part of the room. Some other strategies include the following:

Require meticulously organized assignment books. For every class, the student with ADHD must have each day's homework recorded. When the teacher doesn't assign homework, the student writes "no homework" in the appropriate place. If the student fails to keep the log current, he or she must get the teacher's signature in the assignment book at the end of class. The teacher should also both write the assignment on the board and repeat the assignment aloud. This time-honored teaching technique of appealing to multiple senses works well for children with ADHD.

Teach students with ADHD to break down assignments into smaller, less overwhelming components. When reading textbooks, for example, we have found a variation of Robinson's SQ3R method to be effective (Robinson, 1961). The student surveys each section of the text by first reading the boldfaced print, looking at the visuals, and reading the captions under the visual displays. The student then generates a general statement about what he or she will be reading, allowing him or her to focus on the content of the reading material. After each section, the student stops to recap the main idea of the completed segment. This strategy helps the student become actively engaged with and focused on the text.

Use flash cards. After students give themselves a pretest to determine what they have already mastered, they make flash cards of all of the material that they don't know. They then can separate the cards into three piles: mastered material that they know without hesitation, material that they've guessed correctly but without confidence, and material that they don't know. In this way, the students gain a sense of control over the learning situation and learn to transfer these strategies to other academic and non-academic learning settings. The corresponding sense of accomplishment for both teacher and students can be enormously rewarding.

Experienced teachers will note that many of these strategies have been around for years—long before we reached our present understanding of ADHD. We know now that ADHD leaves the student with deficits in executive functioning and that the time-honored classroom techniques create for the student a kind of external frontal lobe. Good teachers have simply hit upon these techniques in their quests to engage and teach their students.

Teachers need not be overwhelmed by the growing complexity of psychiatric and psychological diagnoses that follow their beleaguered students. As always, good educators remain central to a child's development.

Teachers should never hesitate to contact a child's clinician. If a student appears different or suffers a behavioral change, a physician or psychologist will use this valuable information to determine a diagnosis and treatment. Although clinicians and teachers have just begun to work together, educational and clinical collaborations need to evolve and prosper. The teacher, the clinician, and most important, the student, will benefit enormously.

References

American Psychiatric Association. (1994). *Diagnostic and statistical manual for mental disorders* (4th ed.). Washington, DC: Author.

Barkley, R. A. (Ed.). (1990). *Attention deficit hyperactivity disorder: A handbook for diagnosis and treatment.* New York: Guilford.

Biederman, J., Faraone, S. V., Keenan, K., Benjamin, K., Krifcher, B., Moore, C., Sprich-Buckminster, S., Ugaglia, K., Jellinck, M. S., & Steingard, R. (1992). Further evidence for family-genetic risk factors in attention deficit hyperactivity disorder: Patterns of comorbidity in probands and relatives in psychiatrically and pediatrically referred samples. *Archives of General Psychiatry,* 49, 728–38.

Biederman, J., Wilens, T., Mick, E., Spencer, T., & Faraone, S. V. (1999). Pharmacotherapy of attention deficit hyperactivity disorder reduces risk for substance use disorder. *Pediatrics,* 104, e20.

Cantwell, D. P. (1996). Attention deficit disorder: A review of the past 10 years. *Journal of the American Academy of Child and Adolescent Psychiatry,* 35, 978–87.

Dulcan, M. (1997). Practice parameters for the assessment and treatment of children, adolescents and adults with attention deficit/hyperactivity disorder. *Journal of the American Academy of Child and Adolescent Psychiatry,* 36 (Suppl. 10), 85S–121S.

Robinson, F. P. (1961). *Effective study.* New York: Harper and Row.

Rubia, K., Overmeyer, S., Taylor, E., Brammer, M., Williams, S. C., Simmons, A., & Bullmore, E. T. (1999). Hypofrontality in attention deficit hyperactivity disorder during higher order motor control: A study with functional MRI. *American Journal of Psychiatry,* 156, 891–6.

Weiss, G. (1996). Attention deficit hyperactivity disorder. In M. Lewis (Ed.), *Child and adolescent psychiatry: A comprehensive textbook* (pp. 544–63). Baltimore, MD: Williams and Wilkins.

Zametkin, A. J., & Monique, E. (1999). Current concepts: Problems in the management of attention deficit hyperactivity disorder. *New England Journal of Medicine,* 340, 40–46.

Steven C. Schlozman, M.D., is Clinical Instructor in Psychiatry, Massachusetts General Hospital/Harvard Medical School, 15 Parkman St., WACC-725, Boston, MA 02114; and Lecturer in Education, Harvard Graduate School of Education; 617-724-6300, ext. 133-1114; sscholzman@partners.org. **Vivien R. Schlozman** is a private practice educator at the Pembroke Hill School. She may be reached at 6600 Overhill Rd., Shawnee Mission, KS 66208.

UNIT 10
Giftedness

Unit Selections

Key Points to Consider

• How can preschool teachers meet the needs of all students, including those with special gifts or talents?

• Is the Internet a useful tool for students with special gifts to communicate, collaborate, and develop higher-level thinking skills?

• How should gifted programs be assessed and how should schools change to meet the needs of high-ability students?

 **Links: www.dushkin.com/online/**
These sites are annotated in the World Wide Web pages.

The Council for Exceptional Children
http://www.cec.sped.org/index.html

Kenny Anthony's Gifted and Talented and General Educational Resources
http://www2.tsixroads.com/~kva/

National Association for Gifted Children (NAGC)
http://www.nagc.org/home00.htm

The Individuals with Disabilities Education Act (IDEA) mandates special services for children with disabilities, but not for children with exceptional gifts or talents. The monies spent to provide special services for three children with high-cost disabilities could pay for accelerated lessons for a classroom full of college-bound students with intellectual giftedness. Should schools in the twenty-first century be more egalitarian? IDEA mandates appropriate education but not sameness of quantity or degree of knowledge to be imported to every child. Are we inclined to push compensatory education of students with shortcomings in learning, while leaving students with a gift for learning to cope for themselves to counterbalance the equation? Do we want educational parity?

Since many textbooks on exceptional children include children with special gifts and talents, and since these children are exceptional, they will be included in this volume. Instructors who deal only with the categories of disabilities covered by IDEA may simply omit coverage of this unit.

The Omnibus Education Bill of 1987 provided modest support for gifted and talented identification and the education of students with giftedness in the United States. It required, however, that each state foot the bill for the development of special programs for children with exceptional gifts and talents. Some states have implemented accelerated or supplemental education for the gifted. Most states have not.

Giftedness can be viewed as both a blessing and a curse. Problems of jealousy, misunderstanding, indignation, exasperation, and even fear are often engendered in people who live with, work with, or get close to a child with superior intelligence. Are children with giftedness at a disadvantage in our society? Do their powerful abilities and potentialities in some area (or areas) leave them ridiculed or bored in a regular classroom? Children with special gifts and talents are deprived of some of the opportunities with which less exceptional children are routinely provided.

Students who are gifted tend to ask a lot of questions and pursue answers with still more questions. They can be incredibly persistent about gathering information about topics that engage them. They may, however, show no interest at all in learning about topics that do not. They may be very competitive in areas where they are especially skilled, competing even with teachers and other adults. They may seem arrogant about their skills, when, in their minds, they are only being honest.

Many children and youth with special gifts and talents have extraordinary sensitivity to how other people are reacting to them. As they are promoted through elementary school into middle school and high school, many such children learn to hide their accomplishments for the secondary gain of being more socially acceptable or more popular. Because they have not been challenged or have been discouraged from achieving at their highest potentialities, underachievement becomes a problem. They have poor study habits as a result of not needing to study. They are unmotivated, intensely bored, and discouraged by the educational programs available to them.

Researchers who have studied creative genius have found that most accomplished high achievers share one childhood similarity. Their parents recognized their special abilities early and found tutors or mentors who would help them develop their skills. This is true not only of mathematicians and scientists but also of world-class sports players, musicians, artists, performers, writers, and other producers of note.

Educational programs that refuse to find tutors or mentors, to encourage original work, or to provide special education in the skill areas of students with gifts are depriving the future of potential producers.

The earlier that children with special gifts and talents are recognized, the better. The sooner they are provided with enriched education, the more valuable their future contributions will become. Children from all ethnic backgrounds, from all socioeconomic levels, and from both sexes can have exceptional gifts and talents. Researchers have reported that parents of gifted persons seldom have any special creative skills or talents of their own.

The assessment of children with special gifts and talents, especially in the early childhood years, is fraught with difficulties. Should parents nominate their own children when they see extraordinary skills developing? How objective can parents be about their child's ability as it compares to the abilities of other same-aged children? Should measures of achievement be used (recitals, performances, art, reading levels, writings)? Many parents are embarrassed by their child's extraordinary aptitudes. They would rather have a popular child or a child more like his or her peers.

The first article in this unit describes the uncommon talents of children who have been productive in exceptional ways—Mozart, Edison, Wang Yani, and some individuals with autistic savant syndrome. Ellen Winner reviews studies of giftedness, such as Terman's famous study at Stanford University early in the twentieth century, and more contemporary research such as that by Csikszentmihalyi of the University of Chicago and Geschwind and Galaburda at Harvard University. The author points out the uneven development of many exceptionally gifted students. They may, for example, excel in spatial skills but have verbal deficits or be high achievers in one area and unremarkable in others. In addition, many uncommonly talented youngsters suffer social problems and low self-esteem. They need help dealing with the bullies who ridicule them as oddballs or nerds.

Angela Guptill, in the second article, describes how the Internet can be used to challenge and improve the performance of students with intellectual giftedness. Computer-based lessons allow students to pursue more work, find answers to questions, and spend evenings and weekends on learning adventures when and if they choose.

In the last article Susan Winebrenner gives strong arguments for spending the time, effort, and money to assure that our children with gifts and talents get all the education they need. Many students with special gifts and talents become underachievers. They rarely are challenged to learn above their current abilities. Because they score high on achievement tests, it is assumed that they must be learning. An alternate explanation is that they already possessed these abilities. When they are not given a chance to pursue their special interests, or are not requested to demonstrate increased excellence in an area, they lose confidence in their abilities to perform. This article urges that they be given a stimulating learning environment of their own.

Uncommon Talents:
Gifted Children, Prodigies and Savants

Possessing abilities well beyond their years, gifted children inspire admiration, but they also suffer ridicule, neglect and misunderstanding

by Ellen Winner

One evening a few years ago, while I was attending a concert, a young boy in the audience caught my attention. As the orchestra played a Mozart concerto, this nine-year-old child sat with a thick, well-thumbed orchestral score opened on his lap. As he read, he hummed the music out loud, in perfect tune. During intermission, I cornered the boy's father. Yes, he told me, Stephen was really reading music, not just looking at it. And reading musical scores was one of his preferred activities, vying only with college-level computer programming manuals. At an age when most children concentrate on fourth-grade arithmetic and the nuances of playground etiquette, Stephen had already earned a prize in music theory that is coveted by adults.

Gifted children like Stephen are fascinating but also intimidating. They have been feared as "possessed," they have been derided as oddballs, they have been ridiculed as nerds. The parents of such young people are often criticized for pushing their children rather than allowing them a normal, well-balanced childhood. These children are so different from others that schools usually do not know how to educate them. Meanwhile society expects gifted children to become creative intellectuals and artists as adults and views them as failures if they do not.

Psychologists have always been interested in those who deviate from the norm, but just as they know more about psychopathology than about leadership and courage, researchers also know far more about retardation than about giftedness. Yet an understanding of the most talented minds will provide both the key to educating children and a precious glimpse of how the human brain works.

The Nature of Giftedness

Everyone knows children who are smart, hard-working achievers—youngsters in the top 10 to 15 percent of all students. But only the top 2 to 5 percent of children are gifted. Gifted children (or child prodigies, who are just extreme versions of gifted children) differ from bright children in at least three ways:

- *Gifted children are precocious.* They master subjects earlier and learn more quickly than average children do.
- *Gifted children march to their own drummer.* They make discoveries on their own and can often intuit the solution to a problem without going through a series of logical, linear steps.
- *Gifted children are driven by a "rage to master."* They have a powerful interest in the area, or domain, in which they can readily focus so intently on work in this domain that they lose sense of the outside world.

These are children who teach themselves how to read as toddlers, who breeze through college mathematics in middle school or draw more skillfully as second-graders than most adults do. Their fortunate combination of obsessive interest and an ability to learn easily can lead to high achievement in their chosen domain. But gifted children are more susceptible to interfering social and emotional factors than once was thought.

The first comprehensive study of the gifted, carried out over a period of more than 70 years, was initiated at Stanford University in the early part of this century by Lewis M. Terman, a psychologist with a rather rosy opinion of gifted children. His study tracked more than 1,500 high-IQ children over the course of their lives. To qualify for this study, the "Termites" were first nominated by their teachers and then had to score 135 or higher on the Stanford-Binet IQ test (the average score is 100). These children were precocious: they typically spoke early, walked early and read before they went to school. Their parents described them as being insatiably curious and as having superb memories.

Terman described his subjects glowingly, not only as superior in intelligence to other children but also as superior in health, social adjustment and moral attitude. This conclusion easily gave rise to the myth that gifted children are happy and well adjusted by nature, requiring little in the way of special attention—a myth that still guides the way these children are educated today.

In retrospect, Terman's study was probably flawed. No child entered the study unless nominated by a teacher as one of the best and the brightest; teachers probably overlooked those gifted children who were misfits, loners or problematic to teach. And the shining evaluations of social adjustment and personality in the gifted were performed by the same admiring teachers who had singled out the study subjects. Finally, almost a third of the sample came from professional, middle-class families. Thus, Terman confounded IQ with social class.

The myth of the well-adjusted, easy-to-teach gifted child persists despite more recent evidence to the contrary. Mihaly Csikszentmihalyi of the University of Chicago has shown that children with exceptionally high abilities in any area—not just in academics but in visual arts, music, even athletics—are out of step with their peers socially. These children tend to be highly driven, independent in their thinking and introverted. They spend more than the usual amount of time alone, and although they derive energy and pleasure from their solitary mental lives, they also report feeling lonely. The more extreme the level of gift, the more isolated these children feel.

Contemporary researchers have estimated that about 20 to 25 percent of profoundly gifted children have social and emotional problems, which is twice the normal rate; in contrast, moderately gifted children do not exhibit a higher than average rate. By middle childhood, gifted children often try to hide their abilities in the hopes of becoming more popular. One group particularly at risk for such underachievement is academically gifted girls, who report more depression, lower self-esteem and more psychosomatic symptoms than academically gifted boys do.

The combination of precocious knowledge, social isolation and sheer boredom in many gifted children is a tough challenge for teachers who must educate them alongside their peers. Worse, certain gifted children can leap years ahead of their peers in one area and yet fall behind in another. These children, the unevenly gifted, sometimes fall hopelessly out of sync.

The Unevenly Gifted

Terman was a proponent of the view that gifted children are globally gifted—evenly talented in all academic areas. Indeed, some special children have exceptional verbal skills as well as strong spatial, numerical and logical skills that enable them to excel in mathematics. The occasional child who completes college as an early teen—or even as a preteen—is likely to be globally gifted. Such children are easy to spot: they are all-around high achievers. But many children exhibit gifts in one area of study and are unremarkable or even learning disabled in others. These may be creative children who are difficult in school and who are not immediately recognized as gifted.

Unevenness in gifted children is quite common. A recent survey of more than 1,000 highly academically gifted adolescents revealed that more than 95 percent show a strong disparity between mathematical and verbal interests. Extraordinarily strong mathematical and spatial abilities often accompany average or even deficient verbal abilities. Julian Stanley of Johns Hopkins University has found that many gifted children selected for special summer programs in advanced math have enormous discrepancies between their math and verbal skills. One such eight-year-old scored 760 out of a perfect score of 800 on the math part of the Scholastic Aptitude Test (SAT) but only 290 out of 800 on the verbal part.

In a retrospective analysis of 20 world-class mathematicians, psychologist Benjamin S. Bloom, then at the University of Chicago, reported than none of his subjects had learned to read before attending school (yet most academically gifted children do read before attending school) and that six had had trouble learning to read. And a retrospective study of inventors (who presumably exhibit high mechanical and spatial aptitude) showed that as children these individuals struggled with reading and writing.

Indeed, may children who struggle with language may have strong spatial skills. Thomas Sowell of Stanford University, an economist by training, conducted a study of late-talking children after he raised a son who did not begin to speak until almost age four. These children tended to have high spatial abilities—they excelled at puzzles, for instance—and most had relatives working in professions that require strong spatial skills. Perhaps the most striking finding was that 60 percent of these children had engineers as first- or second-degree relatives.

The association between verbal deficits and spatial gifts seems particularly strong among visual artists. Beth Casey of Boston College and I have found that college art students make significantly more spelling errors than college students majoring in either math or in verbal areas such as English or history. On average, the art students not only misspelled more than half of a 20-word list but also made the kind of errors associated with poor reading skills—nonphonetic spelling such as "physicain" for "physician" (instead of the phonetic "fiscian").

The many children who posses a gift in one area and are weak or learning disabled in others presents a conundrum. If schools educate them as globally gifted, these students will continually encounter frustration in their weak areas; if they are held back because of their deficiencies, they will be bored and unhappy in their strong fields. Worst, the gifts that these children do possess may go unnoticed entirely when frustrated, unevenly gifted children wind up as misfits or troublemakers.

Savants: Uneven in the Extreme

The most extreme cases of spatial or mathematical gifts coexisting with verbal deficits are found in savants. Savants are retarded (with IQs between 40 and 70) and are either autistic or show autistic symptoms. "Ordinary" savants usually possess one skill at a normal level, in contrast to their otherwise severely limited abilities. But the rarer savants—fewer than 100 are known—display one or more skills equal to the prodigy level.

Savants typically excel in visual art, music or lightning-fast calculation. In their domain of expertise, they resemble child prodigies, exhibiting precocious skills, independent learning and a rage to master. For instance, the drawing savant named Nadia sketched more realistically at ages three and four than any known prodigy of the same age. In addition, savants will also surpass gifted children in the accuracy of their memories.

Savants are just like extreme versions of unevenly gifted children. Just as gifted children often have mathematical or artistic genius and language-based learning disabilities, savants tend to exhibit a highly developed visual-spatial ability alongside severe deficits in language. One of the most promising explanations for this syndrome posits atypical brain organization, with deficits in the left hemisphere of the brain (which usually controls language) offset by strengths in the right hemisphere (which controls spatial and visual skills).

According to Darold A. Treffert, a psychiatrist now in private practice in Fond du Lac, Wis., the fact that many savants were premature babies fits well with this notion of left-side brain damage and resultant right-side compensation. Late in pregnancy, the fetal brain undergoes a process called pruning, in which a large number of excess neurons die off [see "The Developing Brain," by Carla J. Shatz; SCIENTIFIC AMERICAN, September 1992]. But brain of babies born prematurely may not have been pruned yet; if such brains experience trauma to the left hemisphere near the time of birth, numerous uncommitted neurons elsewhere in the brain might remain to compensate for the loss, perhaps leading to a strong right-hemisphere ability.

Such trauma to a premature infant's brain could arise many ways—from conditions during pregnancy, from lack of oxygen during birth, from the administration of too much oxygen afterward. An excess of oxygen given to premature babies can cause blindness in addition to brain damage; many musical savants exhibit the triad premature birth, blindness and strong right-hemisphere skill.

Gifted children most likely possess atypical brain organization to some extent as well. When average students are tested to see which part of their brain controls their verbal skills, the answer in generally the left hemisphere only. But when mathematically talented children are tested the same way, both the left and right hemispheres are implicated in controlling language—the right side of their brains participates in tasks ordinarily reserved for the left. These children also tend not to be strongly right-handed, and indication that their left hemisphere is not clearly dominant.

The late neurologist Norman Geschwind of Harvard Medical School was intrigued by the fact that individuals with pronounced right-hemisphere gifts (that is, in math, music, art) are disproportionately nonright-handed (left-handed or ambidextrous) and have higher than average rates of left-hemisphere deficits such as delayed onset of speech, stuttering or dyslexia. Geschwind and his colleague Albert Galaburda theorized that this association of gift with disorder, which they called the "pathology of superiority," results from the effect of the hormone testosterone on the developing fetal brain.

Geschwind and Galaburda noted that the elevated testosterone can delay development of the left hemisphere of the fetal brain; this in turn might result in compensatory right hemisphere growth. Such "testosterone poisoning" might account for the larger number of males than females who exhibit mathematical and spatial gifts, nonright-handedness and pathologies of language. The researchers also noted that gifted children tend to suffer more than the usual frequency of immune disorders such as allergies and asthma; excess testosterone can interfere with the development of the thymus glad, which plays a role in the development of the immune system.

Testosterone exposure remains a controversial explanation for uneven gifts, and to date only scant evidence from the study of brain tissue exists to support the theory of damage and compensation in savants. Nevertheless, it seems certain that gifts are hardwired in the infant brain, as savants and gifted children exhibit extremely high abilities from a very young age—before they have spent much time working at their gift.

Emphasizing Gifts

Given that many profoundly gifted children are unevenly talented, socially isolated and bored with school, what is the best way to educate them? Most gifted programs today tend to target children who have tested above 130 or so on standard IQ tests, pulling them out of their regular classes for a few hours each week of general instruction or interaction. Unfortunately, these programs fail the most talented students.

Generally, schools are focusing what few resources they have for gifted education on the moderately gifted. These children make up the bulk of current "pull-out" programs: bright students with strong but not extraordinary abilities, who do not face the same challenges of precocity and isolation to the same degree as the profoundly gifted. These children—and indeed most children—would be better served if schools instead raised their standards across the board.

Other nations, including Japan and Hungary, set much higher academic expectations for their children than the U.S. does; their children, gifted or not, rise to the challenge by succeeding at higher levels. The needs of moderately gifted children could be met by simply teaching them a more demanding standard curriculum.

The use of IQ as a filter for gifted programs also tends to tip the programs toward the relatively abundant, moderately academically gifted while sometimes overlooking profoundly but unevenly gifted children. Many of these children do poorly on IQ tests because their talent lies either in math or language, but not both. Students whose talent is musical, artistic or athletic are regularly left out as well. It makes more sense to identify the gifted by examining past achievement in specific areas rather than on plain-vanilla IQ tests.

Schools should then place profoundly gifted children in advanced courses in their strong areas only. Subjects in which a student is not exceptional can be taught to the student in the regular classroom. Options for advanced classes include arranging courses especially for the gifted, placing gifted students alongside older students within their schools, registering them in college courses or enrolling them in accelerated summer programs that teach a year's worth of material in a few weeks.

Profoundly gifted children crave challenging work in their domain of expertise and the companionship of individuals with similar skills. Given the proper stimulation and opportunity, the extraordinary minds of these children will flourish.

ELLEN WINNER was a student of literature and painting before she decided to explore developmental psychology. Her inspiration was Harvard University's Project Zero, which researched the psychological aspects of the arts. Her graduate studies allowed her to combine her interests in art and writing with an exploration of the mind. She received her Ph.D. in psychology from Harvard in 1978 and is currently professor of psychology at Boston College as well as a senior research associate with Project Zero.

One of Winner's greatest pleasures is writing books; she has authored three, one on the psychology of the arts, another on children's use of metaphor and irony and, most recently, *Gifted Children, Myths and Realities*. "I usually have several quite different projects going on at once, so I am always juggling," she remarks. She is especially intrigued by unusual children—children who are gifted, learning disabled, gifted and learning disabled, nonright-handed or particularly creative. "The goal is to understand cognitive development in its typical and atypical forms."

When she has time to play, Winner devours novels and movies and chauffeurs her 13-year-old son on snowboarding dates. She is married to the psychologist Howard Gardner and has three grown stepchildren.

USING THE INTERNET
to Improve Student Performance

Angela M. Guptill

> Use a search of the Web to draw associations between prior knowledge and new information
>
> Individual or team collection of information
>
> Classify information
>
> Predict outcomes based on Web site search
>
> Refine online search, as needed

Activities like these are essential parts of Internet-based lessons, and the activities are related to a well-known standard that teachers have relied on for years: *Bloom's Taxonomy*. These particular activities can be categorized as "application of knowledge," and teachers can assess the breadth and depth of their own lessons—and the performance of their students—by using a checklist like this one. This article shows how.

Challenges of New Technologies

Technology in the classroom creates new opportunities and challenges for educators. Skill-and-drill computer programs are being replaced by access to sites on the World Wide Web that allow students to use collaboration and multi-media to gather and demonstrate knowledge. Technological resources have made it possible to develop lessons that promote critical, analytic, higher-order thinking skills and real-world problem-solving that are frequently found on assessments today (Blasi, Heinecke, Milman, & Washington, 1999). With the proper tools to monitor student performance, special educators have the opportunity to target individual needs and monitor progress as students progress through the curriculum using the Internet as a resource.

Challenges of the Standards Movement

As the focus on learning standards and outcomes prevails, educator concern has shifted from the multiple-choice standardized test to performance-based assessments. The possibilities for developing and strengthening higher-order thinking skills using the Internet has increased with the availability of interactive sites and classroom collaboration found on the Internet. Although research is inconclusive about the effect of technology on student performance, studies suggest that several outcome areas may be enhanced. According to Blasi et al. (1999), "These areas include higher order thinking skills, more sophisticated communication skills, research skills, and social skills" (p. 5).

This focus has challenged educators to develop lesson plans using the Internet that target the development of higher-order thinking skills required on many state assessments. For instance, the

Figure 1 Sample Internet Lesson Plan

The Structure of Matter   Grade 8

Unit Goals:
- Students will analyze the structures of matter by accessing their Hyperstudio stack titled "The Structure of Matter" and finding 3 Web sites that provide supporting information.
- Utilize Language Arts Skills—Complete Web site evaluation forms for 3 Web sites. Use information to prepare a newspaper article on the structure of matter. Send a copy to the assigned collaborative classroom. Respond to feedback and provide feedback to your collaborative partner.
- Prepare a multimedia presentation using your findings and the findings of your collaborative partner.
- Students will utilize technology skills—accessing programs, evaluating Web sites, toggle between programs, collaborate with other classrooms, prepare multimedia presentation.

Length of Unit: 8-12 days
Students should be able to:
- Classify objects by their properties
- Understand that matter exists in 3 states: solids, liquids, gases
- Understand the difference between chemical change and physical change (demonstrated through the newspaper article and presentation)
- Successfully collaborate with partner and provide feedback
- Prepare and present multimedia presentation
- Respond to questions from classmates and collaborative partner

Materials:
- Classroom computer lab with Internet access
- Software: Hyperstudio
- Web site evaluation form
- Technology taxonomy for assessment
- Web addresses for collaboration with other classrooms

Figure 2 Lesson Development and Assesment

1. For a lesson plan such as that in Figure 1, locate a collaborative classroom with a site on the Internet. This is a classroom working on the same topic in the same grade. Students can send and receive information (see http://www.epals.com/index.html).
2. Use a Web site evaluation form. Such a form gives the student the opportunity to critically analyze the information present on each Web site for timeliness and accuracy. These skills are addressed in the evaluation section of the technology taxonomy in Figure 3. See Web Site Evaluation form (Figure 2a).
3. Before presenting the lesson, assess whether it will provide students with the opportunity to progress up the technology taxonomy (Figure 3). Each lesson should facilitate demonstration of higher-level thinking skills.
4. Conduct performance measurement. At least quarterly, monitor the progress each student has made. This includes an assessment of progress using technology to develop critical-thinking and higher-order thinking skills. Careful documentation and charting of performance and progress is helpful for the student, parent, and the teacher. Use the technology taxonomy in Figure 3 to measure individual growth and performance.

ity of interactive sites and collaboration with other teachers and classrooms across all subjects and grades has made lesson planning easier (see Figures 1 and 2). More difficult has been the assessment of student performance using critical, higher-order, and problem-based inquiry skills. "It is clear that teaching and learning processes are embedded within complex systems. The challenge is to develop evaluation models that reflect this complexity" (Blasi et al., p. 4).

Figure 2a Web Site Evaluation: Junior High School

Student Information

Name: _____ Today's Date: _____

Topic: _____

Presentation of Information

URL of Web Page: _____
Name of Web Page: _____
Date the Web Page Was Made: _____
E-Mail Address of Author: _____
Was it easy to locate the Web Page? __ Yes __ No
Did the Web Page give you a list of other good sites?
__ Yes __ No
Did the pictures and sound help you to understand the information?
__ Yes __ No
Did you find any spelling errors? __ Yes __ No
If yes, explain what errors you found:

Did you think that the information that you found was accurate?
Explain why or why not.

Notes

Notes:

Would you recommend this site to a classmate? __Yes __ No

World Wide Web can be used as a source of information for teachers and students to enhance classroom instruction and present knowledge using multimedia. Educators can evaluate these outcomes, but it is more complicated than the standardized testing route. According to Blasi et al. (1999), "Standardized tests are an efficient means for measuring certain types of learning outcomes but educators must ask if these are the outcomes valuable for the new millennium" (p. 3).

Classroom Collaboration

To share classroom ideas, projects, and communicate with teachers and students from around the world try... http://www.epals.com/index.html.

This Web site allows educators to locate classrooms to collaborate with by grade, location, and subject area.

Access to sites on the World Wide Web allows students to use collaboration and multimedia to gather and demonstrate knowledge.

Honey, McMillan, and Spielvogel (1995) have emphasized the real-world applications of modern technology: "Evidence indicates that when used effectively, technology applications can support higher-order thinking by engaging students in authentic, complex tasks within collaborative learning contexts" (p. 3). The availabil-

Benefits and Outcomes of Internet-Based Instruction

What are the benefits of Internet-based instruction, and what type of outcomes can be realized over traditional instruction? Accord-

Figure 3 Technology Taxonomy

Measuring Student Performance

Competence	Learning Hierarchy/Computer Application
Knowledge	• Search and reinforce . . . • Knowledge of major ideas • Knowledge of dates, events, places • Technological and academic concepts
Comprehension	• Surf (and sift) through information on the Web, and read for understanding • Identify valuable Web sites, record sites • Group Web sites into categories • Interpret, compare, and contrast facts • Predict consequences—use interactive Web sites to develop understanding of concepts • Contact experts to clarify understanding • Interpret information, provide perspectives
Application	• Draw together associations between prior knowledge and a search of the Web • Individual or team collection of information • Classify information • Predict outcomes based on Web site search • Refine online search, as needed • Select photographs, quotations, sound clips, virtual reality tours for use in presentation • Select format of presentation: newspaper, collage, Web page
Analysis	• Organization of information . . . (text, graphics, sound clips) • Sort and discern quality information from outdated or biased information • Find solutions to questions using collaboration and investigations with peers and experts
Synthesis	• Combine information from different Web sites • Modify information to meet assignment guidelines • Create and design Web sites, interactive projects, visual displays, and written text • Prepare essays, projects, visual displays, interactive presentations • Compose meaningful text from information gathered • Explain findings/synthesize findings
Evaluation	• Assess value and quality of presentation • Compare and discriminate between information from different sites • Verify value of information from various sources • Recognize the difference between subjective vs. objective information • Support information with prior knowledge • Summarize findings

Measuring individual growth and performance of students is a necessity when working with students with disabilities. To measure these elements when incorporating the use of technology into lessons, a taxonomy checklist is useful. This makes it possible to visualize student progress and provides excellent documentation.

Note: Adapted from *Bloom's Taxonomy* (adapted from Learning Skills Program, 1999. Available: http://www.coun.uvic.ca/learn/program/hndouts/ bloom.html).

Teachers and students can use the Internet to obtain feedback from other students—worldwide as well as to provide feedback to others.

Developing Internet-Based Lessons and Assessments

Access to the Internet provides educators with the opportunity to develop and implement lessons similar to the one that appears in Figure 1—a technology/science/language arts lesson selected from the Internet (http://www.d261.k12.id.us/tip/index.htm). The lesson was adapted to cover all levels on the "technology taxonomy" (adapted from *Bloom's Taxonomy*) in Figure 3. The lesson challenges students to use higher-level thinking skills as they use the World Wide Web to perform assignments and participate in activities.

Internet Resources for Educators

Awesome Library for Teachers, Students, and Parents
   http://www.neat-schoolhouse.org/awesome.html
Yahooligans!
   http://www.yahooligans.com/
The Global Classroom
   http://www/globalclassroom.org/projects.html
Index to Internet Lesson Plan Sites for K–12 Educators
   http://falcon.jmu.edu/~ramseyil/lesson.htm
Links to Educational Web Sites
   http://windsor.k12.co.us/links.htm
Internet Resources: Education Resources
   http://www.mcneese.edu/depts/library/int/educ.htm

The internet can help learners explore the world... by providing access to vast resources and information.

Educators can select similar lessons and adapt them for their own use (see Figure 2). Teachers can measure students' progress on the lesson by completing the "technology taxonomy" (Figure 3). This assessment model can be used to chart progress as students perform activities incorporated in the lesson using the Internet to access the World Wide Web.

Another boon to evaluation is the use of the Internet to obtain feedback from other students—worldwide—through collaboration, as well as to provide feedback to others. Teachers can access Web sites that provide instructional guidelines and can visit chat rooms that address Internet use in the classroom (see box, "Internet Resources"). Teachers can use the technology taxonomy in Figure 3 to check their lessons before class to ensure that learners gain exposure to each level of the taxonomy.

ing to Owston (cited in Pea & Roschelle, 1999), the Web can improve learning in three ways: "(a) by appealing to the learning styles of students, presumably increasing their motivation to learn; (b) by offering greater convenience through asynchronous communication; and (c) by providing a fertile ground for developing higher order thinking skills which are required to overcome the general lack of organization of knowledge in the Web" (p. 23). And don't forget the real-world applications: "The Internet can help learners explore the world beyond the classroom by providing access to vast resources and information, promoting scientific inquiry and discovery, and allowing students to communicate with experts" (Honey et al., 1995, p. 5).

Internet for Success

The Internet is an educational tool that can be used to expand learning opportunities and develop higher-order thinking skills. By adapting lessons found on the Web, collaborating with other classrooms, and obtaining feedback from other teachers and students, teachers can greatly expand their instructional strategies. Using a visual checklist such as the technology taxonomy (Figure 3) makes it possible to bring a level of classroom accountability to the application of advanced technology. It also serves as an instrument to measure individualized progress that may be incorporated in quarterly student progress reports to parents. Using the supports available on the Internet (see boxes), teachers have opportunities to develop lessons that provide students with effective instruction and enriched experiences.

"When used effectively, technology applications can support higher order thinking by engaging students in authentic, complex tasks within collaborative learning contexts."

References

Blasi, L., Heinecke, W., Milman, N., & Washington, L. (1999). New directions in the evaluation of the effectiveness of educational technology. The Secretary's Conference on Educational Technology 1999 [online]. Available: http://www.ed.gov/Technology/Techconf/1999/whitepapers/ paper8.html.

Honey, M., McMillan, K., & Spielvogel, R. (1995). Critical issue: Using technology to improve student achievement. The Center for Children and Technology [online]. Available:http://www/ncrel.org/sdrs/areas/issues/methods/technlgy/te800.htm.

Joint Jerome School District #261. (1999). Technology Integration Project: The structure of matter. Available: http://www/d261.id.us/tip/index.htm.

Learning Skills Program, Bloom's Taxonomy [online]. Available: http://www.coun.uvic.ca/learn/program/hndouts/bloom.html.

Pea, R., & Roschelle, J. (1999). Trajectories from today's WWW to a powerful educational infrastructure. Educational Researcher, 26, 22–26.

Angela M. Guptill *(CEC Chapter #402), special education teacher, Shaker Junior High School, North Colonie Central School District, Latham, New York, and candidate, Certificate of Advanced Study in Educational Administration, State University of New York at Albany.*

Address correspondence to the author at 1260 Loudon Road, Apt. #C3, Cohoes, NY 12047 (e-mail: ANG111@aol.com).

This article was made possible in part by a grant from the AAUW Educational Foundation.

Gifted Students Need an Education, Too

Gifted children have the right to an education that takes into account their special needs. Here are suggestions for how to provide it.

Susan Winebrenner

Math time is beginning in Kate Ahlgren's primary grade classroom. Her objective is to teach several concepts relating to the base 10 method of counting and computing. Her first task is to assess her students' previous mastery of these concepts. She plans to allow those students who already have a clear understanding of this week's work to spend their math time applying what they have mastered about base 10 to learning about base 5.

Kate conducts a hands-on assessment by giving all students several tasks to complete with Cuisenaire rods. As she directs students to demonstrate what happens when they count past 10, she watches specifically for students who complete each directed task quickly and correctly. Fifteen minutes later, she has identified four children who clearly need more challenging content for the rest of this week's math work. She assigns a base 10 application task for most of the students to complete with partners and takes those four youngsters aside to briefly teach them the essential elements of base 5.

The four students practice excitedly for a few minutes under Kate's supervision. She explains that they will be working together for the rest of this week on learning about base 5 because that will challenge them. She assures them that all students should be working on challenging learning tasks.

Kate gives the four advanced students several tasks similar to those she has demonstrated. They practice together while she works with the rest of the students for the duration of the math period. Just before her instruction ends, she explains to the whole class that they will notice that not all students are working on the same tasks in math. She reassures them that this is perfectly all right and that her job is to make sure that all students are working on tasks that will help them move forward in their own learning. In this way, Kate makes differentiation the normal and acceptable condition of her classroom. She

knows that when her students know something is all right with her, it will generally be all right with them, too.

Differentiated learning for high-ability students in heterogeneous classrooms is as important as it is for other children, yet the needs of the gifted are often misunderstood. Here are reasons why and suggestions for how teachers and administrators can differentiate the prescribed grade-level curriculum to meet the needs of high-ability students.

Why Provide Differentiated Learning for Gifted Students?

For the past 10 years, students who were not learning successfully were targeted for special attention. Sadly, during that same time, the needs of our most capable students have been overlooked. One reason for this neglect is the ability of gifted students to score high on assessments, which has led to the erroneous assumption that they must be learning. Another reason for ignoring their needs is that many educational leaders have misunderstood research on role modeling to mean that some gifted students should be present in all classrooms to facilitate forward progress for other students. Although students who struggle to learn can benefit from mixed-ability classes, they have plenty of positive role models in students who function well at the appropriate grade level, who are capable but not gifted learners. The discrepancy in learning ability between students who struggle to learn and gifted students is simply too wide to facilitate positive role modeling (Schunk, 1987).

Consider the range of abilities present in most classrooms. Visualize that both extremes of a learning curve are equally far removed from the norm. Students who fail to achieve the designated standards have received unprecedented attention during the past several years. They are identified for special services before they start kindergarten, experience lower student-teacher ratios, and may even have a full-time aide assigned to them for the entire school day. School districts spend much more money educating this population than they designate for the usual per-pupil expenditure.

© SUSIE FITZHUGH

Teachers are expected to create numerous differentiation adjustments for low-achieving students by modifying the amount of work, depth, complexity, and content of the curriculum and by linking students' learning styles and interests to the prescribed learning tasks. Politicians, community members, and teachers avidly follow the progress of these students' learning for evidence that these students are indeed moving forward.

Contrast this with the situation for gifted students, whose natural learning abilities place them as far from average as their classmates who struggle to learn. In September, many of these youngsters could take the assessments that all students in their grade will take at the end of the year and still score at or above the 95th percentile. Simply in the interests of equity, these students are as entitled to receive the same types of differentiation so readily provided to the students who struggle to learn.

To assume that gifted students are learning because they achieve acceptable standards on state assessments is unrealistic. In Colorado, Oregon, and several other states,

educators have realized that the learning progress of gifted students cannot be adequately measured simply because the students meet or exceed minimum standards, so these states have specified learning expectations at exemplary levels. By setting exemplary standards, they can document the learning progress of gifted students.

Does the Promise of Education for All Apply to Gifted Students?

Every school district's mission statement promises its parents that "[a]ll students, including those who are exceptional, are entitled to a public-supported education in which instruction is geared to their needs, interests, and developmental levels" (Reis, Burns, & Renzulli, 1992, p. 3). Unfortunately, those at greatest risk of learning the least in classrooms are those at the top range of ability. Because a sense of confidence comes primarily from being successful at something perceived to be difficult (Rimm, 1990), gifted students who rarely undergo demanding learning experiences may lose confidence in their ability to perform well on challenging learning tasks. Many of these students learn to find the easiest way out, postponing their exposure to challenge in many patterns of underachievement (Rimm, 1990; Schmitz & Galbraith, 1985).

Either we must explain to parents that the promise of the school's mission statement does not apply to high-ability students, or we must commit ourselves to providing these students with appropriate and differentiated learning experiences. Whatever has been designated as suitable for students who are learning at a level commensurate with their age is not equally appropriate for students who learn at levels more typical of students several years older.

What Are the Characteristics and Needs of Gifted Students?

Gifted students learn differently from their classmates in at least five important ways. They learn new material in much less time. They tend to remember what they have learned, making spiral curriculums and reviewing previously mastered concepts a painful experience. They perceive ideas and concepts at more abstract and complex levels than do their peers. They become passionately interested in specific topics and have difficulty moving on to other learning tasks until they feel satisfied that they have learned as much as they possibly can about their passionate interest. Finally, gifted students are able to operate on many levels of concentration simultaneously, so they can monitor classroom activities without paying direct or visual attention to them.

Gifted students have already mastered much of the grade-level work, so they should have opportunities to function at more advanced levels of complexity and depth and to tie their own passionate interests into their schoolwork.

Why Are Many Educators Reluctant to Help Gifted Students?

Many teachers are reluctant to facilitate the needs of gifted students because of the lack of teacher training in this type of differentiation, a concern that other students or parents will accuse them of unfairness, or their belief that providing differentiation for this population is elitist.

Most preservice teachers take at least one course about meeting the needs of special–education students, but few states require teachers to take any courses in how to recognize and teach gifted students. Many teachers assume that gifted kids are highly productive, always complete their work on time, get consistently high grades, and will make it on their own without much assistance. Many educators believe that a student who is unproductive in school could not possibly be gifted.

Such misconceptions about how gifted students do their work are sources of great frustration for the students, their parents, and their teachers. Most teachers in my workshops are surprised when I tell them that gifted students often resist doing their assigned work because it is designed for age-appropriate learners and usually cannot provide the challenge and sense of accomplishment that would keep gifted learners motivated to work.

Another part of the problem is confusion about whether the mandated goals must actually be *taught* to students. Realistically, teachers are only required to demonstrate that all their students have *learned* the designated standards. Students who have already mastered the required content should be allowed to demonstrate their mastery before test-preparation sessions begin and to work on alternative activities because they already know the required content. When teachers learn how to plan and provide these alternative activities routinely to students who demonstrate prior mastery, these students can make progress in their own learning during more of their time in school.

How Can Teachers Provide Differentiation for Gifted Students?

The typical approach to differentiation for gifted students in heterogeneous classes has been to offer extra credit, an expectation that doesn't work because the only students eligible for extra credit are those who often have more than enough earned credit. The practice of offering extra credit should be replaced with approaches that can motivate gifted students to become enthusiastic learners.

Compact the curriculum. The most important needs of gifted students are to have regular opportunities to demonstrate what they already know, to receive full credit for content they have already mastered, and to spend their own learning time on challenging activities that accelerate and enrich the regular curriculum (Reis, Burns, & Renzulli, 1992). Compacting the curriculum can answer these needs.

To ascertain who would benefit from a compacted curriculum for a specific topic, teachers will want to provide interested students with pre-assessment opportunities for all learning activities. Teachers should use the same methods of assessment that they plan to use at the end of a learning unit, including written tests or observed performance on designated tasks. Because the preassessment is open to all students, the learning task itself can identify those who could benefit from the specific differentiated tasks regardless of whether particular students have been designated as gifted.

Students who can demonstrate previous mastery of upcoming content are expected to pay attention to direct instruction only when instruction includes concepts they have not yet mastered. On days when the lesson content is based on what these students have already mastered, they work instead on extension activities provided by the teacher or suggested by the students themselves. They receive full credit for what they have already mastered and earn daily credit for following the teacher's expectations about on-task behavior and productivity and by developing alternative projects and activities.

Design alternative learning experiences. As part of their regular lesson planning, teachers design alternative learning experiences. These provide differentiation opportunities in terms of *content, learning processes, products, learning environment*, and *assessment*.

The *content* is different because it moves students beyond grade-level standards or is connected to students' passionate interests. The *learning processes* called upon are different because they provide depth and complexity appropriate to these students' learning abilities. *Products* differ in that they demonstrate the students' learning at advanced levels, moving beyond typical research activities to the development of individual students' talents and curiosities and the presentation of their findings to appropriate audiences. Sometimes the *learning environment* is also different; students may pursue interests outside the regular classroom, work more independently on self-directed projects, or collaborate with other students. Even the *assessment process* is different because students receive full credit for what they have already mastered and do not have to complete all the work assigned to the rest of the class.

One particularly striking opportunity to provide alternative learning experiences presented itself when I discovered that James, one of my exceptionally gifted 6th graders, was writing a book at home on the anatomy and physiology of the human body. I pretested him and other interested students at the beginning of all language arts, reading, and writing units. James experienced differentiation in *content* because he wrote his book in class, in *learning processes* because he used sophisticated writing techniques, and in *assessment* because his grades for each unit were earned at the time of the pretest rather than at the end of the unit, with an overall grade that included an evaluation of his on-task behavior and project.

Allow differentiated pacing. For a curriculum that cannot be assessed beforehand because it is unfamiliar to all, gifted students work at their own pace to learn the required concepts and spend more time developing an expertise on a related topic of their choice.

Agree on expectations. Teachers and students work together to set up standards for evaluating productivity, behavior, and differentiated products and then agree to these standards in writing. Teachers should arrange to spend time with these students. It is important that gifted students not feel abandoned by the teacher and that they learn that everyone needs help on challenging tasks.

What Can Administrators Do to Facilitate Differentiation for Gifted Students?

Acknowledge the needs of gifted students. Acknowledge that the precedent for differentiation has been firmly set by the differentiation opportunities always available for students who struggle to learn. Because gifted learners are just as far removed from average as are children with learning problems, the differentiation that gifted students need is highly defensible and equitable.

Facilitate gifted education training for staff. Any strategies teachers learn for the benefit of their gifted students are applicable to many other students and tend to raise the learning bar for all students. One strategy, for example, is to allow students to get credit for an entire assignment by answering correctly at least four of the five most difficult problems first. This challenge motivates many students to listen more carefully to instructions so they can also qualify.

Investigate cluster grouping. Look into the practice of cluster grouping for gifted students. Cluster grouping is the practice of purposefully placing four to six gifted students together in an otherwise heterogeneous class. Their teacher must have some training in how to differentiate the curriculum for students who demonstrate previous mastery or who can learn new content faster than their classmates. Studies have demonstrated that cluster grouping can lead to improved achievement for many

students at all levels of learning ability (Gentry, 1999; Winebrenner & Devlin, 1996).

Communicate your expectations. Make clear your pledge that all students, including the most capable, will be able to learn something new and challenging every day. Clarify your commitment to the goal that all students will be expected to make continuous progress in their own learning. To that end, expect gifted students to demonstrate competencies that exceed those designated as basic.

Keep the Promise

Parents of gifted learners have a right to expect that schools will fulfill the promise made to all students that children will have consistent and daily opportunities for challenging learning experiences and will demonstrate continuous forward progress in their learning. This expectation requires providing gifted students with differentiation of the regular curriculum. To complacently accept their performance at regular competency levels is to deny their equal right to an appropriate education.

References

Gentry, M. L. (1999). *Promoting student achievement and exemplary classroom practices through cluster grouping: A research-based alternative to heterogeneous elementary classrooms.* Storrs, CT: National Research Center on the Gifted and Talented.

Reis, S. M., Burns, D. E., & Renzulli, J. S. (1992). *Curriculum compacting: The complete guide to modifying the regular curriculum for high ability students.* Mansfield Center, CT: Creative Learning Press.

Rimm, S. (1990). *How to parent so children will learn.* Watertown, WI: Apple Publishing.

Schunk, D. H. (1987). Peer models and children's behavioral change. *Review of Educational Research, 57,* 149–174.

Schmitz, C., & Galbraith, J. (1985). *Managing the social and emotional needs of the gifted.* Minneapolis, MN: Free Spirit Publishing.

Winebrenner, S., & Devlin, B. (1996). *Cluster grouping of gifted students: How to provide full-time services on a part-time budget.* Reston, VA: ERIC Clearinghouse on Disabilities and Gifted Education (ERIC Digest Document Reproduction Service No. 397618).

Susan Winebrenner is an educational consultant and author of *Teaching Gifted Kids in the Regular Classroom* (Free Spirit Publishing, 2000). She may be reached at P.O. Box 398, Brooklyn, MI 49230–0398 (e-mail: ecsfirst @aol.com)

UNIT 11
Transition

Unit Selections

Key Points to Consider

- What are some of the collaborative efforts needed to help students with severe disabilities make the transition from a sheltered setting to the outside world?

- What services are needed to make the transition smoother from high school to postsecondary programs for students with disabilities?

- What are the eight curricular components of a self-determination curriculum?

 **Links: www.dushkin.com/online/**
These sites are annotated in the World Wide Web pages.

Building Partnerships Between Centers for Independent Living and Schools
http://cdrc.ohsu.edu/csd1/home/Projects_at_the_Center/Networks/BUILDING_PARTNERSHIPS

National Center on Secondary Education and Transition
http://www.ncset.org

Special educational services are now required by law for students from the completion of their public school education through age 21 if they have a diagnosed condition of disability. The U.S. Individuals with Disabilities Education Act (IDEA), when it was reauthorized in 1997, made transitional services mandatory. These additional benefits for students with exceptional conditions are to help them transfer from their relatively protected life as students into the more aggressive world of work, driven by forces such as money and power. The services that the educational system needs to give to students with disabilities to help them prepare for the world of work start with an assessment of their interests, abilities, and aptitudes for different types of work. Career counseling about what they need to do to prepare for such employment, and its feasibility, comes next. Counselors must remember to allow students to dream, to think big, and to have optimistic visions of themselves. They also need to inculcate the idea that persistence pays: It takes a lot of little steps to achieve a goal.

The implementation of transitional services has been slow. The U.S. government defined transitional services as outcome-oriented, coordinated activities designed to move students with disabilities from school to activities such as college, vocational training, integrated employment, supported employment, adult education, adult services, independent living, and community participation. Choices are not either/or but rather multiple: to help students with disabilities move from school to successful adulthood. While some students may only be able to achieve partial independence and supported employment, others may achieve professional degrees and complete self-sufficiency.

Every student with a disability should have an individualized transition plan (ITP) added to his or her individualized education plan (IEP) by age 16 the upper limit for beginning transition planning. Transitional services are more difficult to design than educational plans because of the nearly unlimited possibilities for the rest of one's life compared to the defined academic subjects it is possible to learn while in school.

The first step is to determine an appropriate individualized transition plan (ITP) for each unique student. Many teachers, special educators, vocational counselors, and employment mentors (job coaches) are not sure what kind of vocational preparation should be given in the public schools or when. Should children with disabilities start planning for their futures in elementary school, in middle school, in high school, throughout their education, or just before they finish school? Should there be a trade-off between academic education and vocational education for these students? Should each student's vocational preparation be planned to meet the kind of needs and abilities of the individual, with no general rules about the wheres and whens of transitional services? Should students with disabilities be encouraged to seek out postsecondary education? The choices are legion. The need to rule out some possibilities and select others is frightening. Nobody on a team wants to make a mistake. Often the preferences of the student are quite different from the goals of parents, teachers, counselors, or significant others. Compromises are necessary but may not please everyone, or anyone.

The transition to the world of work may take the form of supported employment (mobile work crew, clustered or enclave placement, on-site training and supervision by a job coach, group providing a specific service product) or sheltered employment (in a workshop). Many students with disabilities can make a transition from school to competitive employment. If they will eventually work side-by-side with nondisabled coworkers, they may need transitional services such as assertiveness training, conflict resolution, negotiating skills, and personal empowerment counseling.

Just a few years ago, adults with disabilities were expected to live in institutions or with parents, siblings, or extended family members. This is no longer considered appropriate. Each individual with a disability should be encouraged to be as autonomous as possible in adulthood. Self-sufficiency is enhanced by providing education in life skills such as meal preparation and cleanup, home deliveries (for example, mail) and delivery pickups (for example, trash), using money and paying bills, making household repairs, and following home safety precautions.

The transition from noncommunity participant to fully participating member of society requires ITP modifications quite different from IEP academic goals. Students with exceptional conditions may need more than the usual amount of assistance in learning to drive a car or to use public transportation. They need to know how to read maps and schedules. They must be able to assert their right to vote in secret (for instance, ballot in braille or computerized for their software) and to marry, divorce, reproduce, sue, defend themselves, or even run for public office. They should know social conventions (greetings, conversation skills, manners), grooming fashions, and clothing styles. They deserve to have the same access to health settings, religious locales, social activities, and information services (telephone, television, computer networks) as do persons without disabilities.

The first article in this unit offers insights into the collaborative efforts required of administrators, staff, regular and special education teachers, employment specialists, and students with severe disabilities. The authors emphasize the need for rigorous employment-training programs. Students who lack communication skills and academic skills pose special challenges. The development of partnerships with potential employers of disabled students in the area surrounding the school can make each ITP voyage a smoother sail.

In the second article, Jean Lehmann, Timothy Gray Davies, and Kathleen Laurin report on the transition needs of students with disabilities who go on to postsecondary institutions. Thirty-five such students attended a summit to discuss what would best meet their requirements in higher education. The ideas expressed most frequently were for more understanding of their disabilities, more services, more financial resources, and more self-advocacy training.

The last article in this transition unit deals with self-determination. This is one of the most important considerations for any ITP, yet one that is often forgotten as experts (parents, teachers, counselors, and so on) debate what would be most appropriate for a student with a disability. This selection describes a project whose goal was to promote each student's self-determination.

Transition Planning for Students with Severe Disabilities:

Policy Implications for the Classroom

CHRISTY HOLTHAUS STUART AND STEPHEN W. SMITH

The reauthorization of the Individuals with Disabilities Education Act Amendments (IDEA, 1997) is the cornerstone for disability legislation entitling students to a free appropriate public education. Within the law, students with disabilities are afforded an Individualized Education Program (IEP) that provides an appropriate education in the least restrictive environment. The reauthorization of IDEA included several specific components addressing transition issues (e.g., career planning, job training, functional skill development) beginning at age 14 for students receiving special education services. The transition components for students with disabilities included (a) a coordinated set of activities (e.g., real work experience) specific to the individual, (b) activities for movement from school to postschool environments (e.g., supported employment, adult services), (c) assessment of students' individual needs, (d) identification of student preferences and interests, and (e) development of employment objectives.

The IDEA transition components are intended for all students with disabilities; however, some professionals may disregard students with more severe disabilities, such as profound mental retardation and deaf-blindness. Under the Rehabilitation Act (1973), when students with severe disabilities leave school, they are entitled to continued services for supported living and employment services. The Rehabilitation Act promotes individuals with severe disabilities and their rights to gainful employment. Specifically, the Act defines *a person with a severe disability* as an individual whose ability to function independently in family or community or whose ability to become gainfully employed is limited due to the severity of his or her disability. Both the IDEA and the Rehabilitation Act are equally important in providing support, such as supported employment and educational training programs, for individuals with disabilities, yet for individuals with severe disabilities there continue to be significant problems.

Individuals with severe disabilities have unique learning characteristics, such as difficulty in generalizing learned skills to new work situations. Further, individuals with more significant disabilities learn more slowly, which in turn means that they learn less and have difficulty generalizing learned skills to other settings, putting together isolated activities that make a skill, and maintaining what they have learned over time (Ryndak & Alper, 1996). These learning characteristics may lead some people to believe that per-

sons with severe disabilities are incapable of learning necessary job skills. Consequently, persons with severe disabilities are caught in a difficult cycle. They have difficulty learning the job skills, resulting in perceptions of being incapable of successful employment, which causes them to be further stigmatized and reduces the possibility that employers will hire them. Despite the legislative support that has evolved over the years, outcome data such as long-term employment continue to show poor results for individuals with severe disabilities.

Educator's General Role

Teachers of secondary students with severe disabilities play a significant role in developing and implementing effective transition plans to help students plan for the future and obtain gainful employment. For example, a student may indicate that following school, he or she wishes to live in an apartment with friends and have a job that involves sports. The student's interests can be gathered from a variety of sources, such as student, parents, and family members, and used as a stepping stone to prepare the student for the skills necessary to achieve future goals. Specifically, exposing the student to a variety of sport jobs (e.g., greeter/usher using a communication device or an equipment manager paired with a peer) and encouraging the student to develop goals assists the student in eventually maintaining employment and living as independently as possible. Because of poor outcomes, such as low full-time employment rates, and decreased competitive wages and hours, policymakers need knowledge and direction from practitioners at the implementation level (i.e., school-based vocational programs) to compose effective policies that, in turn, promote effective practice.

Promoting Employment Skills Through Transition Planning

Secondary educators must do their part in facilitating a meaningful transition for their students with severe disabilities to create a link between school setting services and services provided in the postschool employment setting. McDonnell, Mathot-Buckner, and Ferguson (1996) emphasized the need for an effective and rigorous employment-training program that would identify the skills students need to participate successfully in the postschool employment setting. Students need

- work experience and work-related behaviors,
- work interests and preferences, and
- supports necessary to ensure success in employment settings.

Because common work and work-related behaviors are necessary for success in every job, the goal for every student during high school is to develop employment skills (e.g., manage one's time, stay on task, complete step-by-step directions), communicate effectively, demonstrate social and interpersonal skills, and tend to personal hygiene. The behaviors that accompany the skills are paired with a successful transition for the student with disabilities.

Employment training must incorporate a job sampling process that provides students with the basis for determining their work interests and preferences. Exposure to a wide range of employment options is a key component for the future job matching process (Chadsey-Rusch & Heal, 1995). Students with severe disabilities who may lack adequate communication and academic skills pose a special challenge because the information traditionally gathered (student interests and preferences) regarding career alternatives must be gathered from sources other than the student (e.g., parents, peers, service coordinators from agencies).

Identifying the nature and amount of supports depends on the individual needs of the student, but coordinating the supports to be as least restrictive as possible is the challenge. During the employment-training phase, a variety of supports can be tested. For example, a student with severe disabilities may respond more effectively with supports from a peer rather than a paraprofessional. This information may be used for future interactions with service agencies that use peers on the job versus job coaches from an agency.

Obtaining meaningful employment is crucial to the successful transition of students from school to community/employment life. This outcome is achieved most effectively when an educational program is designed to develop skills and routines that better prepare individuals with disabilities for life after school. It is up to secondary educators to develop and implement meaningful training programs that equip their students with skills and prepare them for employment and community involvement outside the educational arena. Several guidelines are recommended for secondary education teachers to follow while developing individual transition programs:

- Promote individual choice and self-determination activities (e.g., self-directed IEPs);
- include a variety of participants who have contact with the student (special education and general education) in the development of the transition IEP;
- develop partnerships with community establishments and potential job training or employment sites;
- extend agency collaboration as part of the transition process;

- make significant changes to traditional prevocational training programs to include job training in natural work environments and to include all students, especially those with the most severe disabilities in the program; and
- incorporate placement models at the secondary level to ease the transition to postschool employment activities (individual placement model, clustered placement model, mobile crew model, and the entrepreneurial model).

Summary

The increase in responsibility for educators to collaborate and develop effective transition plans should also empower educators to become stakeholders in the transition process (Kohler, 1998). As stakeholders, the secondary educators should be encouraged to

- participate in program-level planning;
- serve on curriculum development teams;
- participate in teacher or family training, technical assistance, and staff development activities; and
- play a role in strategic planning and resource allocation.

Although transition planning is to be included on a student's IEP, all professionals, otherwise known as stakeholders (general education teachers, special education teachers, transition specialists, employment specialists), need to be prepared to participate in an ongoing process that begins in secondary schools and continues in the postschool environment. This process needs to be collaborative in nature. Feedback from stakeholders proves to be an effective tool in making changes or improvements to current practices. The expertise of those individuals at the grass roots level, in this case the educators themselves, should prove to be a source of knowledge and information that will drive best practice in transition planning.

References

Chadsey-Rusch, J., & Heal, L. (1995). Building consensus from transition experts on social integration outcomes and interventions. *Exceptional Children, 62(3),* 165–187.

Individuals with Disabilities Education Act Amendments of 1997, 20 U.S.C. § 1401 (26).

Kohler, P. D. (1998). Implementing a transition perspective of education. In F. R. Rusch & J. G. Chadsey (Eds.), *Beyond high school: Transition from school to work* (pp. 179–205). Boston: Wadsworth.

McDonnell, J., Mathot-Buckner, C., & Ferguson, B. (1996). *Transition programs for students with moderate/severe disabilities.* Baltimore: Brookes.

Rehabilitation Act of 1973, 29 U.S.C. § 701 *et seq.*

Ryndak, D. L., & Alper, S. (1996). *Curriculum content for students with moderate and severe disabilities in inclusive settings.* Boston: Allyn & Bacon.

Christy Holthaus Stuart, MS, is a doctoral candidate in the Department of Special Education at the University of Florida. **Stephen W. Smith**, PhD, is a professor in the Department of Special Education at the University of Florida. Address: Christy Holthaus Smart, Dept. of Special Education, G315 Norman Hall, University of Florida, Gainesville, FL 32611.

From *Intervention in School and Clinic,* March 2002, pp. 234–236. © 2002 by The Council for Exceptional Children. Reprinted by permission.

Listening to Student Voices About Postsecondary Education

Jean P. Lehmann • Timothy Gray Davies • Kathleen M. Laurin

Every year an increasing number of students with disabilities enter postsecondary education. Many of these students fail to successfully compete academically or simply leave before they complete their planned programs of study (Fairweather & Shaver, 1991; Wagner, 1989). In an effort to change the status quo, one community college and a university school of education program formed a collaborative support team to:

- Identify and systematically eliminate barriers to postsecondary education.
- Improve students' potential for having successful postsecondary experiences.

"Aiming for the Future," the project described here, is housed in a Midwestern community college in a rural area.

Using a systems-change model borrowed from Fullan (1993) that emphasizes the importance of listening to and acting on the ideas expressed by those most likely to be affected by change efforts, the collaborative support team sought information from the students' perspective. We asked students with disabilities currently attending postsecondary programs at the community college and university what they felt they needed to succeed. The process used to elicit these students' perceptions and ideas, which resulted in plans developed by the support team, is the focus of this article.

A Summit on "Aiming for the Future"

We invited 35 college students with a variety of disabilities—including hearing impairment, deafness, low vision, blindness, learning disabilities, traumatic brain injury, cerebral palsy, and paraplegia and quadriplegia—to attend a half-day focus group, which we called a *summit*. We asked the students to give us their perspectives on their personal and academic needs, barriers to their success, their support needs, and their visions for their future.

Using a nonthreatening group process designed to elicit a wealth of information in a short time, we ran-domly placed the students in seven groups of five people each. We then asked each group to discuss questions aimed at helping students identify the barriers they have experienced as they attempt to successfully complete their educational and career goals. Students considered barriers encountered with admissions, financial assistance, and classes. They were asked to answer the following three questions:

- What are the most substantial barriers to your college experience?
- Are there special problems for students whose disability is not identified until posthigh school?
- What problems are encountered when making the transition from one college/university setting to another or into a job?

As students discussed their experiences, it became evident that the first question was central to understanding the realities and hopes of students receiving postsecondary training. Students perceived similar problems regardless of when their disability was identified, their year in college, or if they had entered the job market.

Next, we asked students to browse through magazines we placed on their table and select pictures representing barriers to their success in their current postsecondary institutions. We also asked them to select a second group of pictures representing strategies to support them in reaching their academic and career goals. Finally, we asked them to arrange these pictures to form a collage communicating their thoughts and ideas. Each group chose a spokesperson who interpreted the collage to the entire summit audience.

Student Barriers

As the students explained the experiences represented in their collages, four dominant themes emerged (see "Theme" boxes).

1. The lack of understanding and acceptance concerning disabilities in general, and their disabilities in

particular, on the part of people in general, fellow students, staff, and even faculty.

2. The lack of adequate services to assist in tackling academic and nonacademic responsibilities.
3. The lack of sufficient financial resources and the knowledge of how to acquire them, to live a more self-sufficient life.
4. The lack of self-advocacy skills and training needed to live independently.

Lack of Understanding and Acceptance

All the student groups emphasized two elements: the lack of acceptance and the lack of understanding of those with disabilities. One group's members strikingly portrayed how they felt about this lack of acceptance by placing a large picture of Tom Hanks in a trendy two-piece dress suit in its collage. Rather than leave the familiar face in place, however, they replaced it with a head disproportionately smaller. According to students, this picture "represents for us the small-minded people, small-minded students on campus; and every once in a while you run into a professor like that, too."

One member of the "summit" looks through magazines and selects pictures representing barriers to her success in her current postsecondary institution.

As groups shared their collages with other summit participants, they elaborated on their frustrations. For ex-

ample, another group shared that this lack of understanding and acceptance often resulted in a "crash and burn effect with the teachers; they don't understand you, and it gives you a sense of being out of order." Particularly troubling to students was the perception they had that society generally viewed disability to be associated with incompetence. Typifying this perception is the remark of one student, who stated: "Because of the problems we have, a lot of times people get mad that we are not doing things the way they do it and you always want to say, 'Yes, I will do it!'"

Theme 1. The lack of understanding and acceptance concerning disabilities by fellow students, staff, and faculty

- Small-mindedness.
- Disability viewed as incompetence.
- Instructor frustration.
- Instructors can damage students.

Several groups of students expressed the difficulties they experience when instructors are not knowledgeable or experienced in modifying classroom environments, instructional strategies, or grading methods, For example, one group noted:

> We have to deal with professors, but they don't deal with us. They deal with the norm, and some are frustrated with us.

Another student expanded on this remark by saying: "Not only do we have a problem, we then have to alleviate accommodation anxiety [of instructors]." Perhaps the most poignant remark relative to this first barrier was from a student who stated:

> Some teachers and TA's [teaching assistants] don't have an understanding of students' needs. They cause damage to students with disabilities through their lack of understanding. It makes me think sometimes, so who has the real problem? Me or them?

Lack of Adequate Services

The second barrier identified by the students was the lack of adequate services available to assist them in tackling both academic and nonacademic challenges. These summit students realized that they were not alone in needing academic support outside the postsecondary classroom. Many of these students perceived that college educators and college-services staffs needed information, training, and ongoing support themselves to effectively teach students with disabilities. Perhaps that is why students expressed such disappointment in their traditional academic support laboratories, where tutoring in math, reading, writing, and computer literacy skills are available to all students. Their disappointments stem from the examples mentioned previously—that the staff and tutors knew little about these students' disabilities and thus could not communicate with them effectively.

Theme 2. The lack of adequate services to assist in tackling academic and non-academic responsibilities

- Teachers and support staff need information, training, and ongoing support themselves to effectively teach students with disabilities.
- Documentation of disability is not forwarded to postsecondary institutions.
- Students are unable to acquire medical and dental services because communication was difficult.
- Students felt need for increased access to transportation, buildings, and adaptive computers.

Further, students indicated that they literally were "searching for services" that were more appropriate to their needs but were beyond the scope of the support traditionally provided on campus. Examples of these needs included having adequate, reliable transportation to campuses, as well as on campus, and the need for networking and mentoring so that students could "learn from each other and reach their potential."

Theme 3: Lack of sufficient financial resources and the knowledge of how to acquire them to be self-sufficient

- Need reliable income to move out on their own and become more self-sufficient.
- Less on-campus opportunity to work compared to other students.
- Feeling insecure in their knowledge of time and money management.

Disabilities documentation was a major issue for many students. High school records of special education services received were not routinely given to students or passed along to the postsecondary institutions. Without this documentation, students were faced with several dilemmas, including having to prove their eligibility for postsecondary services. Often, students felt themselves to be unable to explain fully or even identify strategies previous educators had found to be helpful for enhancing their learning processes. Thus, students in several groups pointed out the need for more assessment opportunities at the postsecondary level so that incoming students could learn more about the extent of their disability and what assistance the support laboratories can provide on

an individual and group basis. Students reported that "disability changes the way you see life," but they needed to learn the accommodations and compensatory skills that might enhance their success.

It was not only the lack of academic support services and inadequate knowledge of their individual files that these students decried. For example, some students were upset at being unable to obtain service at local medical centers where neither doctors nor their staff could understand even basic signing, thus causing frustration and anxiety during examinations. Students said that there was no systematic career-services network to assist them in obtaining full-time employment. One student shared his appreciation for a counselor who was well connected with community employers; but when the counselor left, the contacts seemed to disappear.

Finally, students discussed the need for environmental support on campus and in the community so that they could more easily manage access to dependable transportation, buildings, restrooms, and adaptive computer technology on their campuses and at their banks.

Need for Financial Resources

The third barrier, insufficient financial resources, was a universal concern among students at the summit. They knew they needed a steady, reliable income for food, clothing, housing, transportation, and medical insurance so they could "move out on our own and be self-sufficient." Yet they were not sure they had the knowledge base to independently manage their time and budget their money effectively.

In addition, students' postsecondary experiences had taught them that, as students with disabilities, their opportunities for employment to work-study positions or student assistantships were limited and not on a par with their peers without disabilities. Further, the consequences of their disability often precluded the possibility of employment due to complicating factors of Social Security Disability Income (SSDI), Medicaid, or Vocational Rehabilitation Services. Often students' time was limited by constraints related to their disability, such as time scheduled for tutoring sessions and the need to reserve as much time as possible to studying.

Need for Self-advocacy Skills

The fourth barrier is a theme unto itself, yet is also a thread connecting the first three barriers. The students feel they lack self-advocacy skills. A constant cry from each of the groups at the summit was the need for respect: from their peers, their community, their professors, and from themselves. Students, however, also indicated that they had no training or experience in describing their disability to others. They wanted to learn how to advocate for themselves; to help educate their college community;

to be more assertive in gaining knowledge of their disability; to be forceful in communicating their strengths and weaknesses, abilities and inabilities; and to gain the necessary strength and courage to ask for what they needed to be able to succeed. In learning to advocate for themselves, they would continue to deepen their own self-understanding, increase their self-esteem and self-worth, and begin to develop "a positive attitude to live life to its potential!"

Theme 4. The lack of self-advocacy skills and training to live independently

- Need to gain respect from the college community.
- Need to learn to advocate for themselves.
- Need to be more assertive in gaining knowledge of their disability.
- Need to deepen their own self-understanding, self-esteem, and self-worth.

Visions for the Future

Although students expressed enormous frustration with the multiple barriers they encounter, they were positive in their outlook as they begin the "journey" to their futures. One student expressed this optimism by telling the group, "The dream begins as soon as you open the door." In describing their visions for the future, the students' statements signified the importance of self-advocacy skills. One group related that the key to breaking free of barriers was having "confidence, family, self-esteem, strength, and support." Another student stated that each day, "you get up in the morning, and you have to encourage yourself somehow." Other students discussed the importance of surrounding themselves with a supportive network of people. One student stated, "I didn't want to go to school, but I found out [that] more learning and knowledge make life easier."

Self-responsibility, interdependence, realistic goals, self-acceptance, positive self-esteem, knowledge of disability, communication skills, the ability to self-advocate, a supportive network of people, and a positive attitude—these were the elements that defined the students' perspective on self-determination.

Recommendations for Eliminating Barriers

In response to students' statements, the postsecondary education support team has planned a three-pronged approach that supports students, secondary teachers, and postsecondary faculty. The plan also addresses larger institutional issues regarding receptivity to recruiting and serving students with disabilities (see box, "Tips for Eliminating Barriers").

The support team provides tuition waivers (using federally granted funds) for students who need financial assistance. The team also provides students with more intensive academic and nonacademic support. Specifically, the support team holds workshops throughout the state to recruit students with disabilities and inform them about higher education requirements. These workshops, for students, secondary teachers, and parents, are held on college and community college campuses. The workshops also help students gain insight into their responsibilities as college students, help them explore their learning styles, and provide students with self-determination training.

Tips for Eliminating Barriers

- Ask students to conduct workshops that describe the nature of various disabilities to faculty and staff.
- Provide staff development to postsecondary faculty regarding adaptations and accommodations they can implement.
- Reward faculty who are willing to adapt instruction to address the learning needs of students.
- Evaluate transportation availability to campus and on campus.
- Inform students about the documentation requirements of local postsecondary institutions before their senior year at high school.
- Identify potential financial resources for students entering into postsecondary settings.
- Teach high school students time and money management skills.
- Tour the college campus with interested students during transition planning.
- Provide summer classes addressing compensatory strategies on college campuses for high school students interested in obtaining a postsecondary education.
- Role-play with students ways of communicating to college faculty about students' disability and learning needs.
- Encourage networking between college students via focus groups, student meetings, and information workshops.

The support team also invites high school and college faculty members to training sessions regarding laws and accommodations for students with disabilities. To remind and assist institutions of higher education about the level of their commitment to teaching students with disabilities, the team is developing an evaluation instrument for postsecondary faculty members to use. The instrument addresses accessibility in terms of attitudes and architecture of many aspects of higher education: the college admissions office, career center, housing office, library, financial aid office, and student centers.

To gather more information, the team holds focus groups with community members, secondary teachers, and families. We hope to learn more about the specific types of support that these stakeholders perceive they need.

Final Thoughts

Students' perceptions solicited in the summit are consistent with research reported in recent years. Students in studies by Finn (1998) reported that receiving accommodations in courses and during testing were most beneficial to their success in postsecondary education. Finn (1998) concluded, as a result of these findings, that both staff development and student training in self-advocacy were therefore necessary (see box, "Why Involve Students?"). Research regarding faculty attitudes confirms that there is, in fact, a lack of understanding on the part of instructors relative to issues of disabilities (Hill, 1996; West et al., 1993).

One member from each group presented a collage communicating his or her thoughts and ideas to the entire "summit" audience.

What is unusual about the "Aiming for the Future" project? From the beginning, the support team solicited students' concerns and then designed the project's interventions in accordance with project goals *and* student responses generated during the focus group activities. This approach to changing systems is consistent with national efforts to increase self-determination of students with disabilities.

Clearly, it is futile to create new student support services—or even enhance existing services—without gathering the opinions of all stakeholders, particularly students' opinions (Fullan, 1993). Excluding students from opportunities to articulate their needs is a recipe for failure. Not only do students lose a sense of ownership of the services (Smith, et al., 1995), but they also miss opportunities to practice self-determining skills, such a problem-solving and advocating for themselves (see box, "Why Involve Students?"). As noted by the students participating in the "Aiming for the Future" project, having a disability should not prevent you from having dreams and "going the distance."

Why Involve Students?

- *Increases knowledge of and ownership of the services offered.* According to Smith, Edelen-Smith, & Stodden (1995), excluding key participants in planning processes may increase resistance to ideas and decrease cooperation.
- *Enhances students' future success.* Reiff, Gerber, and Ginsberg (1997) found that successful adults with learning disabilities sought to and exerted control over their lives by making decisions about events in their lives. Further, Ward (1988) suggested that people who take control of their lives and can identify future goals will have greater future success.
- *Fosters high self-esteem.* Students whose opinions are valued, listened to, and acted upon become equal partners in the service delivery, thus increasing their sense of accomplishment and dignity (Lovett, 1996).
- *Provides students with opportunities to practice self-determination skills.* In a study by Lehmann, Bassett, and Sands (1999), students lack opportunities to engage in activities that facilitate the development of self-determination skills, such as articulating ideas, expressing needs, and acquiring leadership skills. Powers and her colleagues (1996) concluded that self-determination skills are learned and must be bolstered through application.
- *Encourages responsibility and decision-making skills.* Wehmeyer (1993) found that students who did not have opportunities to practice making choices tended to avoid making decisions and accepting responsibility.

References

Fairweather, J. S., & Shaver, D. M. (1991). Making the transition to postsecondary education and training. *Exceptional Children, 57,* 264–267.

Finn, L. (1998). Student's perceptions of beneficial LD accommodations and services at the postsecondary level. *Journal of Postsecondary Education and Disability, 13*, 46–67.

Fullan, M. (1993). *Change forces: Probing the depths of educational reform.* London: The Falmer Press.

Hill, J. L. (1996). Speaking out: Perceptions of students with disabilities regarding adequacy of services and willingness of faculty to make accommodations. *Journal of Postsecondary Education and Disability, 12*, 22–43.

Lehmann, J. P., Bassett, D. S., & Sands, D. J. (1999). Students' participation in transition-related actions: A qualitative study. *Remedial and Special Education, 20*, 160–169.

Lovett, H. (1996). *Learning to listen: Positive approaches and people with difficult behavior.* Baltimore: Paul H. Brookes.

Powers, L. E., Wilson, R., Matuszewski, J., Phillips, A., Rein, C., Schumacher, D., & Gensert, J. (1996). Facilitating adolescent self-determination: What does it take? In D. J. Sands, & M. L. Wehmeyer (Eds.), *Self-determination across the life span: Independence and choice for people with disabilities* (pp. 257–284). Baltimore: Paul H. Brookes.

Reiff, H. B., Gerber, P. J., & Ginsberg, R. (1997). *Exceeding expectations: Successful adults with learning disabilities.* Austin, TX: PRO-ED.

Smith, G. J., Edelen-Smith, P. J., & Stodden, R. A. (1995). How to avoid the seven pitfalls of systematic planning. A school and community plan for transition. *Teaching Exceptional Children, 27*(4), 42–47.

Wagner, M. (1989). *Youth with disabilities during transition: An overview of descriptive findings from the National Longitudinal Transition Study.* Menlo Park, CA: The National Longitudinal Study of Special Education Students.

Ward, M. J. (1998). *The many facets of self-determination: Transition summary.* Washington, DC: National Information Center for Children and Youth with Handicaps.

Wehmeyer, M. (1993). Perceptual and psychological factors in career decision-making of adolescents with and without cognitive disabilities. *Career Development for Exceptional Individuals, 16*, 135–146.

West, M., Kregel, J., Getzel, E. E., Zhu, M., Ipsen, S. M., & Martin, E. D. (1993). Beyond Section 504: Satisfaction and empowerment of students with disabilities in higher education. *Exceptional Children, 59*, 456–467.

Jean P. Lehmann, *Associate Professor,* **Timothy Gray** Davies, *Associate Professor, School of Education, Colorado State University, Fort Collins, Colorado;* **Kathleen M. Laurin,** *Project Coordinator, Department of Health and Human Services, The University of Northern Colorado, Greeley, Colorado.*

Address correspondence to Jean P. Lehmann, School of Education, Colorado State University, Fort Collins, CO 80523-1588 (e-mail: lehmann@CAHS. colostate.edu).

Preparation of this article was funded in part through the support of Grant HO78C60015 from the U.S. Department of Education, Office of Special Education and Rehabilitation Services. The contents of this article do not necessarily reflect the policies of the funding agency.

Choosing a Self-Determination Curriculum

PLAN *for the Future*

David W. Test • Meagan Karvonen • Wendy M. Wood • Diane Browder • Bob Algozzine

Self-determination. In almost every special education publication, conference, or inservice workshop, someone mentions "self-determination." The popularity of this term is not surprising, considering the urgent need to improve postsecondary outcomes for students with disabilities (see box, "What Does the Literature Say About Self-Determination?"). Self-determination is certainly a factor in the success of all students.

This article describes a project to help educators improve the self-determination of students with disabilities. We conducted this project with support from the U.S. Department of Education, Office of Special Education Programs, to gather, evaluate, and disseminate information about curriculum/assessment materials and strategies on promoting self-determination. In addition, we suggest a process other educators can use to select materials and curricula.

The Self-Determination Synthesis Project

The Self-Determination Synthesis Project (SDSP) has the objective of synthesizing and disseminating the knowledge base and best practices related to self-determination for students with disabilities. To this end, the purpose of the project was to improve, expand, and accelerate the use of this knowledge by the professionals who serve children and youth with disabilities; parents who rear, educate, and support their children with disabilities; and the students themselves.

We found 60 curricula designed to promote self-determination skills.

As part of the SDSP effort, we have conducted a comprehensive literature review of self-determination interventions research, visited school systems that exhibited exemplary self-determination outcomes, and gathered and catalogued published self-determination curricula. For more information on our exemplary sites and literature review visit our Web site at http://www.uncc.edu/sdsp.

Existing Self-Determination Curricula

To identify existing self-determination curricula, we reviewed the literature, conducted Web searches, asked experts in the area, and advertised in newsletters and at conferences. As a result, we found 60 curricula designed to promote self-determination skills. Table 1 shows a sampling of these curricula; other reviews are available from the authors (see Table 1). We compiled the name of each curriculum, the publisher, telephone number, and cost information for each curriculum. Further, we identified, for each curriculum, which of the eight self-determination components the curriculum included, based on the most commonly identified components of self-determination found in the literature (e.g., Field & Hoffman 1994; Mithaug, Campeau, & Wolman, 1992; Ward, 1988; Wehmeyer, 1996). The eight curricular components are as follows:

- Choice/decision-making.
- Goal setting/attainment.
- Problem-solving.
- Self-evaluation, observation, and reinforcement.
- Self-advocacy.
- Inclusion of student-directed individualized education programs (IEP).
- Relationships with others.
- Self-awareness.

Finally, we listed the materials included in each curriculum and the appropriate student audience identified by the author, and noted whether the curriculum had been field-tested.

Table 1. A Sample of Self-Determination Curricula and Components
(For a complete listing, see http://www.uncc.edu/sdsp)

TITLE	Choice/ Decision Making	Goal Setting/ Attainment	Problem Solving	Self Eval	Self Advocacy	IEP Plan	Relationships w/Others	Self Awareness
Next S.T.E.P.: Student transition and educational planning **Product Info:** Pro-Ed (800) 897-3202 Price: $144	X X	X		X		X		X
Contents: Video, Teacher manual, Student workbook Audience: Transition aged students with and without disabilities, and students at-risk Other: Adjustment, Employment, Education, Housing, Daily living, Community *Field Test* X								
Self-advocacy strategy for education and transition planning **Product Info:** Edge Enterprises (785) 749-1473 Price: $15	X X				X	X		X
Contents: Instructor's manual Audience: Audience: Primary and secondary students with mild disabilities, and high risk students Other: Employment, Education, Housing, Daily living, Personal, Community *Field Test* X								
Take action: Making goals happen [Choice-maker] **Product Info:** Sopris West Inc. (800) 547-6747 Price: $95	X X	X		X				
Contents: Teacher's manual, Reproducible lesson masters, Video Audience: Not specified Other: Adjustment, Employment, Education, Housing, Daily living, Personal, Community *Field Test* X								
TAKE CHARGE for the future **Product Info:** OHSU Center on Self-Determination (503) 232-9154 Price: $45	X X	X		X	X	X		X
Contents: Student guide, Companion guide, Parent guide, Class guide Audience: Sophomores and juniors with disabilities Other: Adjustment, Employment, Education, Housing, Daily living, Personal, Community *FieldTest* X								
Whose future is it anyway? A student-directed transition process **Product Info:** The Arc National Headquarters (888) 368-8009 Price $20	X X	X		X	X	X		X
Contents: Student manual with coach's guide Audience: Middle school and transition aged students with mild to moderate cognitive, developmental, or learning disabilities Other: Employment, Education, Housing, Daily living, Personal, Recreation, Community *Field Test* X								

Choosing the Right Curriculum

We found many curricula that address the different components of self-determination. Some curricula teach specific skills, such as decision making or goal setting. Others include content intended to increase students' knowledge about their disabilities or about disability rights. Still others include learning approaches or processes by which students take greater ownership of their IEP planning process. With the variety of materials available, how do teachers know what will be most effective for use with their students? We suggest that the process begin with a careful review of the sampling in Table 1 to become familiar with the variety of resources that are available. In addition, you might want to gather other published descriptions/reviews of self-determination curriculum (see Field, 1996; Field et al., 1998).

What Does the Literature Say About Self-Determination?

Here are the current trends in self-determination research:

- Current research has referred to self-determination as the ultimate goal of education (Halloran, 1993).
- Research has demonstrated a positive relationship between self-determination and improved postsecondary outcomes. These outcomes include a higher rate of employment and higher wages 1 year after graduation for students with mild mental retardation and learning disabilities (Wehmeyer & Schwartz, 1997).
- Classroom teachers are recognizing that self-determination is an important skill to teach students (Agran, Snow, & Swaner, 1999; Wehmeyer, Agran, & Hughes, 2000).

Definition of Self-Determination. Beginning with the "normalization" movement in the early 1970s, many researchers, educators, and self-advocates have developed definitions of self-determination. According to a consensus definition by Field, Martin, Miller, Ward, and Wehmeyer, 1998, self-determination is

a combination of skills, knowledge, and beliefs that enable a person to engage in goal-directed, self-regulated, autonomous behavior. An understanding of one's strengths and limitations together with a belief in oneself as capable and effective are essential to self-determination. When acting on the basis of these skills and attitudes, individuals have greater ability to take control of their lives and assume the role of successful adults. (p. 2)

Conceptual models of self-determination have included knowing and valuing oneself (Field & Hoffman, 1994); skills and knowledge on topics such as choice and decision making, goal setting and attainment, problem-solving, and self-advocacy (Martin & Marshall, 1995; Wehmeyer, 1999); and recognition of the environment's role in supporting self-determination for people with disabilities (Abery & Stancliffe, 1996).

Need for Instruction in Self-Determination. Unfortunately, so far all the rhetoric, research, and recognition is not being translated into classroom instruction. For example, Agran et al. (1999) found that whereas over 75% of middle and secondary teachers rated self-determination skills as a high priority, 55% indicated that self-determination goals were either not included in their students' IEPs or only in some students' IEPs. This finding is supported by: (a) Wehmeyer and Schwartz (1998) who found no self-determination skills in 895 IEP transition goals; and (b) Wehmeyer et al. (2000) who found 31% of secondary-level teachers reported writing no self-determination goals in student IEPs, 47% reported writing self-determination IEP goals for some students, and only 22% reported writing self-determination IEP goals for all students.

Although many explanations may exist for why self-determination skills are not included in student IEPs, we believe a major reason is that teachers are unaware of what resources exist to help with the task. This is supported by Wehmeyer et al. (2000), who reported that 41% of teachers with secondary-aged students indicated that they did not have sufficient training or information on teaching self-determination, and 17% were unaware of curriculum/assessment materials/strategies.

Promoting self-determination also requires training those without disabilities to encourage and respect the decisions made by self-determining individuals with disabilities.

Figure 1 shows a curriculum materials review checklist that we have found useful when deciding what curriculum might be most appropriate. The information included in Figure 1 is summarized in the following set of questions:

Does the intended audience match my students?

Are the materials age-appropriate? Are they designed for use with students who have mild, moderate, or severe disabilities? Some materials that may have been originally designed for use with a specific group of students may have to be modified for use with other groups (including students without disabilities). Check the introductory section of the teacher's manual to see what the authors say.

Do the skills covered in this curriculum meet my students' needs?

You may find that your students are perfectly capable of setting goals, but they do not know enough about their rights under current legislation such as the Individuals with Disabilities Education Act or the Americans with Disabilities Act to be able to ask for reasonable accommodations in their postsecondary setting, or maybe they need a better understanding of how to run their IEP meeting. In some cases, the introduction or overview section of the teacher's manual will state the goals of the curriculum. For example, the Take Action curriculum states: "Students learn to act on their plans, evaluate their plan and results, and make any necessary adjustments" (Marshall, et al., 1999, p. 9). Do the goals of the curriculum match your instructional objectives?

Does the curriculum require prerequisite skills?

Some curricula may require relatively sophisticated reading levels, or assume that the students will already understand how to make choices for themselves. Both the teacher's manual and the student activities will give you a sense of what skill level is required for students to begin using the curriculum.

Figure 1. Curriculum Materials Review Checklist

CURRICULUM MATERIALS REVIEW CHECKLIST

Title:_____

Author:_____

Publisher's name contact/information:_____

Date of publication:_____ Cost of materials:_____

For what type of student is the curriculum designed (e.g., age, disability)?

_____

What types of materials are included (e.g., instructor manual, student workbook, video, alternate formats)

_____

Do the components of self-determination match my students' needs

Students' Needs	Included in Curriculum		Comments
Choice-making	YES	NO	
Decision-making	YES	NO	
Goal setting/attainment	YES	NO	
Problem solving	YES	NO	
Self-evaluation	YES	NO	
Self-advocacy	YES	NO	
Self-awareness	YES	NO	
Person-centered IEP Planning	YES	NO	
Relationship with Others	YES	NO	
Other:_____			

Rate each of the following on a scale from 1 (Excellent) to 4 (Poor) based on your students and yourself as a teacher.

	1 Excellent	2 Good	3 Fair	4 Poor	5 Can't tell
How easy is it to get materials?					
How well do the cost of materials fit my budget?					
Are the materials available in alternative formats?					
Are support materials provided?					
Are the instructions "teacher friendly"?					
Are the prerequisite skills delineated?					
Are there sufficient opportunities for practice?					
How relevant/motivating is the content for my students?					
How age-appropriate is the content for my students?					
How well do the materials match the academic level of my students?					
Is a system for assessing student progress included?					
Is the content based on research/field testing?					
How appealing are the videos and other materials?					
How well does the instructional time (number and length of sessions) fit with my schedule?					
Additional Comments:					

What types of materials are provided?

If you work with students who are visually or hearing impaired, does the curriculum have audiotape, closed-captioned, or Braille formats? Are the materials durable and easy to use? Do they provide enough variety or hold the interest of students? Is an assessment tool included?

How easy is it to follow the lesson plans?

Are the objectives for each lesson clearly stated? Is it easy to tell what materials you will need and how much time each lesson will require? Is the text formatted so you can easily find prompts? Is there flexibility in the order of the lesson plans?

Were the materials field-tested?

Has anyone collected information about whether students who used this curriculum improved their self-determination knowledge, skills, or behaviors? Just because someone is selling a product doesn't mean that it works. Many of the curricula we listed have been field-tested, but not all of them report the results of those tests. Sometimes authors report field-test results in a journal article or book chapter instead of the manual.

What are the time and financial obligations associated with this curriculum?

The costs of materials sampled in Table 1 range from nothing to more than $1,000. The time commitments also vary extensively. Is the financial cost of the curriculum appropriate to the length of instructional time you have available to teach the skills?

Important questions include: Are the materials age-appropriate? Are they designed for use with students who have mild, moderate, or severe disabilities? Do they provide enough variety or hold the interest of students? Is an assessment tool included?

Sample Curricula

We have selected five curricula which have published research documenting their effectiveness to describe in more detail here.

The Self-Advocacy Strategy for Education and Transition Planning

This curriculum was developed using a modified version of the Strategies Intervention Model (Ellis, Deshler, Lenz, Schumaker, & Clark, 1991) at the University of Kansas. The Self-Advocacy Strategy is a motivation strategy that teachers can use to help students prepare for any type of educational or transition planning meeting. The strategy, called I-PLAN, consists of five steps:

- *I*nventory your strengths, areas to improve, goals, needed accommodations, and choices for learning.
- *P*rovide your inventory information.
- *L*isten and respond.
- *A*sk questions.
- *N*ame your goals.

The instructor's manual contains step-by-step lesson plans and cue cards that you can use as transparencies, handouts, or worksheets. Finally, the Self-Advocacy Strategy has been field-tested with students with learning disabilities ages 14–21 (Van Reusen & Bos, 1994; Van Reusen, Deshler, & Schumaker, 1989).

Next S.T.E.P. (Student Transition and Education Planning)

Developed by Andrew Halpern and his colleagues at the University of Oregon, the purpose of the Next S.T.E.P. curriculum is to teach high school students how to begin planning for their lives after they leave school. Materials include a teacher's manual with lesson plans and necessary forms, a student workbook, and a videotape that contains an overview of the curriculum, as well as vignettes that address important issues from specific lessons. The Next S.T.E.P. curriculum has been field-tested with students with mild mental retardation ages 14–19 (Zhang, 2000).

Take Action: Making Goals Happen

Take Action is the last of the three strands of the Choice-Maker Self-Determination Curriculum designed by Laura Huber Marshall and Jim Martin and their colleagues at the University of Colorado at Colorado Springs. The first two strands are Choosing Goals and Expressing Goals (or Self-Directed IEP). Take Action is designed to provide teachers with a set of lessons to teach students a generalizable process for attaining their goals. Materials include a teacher's manual with reproducible lesson masters and a student instructional video. Take Action was field-tested with six students with mild or moderate mental retardation ages 16 to 18 (Jerman, Martin, Marshall, & Sale, 2000). Results indicated that all six students accomplished all goals set during maintenance.

TAKE CHARGE for the Future

This multicomponent curriculum was designed by Laurie Powers and her colleagues at Oregon Health Sciences University to assist students to become more involved in their transition planning process. The four components are coaching, mentorship, parent support, and staff training. Materials include a student guide, companion guide, parent guide, and class guide. TAKE CHARGE for the Future was field-tested with 43 students with specific learning disabilities, emotional disabilities, other health impairments, or orthopedic impairments ages 14–17 years (Powers, Turner, Matuszewski, Wilson, & Phillips, in press). Results indicated significant differences in education planning, transition awareness, family empowerment, and student participation in transition planning.

41% of teachers with secondary-aged students indicated that they did not have sufficient training or information on teaching self-determination.

Whose Future Is It Anyway? A Student-Directed Transition Planning Process

Developed by Michael Wehmeyer and his colleagues at the Arc National Headquarters, this curriculum is designed for middle school and transition-aged students with mild or moderate disabilities. The curriculum consists of a student manual, which includes a cut-out Coach's Guide. While the manual is written for students to read and work through at their own pace, the teacher's role is three part:

- To facilitate student success.
- To teach information requested by students.
- To advocate for a successful transition for students.

This curriculum was field-tested with 53 students with mild or moderate mental retardation ages 15–21 (Wehmeyer & Lawrence, 1995). Results indicate significant increases in self-efficacy and outcome expectancy measures.

For more information on our exemplary sites and literature review visit our World Wide Web site at http://www.uncc.edu/sdsp.

Final Thoughts

Self-determination develops over the life span as students gain self-awareness and learn to make increasingly important decisions about their lives with the guidance of their parents, teachers, and other adult mentors. Because traditionally other people (professionals) have made most major life decisions for them, students with disabilities often require instruction on the skills needed to be self-determining citizens. Promoting self-determination also requires training those without disabilities to encourage and respect the decisions made by self-determining individuals with disabilities.

Fortunately, many self-determination curricula are available from which to choose. We hope that the suggestions provided in this article will help you decide which curriculum will best promote self-determination for your students.

References

Abery, B., & Stancliffe, R. (1996). The ecology of self-determination. In D. J. Sands & M. Wehmeyer (Eds.), *Self-determination across the lifespan: Independence and choice for people with disabilities* (pp. 111–145). Baltimore: Paul H. Brookes.

Agran, M., Snow, K., & Swaner, J. (1999). Teacher perceptions of self-determination: Benefits, characteristics, strategies. *Education and Training in Mental Retardation and Developmental Disabilities, 34*, 293–301.

Ellis, E. S., Deshler, D. D., Lenz, B. K., Schumaker, J. B., & Clark, F. L. (1991). An instructional model for teaching learning strategies. *Focus on Exceptional Children, 23*(4), 1–24.

Field, S. (1996). Self-determination instructional strategies for youth with learning disabilities. *Journal of Learning Disabilities, 29*, 40–52.

Field, S., & Hoffman, A. (1994). Development of a model for self-determination. *Career Development for Exceptional Individuals, 17*, 159–169.

Field, S., Martin, J., Miller, R., Ward, M., & Wehmeyer, M. (1998). *A practical guide for teaching self-determination.* Reston, VA: Council for Exceptional Children.

Halloran, W. D. (1993). Transition service requirements: Issues, implications, challenge. In R. C. Eaves & P. J. McLaughlin (Eds.), *Recent advances in special education and rehabilitation* (pp. 210–224). Boston: Andover.

Jerman, S. L., Martin, J. E., Marshall, L. H., & Sale, P. R. (2000). Promoting self-determination: Using *Take Action* to teach goal attainment. *Career Development for Exceptional Individuals, 23*, 27–38.

Marshall, L. H., Martin, J. E., Maxson, L., Hughes, W., Miller, T., McGill, T., & Jerman, P. (1999). *Take action: Making goals happen.* Longmont, CO: Sopris West.

Martin, J. E., & Marshall L. H. (1995) Choicemaker: A comprehensive self-determination transition program. *Intervention in School and Clinic, 30*, 147–156.

Mithaug, D., Campeau, P., & Wolman, J. (1992). *Research on self-determination in individuals with disabilities.* Unpublished Manuscript.

Powers, L. E., Turner, A., Matuszewski, J., Wilson, R., & Phillips, A. (in press). TAKE CHARGE for the future: A controlled field-test of a model to promote student involvement in transition planning. *Career Development for Exceptional Individuals.*

Van Reusen, A. K., & Bos, C. S. (1994). Facilitating student participation in individualized education programs through motivation strategy instruction. *Exceptional Children, 60*, 466–475.

Van Reusen, A. K., Deshler, D. D., & Schumaker, J. B. (1989). Effects of a student participation strategy in facilitating the involvement of adolescents with learning disabilities in Individualized Education Program planning process. *Learning Disabilities, 1*, 23–34.

Ward, M. J. (1988). The many facts of self-determination. *NICHCY Transition Summary: National Information Center for Children and Youth with Disabilities, 5*, 2–3.

Wehmeyer, M. L. (1996). Self-determination in youth with severe cognitive disabilities: From theory to practice. In L. E. Powers, G. H. S. Singer, & J. Sowers (Eds.), *On the road to autonomy: Promoting self-competence for children and youth with disabilities* (pp. 17–36). Baltimore: Paul H. Brookes.

Wehmeyer, M. L. (1999). A functional model of self-determination: Describing development and implementing instruction. *Focus on Autism and Other Developmental Disabilities, 14,* 53–61.

Wehmeyer, M. L., Agran, M., & Hughes, C. A. (2000). A national survey of teachers' promotion of self-determination and student directed learning. *The Journal of Special Education, 34,* 58–68.

Wehmeyer, M., & Lawrence, M. (1995). Whose future is it anyway? Promoting student involvement in transition planning. *Career Development for Exceptional Individuals, 18,* 69–83.

Wehmeyer, M. L., & Schwartz, M. (1997). Self-determination and positive adult outcomes: A follow up study of youth with mental retardation or learning disabilities. *Exceptional Children, 63,* 245–255.

Wehmeyer, M. L., & Schwartz, M. (1998). The self-determination focus of transition goals for students with mental retardation. *Career Development for Exceptional Individuals, 21,* 75–86.

Zhang, D. (2000). The effects of self-determination instruction on high school students with mild disabilities. *Louisiana Education Research Journal, 25*(1), 29–54.

David W. Test *(CEC Chapter #147), Professor, Special Education Program;* **Meagan Karvonen**, *Project Coordinator, Special Education Program;* **Wendy M. Wood**, *Associate Professor, Special Education Program;* **Diane Browder**, *Snyder Distinguished Professor, Special Education Program; and* **Bob Algozzine**, *Professor, Department of Educational Administration, Research, and Technology, College of Education, University of North Carolina at Charlotte.*

Address correspondence to David Test, Special Education Program, University of North Carolina at Charlotte, 9201 University City Blvd., Charlotte, NC 28223 (e-mail: dwtest@email.uncc.edu; URL: http://www.uncc.edu/sdsp).

From *Teaching Exceptional Children,* November/December 2000, pp. 48-54. © 2000 by The Council for Exceptional Children. Reprinted with permission.

Index

Test Your Knowledge Form

We encourage you to photocopy and use this page as a tool to assess how the articles in *Annual Editions* expand on the information in your textbook. By reflecting on the articles you will gain enhanced text information. You can also access this useful form on a product's book support Web site at *http://www.dushkin.com/online/*.

NAME:

DATE:

TITLE AND NUMBER OF ARTICLE:

BRIEFLY STATE THE MAIN IDEA OF THIS ARTICLE:

LIST THREE IMPORTANT FACTS THAT THE AUTHOR USES TO SUPPORT THE MAIN IDEA:

WHAT INFORMATION OR IDEAS DISCUSSED IN THIS ARTICLE ARE ALSO DISCUSSED IN YOUR TEXTBOOK OR OTHER READINGS THAT YOU HAVE DONE? LIST THE TEXTBOOK CHAPTERS AND PAGE NUMBERS:

LIST ANY EXAMPLES OF BIAS OR FAULTY REASONING THAT YOU FOUND IN THE ARTICLE:

LIST ANY NEW TERMS/CONCEPTS THAT WERE DISCUSSED IN THE ARTICLE, AND WRITE A SHORT DEFINITION:

We Want Your Advice

ANNUAL EDITIONS revisions depend on two major opinion sources: one is our Advisory Board, listed in the front of this volume, which works with us in scanning the thousands of articles published in the public press each year; the other is you—the person actually using the book. Please help us and the users of the next edition by completing the prepaid article rating form on this page and returning it to us. Thank you for your help!

ANNUAL EDITIONS: Educating Exceptional Children 03/04

ARTICLE RATING FORM

Here is an opportunity for you to have direct input into the next revision of this volume.
We would like you to rate each of the articles listed below, using the following scale:

1. **Excellent: should definitely be retained**
2. **Above average: should probably be retained**
3. **Below average: should probably be deleted**
4. **Poor: should definitely be deleted**

Your ratings will play a vital part in the next revision.
Please mail this prepaid form to us as soon as possible.
Thanks for your help!

RATING	ARTICLE	RATING	ARTICLE
	1. Revamping Special Education		21. Making Choices—Improving Behavior—Engaging in Learning
	2. Merry-Go-Round: Using Interpersonal Influence to Keep Inclusion Spinning Smoothly		22. Homeless Youth in the United States
	3. Standards for Diverse Learners		23. Schools for the Visually Disabled: Dinosaurs or Mainstays?
	4. More Choices for Disabled Kids: Lessons From Abroad		24. Seeking the Light: Welcoming a Visually Impaired Student
	5. What's Good? Suggested Resources for Beginning Special Education Teachers		25. Visual Teaching Strategies for Students Who Are Deaf or Hard of Hearing
	6. Emergent Literacy in an Early Childhood Classroom: Center Learning to Support the Child With Special Needs		26. Training Basic Teaching Skills to Paraeducators of Students With Severe Disabilities
	7. Identifying Paraprofessional Competencies for Early Intervention and Early Childhood Special Education		27. Loneliness in Children With Disabilities: How Teachers Can Help
	8. Language Flowering, Language Empowering: 20 Ways Parents and Teachers Can Assist Young Children		28. Using Technology to Construct Alternate Portfolios of Students With Moderate and Severe Disabilities
	9. The Itinerant Teacher Hits the Road: A Map for Instruction in Young Children's Social Skills		29. Mobility Training Using the MOVE Curriculum: A Parent's View
	10. Providing Support for Student Independence Through Scaffolded Instruction		30. Accommodations for Students With Disabilities: Removing Barriers to Learning
	11. Graphic Organizers to the Rescue! Helping Students Link—and Remember—Information		31. Chaos in the Classroom: Looking at ADHD
	12. Successful Strategies for Promoting Self-Advocacy Among Students With LD: The LEAD Group		32. Uncommon Talents: Gifted Children, Prodigies and Savants
	13. For the Love of Language		33. Using the Internet to Improve Student Performance
	14. Literacy-Based Planning and Pedagogy That Supports Toddler Language Development		34. Gifted Students Need an Education, Too
	15. Young African American Children With Disabilities and Augmentative and Alternative Communication Issues		35. Transition Planning for Students With Severe Disabilities: Policy Implications for the Classroom
	16. The Secrets of Autism		36. Listening to Student Voices About Postsecondary Education
	17. Don't Water Down! Enhance: Content Learning Through the Unit Organizer Routine		37. Choosing a Self-Determination Curriculum
	18. Identifying Depression in Students With Mental Retardation		
	19. Scars That Won't Heal: The Neurobiology of Child Abuse		
	20. Wraparound Services for Young Schoolchildren With Emotional and Behavioral Disorders		

(Continued on next page)

ANNUAL EDITIONS: EDUCATING EXCEPTIONAL CHILDREN 03/04

NO POSTAGE
NECESSARY
IF MAILED
IN THE
UNITED STATES

BUSINESS REPLY MAIL
FIRST-CLASS MAIL PERMIT NO. 84 GUILFORD CT

POSTAGE WILL BE PAID BY ADDRESSEE

McGraw-Hill/Dushkin
530 Old Whitfield Street
Guilford, Ct 06437-9989

ABOUT YOU

Name   Date

Are you a teacher? ☐   A student? ☐
Your school's name

Department

Address   City   State   Zip

School telephone #

YOUR COMMENTS ARE IMPORTANT TO US!

Please fill in the following information:
For which course did you use this book?

Did you use a text with this ANNUAL EDITION? ☐ yes ☐ no
What was the title of the text?

What are your general reactions to the *Annual Editions* concept?

Have you read any pertinent articles recently that you think should be included in the next edition? Explain.

Are there any articles that you feel should be replaced in the next edition? Why?

Are there any World Wide Web sites that you feel should be included in the next edition? Please annotate.

May we contact you for editorial input? ☐ yes ☐ no
May we quote your comments? ☐ yes ☐ no